Beyond the Burning Times

Acknowledgments

I want to thank friends and colleagues who read portions of my contributions for clarity, and particularly my Christian friend, Professor Bernie Lammers, who took the time to read the entire manuscript and made many suggestions for improving it. Of course, the final content is my own responsibility.

Gus diZerega

I would like to extend my thanks to my friend John W. Morehead, who has acted as an editor and coordinator of this dialogue, particularly for his patience and understanding throughout the writing of my contributions. It was John who originally contacted Gus about creating a dialogue book. Morag Reeve and Paul Clifford at Lion Hudson deserve special mention first for accepting this text for publication, and then for their patience and understanding during a period of delays in completing the work. Lastly, I am very grateful to my wife Ruth for her support and understanding, and also to my friends Matthew Stone and Simeon Payne, who have been enthusiastic and encouraged me throughout the project.

Philip Johnson

Beyond the Burning Times

A Pagan and Christian in Dialogue

Philip Johnson and Gus diZerega

Edited by John W. Morehead

A Lion Book
an imprint of
Lion Hudson plc
Wilkinson House, Jordan Hill Road,
Oxford OX2 8DR, England
www.lionhudson.com
ISBN 978 0 7459 5272 7

First edition 2008
10 9 8 7 6 5 4 3 2 1 0

This book has been printed on paper and board
independently certified as having been produced
from sustainable forests.

A catalogue record for this book is
available from the British Library

Typeset in 9.75/12 Baskerville BT
Printed and bound in Wales
by Creative Print and Design

CONTENTS

John W. Morehead edited this volume. He is the Director of the Western Institute for Intercultural Studies (www.wiics.org), a senior editor of *Sacred Tribes Journal* (www.sacredtribesjournal.org) and co-editor of *Encountering New Religious Movements* (Kregel, 2004).

Gus diZerega is a Third Degree Wiccan Gardnerian Elder, who studied for six years with a Brazilian shaman and holds a PhD in Political Theory. He has published widely on political, scholarly and spiritual subjects and is a frequent conference lecturer, speaker and writer on topics such as the environment, community and society, contemporary politics, modernity and religion.

Philip Johnson is the founder of Global Apologetics and Mission, a Christian ministry concerned with new religious movements and major religions. He is visiting lecturer in Alternative Religious Movements at Morling College, Sydney, Australia. He holds a Master of Theology degree from the Australian College of Theology and has co-written three other books on theology and new spiritualities.

Don Frew is an Elder in both the Gardnerian and New Reformed Orthodox Order of the Golden Dawn (NROOGD) traditions of Wicca. He is High Priest of Coven Trismegiston in Berkeley, CA. He has attended the University of California, Berkeley, majoring first in Anthropology and then Religious Studies. He has served nine terms on the National Board of the Covenant of the Goddess (www.cog.org), the world's largest Wiccan religious organization, and has represented Wicca in ongoing interfaith work for over twenty years. Don is an internationally recognized spokesperson for the Craft, and interviews with him have appeared on countless radio and television shows and in numerous books.

Lainie Petersen is a lifelong resident of Chicago who has been interested in matters of religion and spirituality for most of her life. While she was an evangelical Christian as a teenager, she later became involved with Western Esotericism, and was eventually ordained a priest in a Neo-Gnostic church. Since that time, she has reverted to orthodox Christianity, and is presently ordained and active in the Independent Sacramental Movement. Lainie holds Master of Divinity and Master of Theological Studies degrees from Garrett Evangelical Theological Seminary, Illinois.

Foreword by Don Frew

In 2002 I attended the Global Assembly of the United Religions Initiative (URI) in Rio de Janeiro. At its conclusion, 300 or so religious representatives engaged in a Peace March the length of Copacabana Beach. Several of us were then asked to address the city of Rio. Two Pagan representatives were included, Rowan Fairgrove and I. I said:

> *Sometimes, people in my faith tradition ask me, 'Why do interfaith work?' And I tell them, 'We all want to see change in the world. We want to see peace, justice and healing for the Earth. Well, the only true change comes through changing people's minds. And nothing has the power over minds and souls that religion has. So any group like the URI, that is working to create understanding and cooperation between religions, to work for the betterment of all, has the potential to be the most powerful force for change on the planet. As a person of faith, called by my Gods to care for and protect the Earth, how can I not be involved?' And then they understand.*

If anyone had told me a few years ago that Wiccans would be asked to bless Rio de Janeiro, I wouldn't have believed it. We've come a long way, and our interfaith efforts have been the reason.

Witches were involved in the creation of the URI almost from the beginning. Its Charter opens with words reflecting our views and beliefs:

> *We, people of diverse religions, spiritual expressions and indigenous traditions throughout the world, hereby establish the United Religions Initiative to promote enduring, daily interfaith cooperation, to end religiously motivated violence and to create cultures of peace, justice and healing for the Earth and all living beings. [www.uri.org]*

The URI now includes almost 400 local and multi-regional interfaith groups in over 70 countries around the world.

At one of the Charter-writing conferences, in Stanford in 1998, representatives of many Earth-based religions, who had previously participated as odd groups on the edges of the core of 'world' religions, got together for lunch. There were practitioners of Wicca, Shinto, North/Central/South American indigenous traditions, Candomble,

Taoism and Hinduism. To our surprise, the environmental scientists also joined in, saying they felt most at home with us. Looking around our circle, we suddenly realized that the Earth-religions comprised 13 per cent of the delegates! We had established an identity in common as a 'way' of being religious – a Pagan identity, broader than the concept of NeoPagan.

That 'Pagan lunch' led to the formation of the *Spirituality & the Earth Cooperation Circle*, a multi-regional group networking Earth-religionists around the world.

For me, the bottom line is what I expressed that day in Rio: a movement to bring the world's religions together to work for the betterment of all is, potentially, the most powerful force for positive change in existence. As a person of faith, called by my Gods to care for and protect the Earth, how can I not be involved?

Interfaith work is, in my opinion, the best hope for the future of the Earth. NeoPagans are active at the heart of the global interfaith movement. This is our opportunity to be part of the change we wish to see.

Here in the United States, we are a small, but growing, religion living under the huge shadow of Christianity. Unlike relations between other faiths, the relationship between Paganism and Christianity has been mythologized into an epic struggle between good and evil, leading on both sides to a continuing demonization of the 'other'. Dialogue between Pagans and Christians is the first, necessary step to building the community of 'peace, justice and healing for the Earth and all living beings' that is the dream of all of us involved in interfaith work.

This small volume is a good beginning from which to extend this dialogue to a wider Pagan and Christian audience.

Foreword by Lainie Petersen

While discussion of religion may seldom be appropriate in polite company, dialogue between religious people is fundamentally necessary in a civil society. Without dialogue, what we know about religions other than our own will be filtered through a detached (and often ignorant) media, projections of outsider 'experts', and noisy ideologues whose views and experiences may not accurately represent those of their co-religionists. These distortions mean that we will possess false assumptions and fears about what our neighbours, friends, co-workers and even family members value, practise and believe.

This reluctance to engage in dialogue (as opposed to debate) about our religious beliefs could be attributed to social convention (i.e., never discuss religion or politics), but I suspect that there are other, deeper reasons for it. For those of us who have friendships with people of a religion different from our own, a mutual exploration of these differences might be frightening. We may fear the pain of encountering our friend's rejection – or so it may seem to us – of what we believe. We may worry that the pain will be so great that we may lose our friendship. Alternatively, we may (secretly) fear that if someone we love and respect believes differently from us, there 'might be something' to their religion: if we learn more about it, we risk having to consider our own faith more deeply. So we avoid the topic, and thus the opportunity to develop greater intimacy with (and empathy for) someone whom we are supposed to care about very deeply.

Similarly, religious leaders/scholars (particularly evangelicals) might be reluctant to publicly 'dialogue' with someone of another religion for fear that they may be seen as 'legitimizing' that 'other' religion. Even private dialogue between religious leaders/scholars becomes complicated and suspect because of what is perceived as a risk to professional integrity: if a 'professional' participant in the dialogue feels challenged by the faith of the other, she may wonder if she is doing her job correctly.

The irony in all this, of course, is that most religious people acknowledge that there is a cosmic/sacred agenda that is of higher importance than their own feelings, desires, fears and concerns. If religious misunderstandings result in social discord, then people of faith have a *responsibility* to prevent misunderstandings before they transform into superstition and slander. This is true even if the process by which this is done (i.e., dialogue) is risky and uncomfortable.

In addition to the problem of fear, dialogue is also undermined by the problem of frustration: for those of us who embrace and honour that which we believe to be sacred, the fact that others do not share our devotion can be troubling, even if our own religious worldview is a pluralistic one. It is painful to encounter indifference, even repugnance, to the God/s that we love and serve. This 'perturbing otherness' can stand in the way of dialogue when it causes us to consider 'the other' unworthy of respectful engagement.

Our fear and perturbation are understandable, yet they must be overcome. True dialogue demands of its participants both vulnerability and willingness to extend a presumption of good will to the other, even if their religious beliefs are antithetical to our own. If we are unable or unwilling to do this, the temptation will be to shift the exchange from dialogue to debate. While there is nothing wrong with debate, its nature demands that one participant wins while the other loses. Neither is expected to walk away from the experience with any increase in understanding. Which brings us back to our initial concern: when religious people fail to dialogue with each other, misunderstandings abound and relationships, communities and even nations can suffer as a result.

As a participant in this book, I have chosen to assume these risks of dialogue. I have chosen to do this because I fear the consequences of religious misunderstanding more than I do hurt feelings and even a possible crisis of faith. It is a privilege to be a part of this engagement, and I hope that it helps to bring healing and clarity to two very diverse religious communities. More importantly, I hope it sparks a desire in readers to take this dialogue *away* from these pages and into the parks, homes, cafés and other spaces where NeoPagans and Christians work and live together.

Introduction

Gus diZerega

Over the last 50 years or so the rise of NeoPaganism in Great Britain, the United States and other modern Western nations has reopened questions many religious people had long regarded as settled. Theologians and modern philosophers alike believed Christianity had triumphed in the first centuries of the modern era, overcoming first Greco-Roman Paganism, and then other Pagan spiritual traditions in Europe and elsewhere, as the church spread its teachings in ever wider circles of influence. Whether the scholar was secular or a believer, the opinion was that monotheism was far more harmonious with modern society than earlier polytheistic practices. The major religious debate was whether modernity had outgrown the spiritual altogether. Pagan religious practices and beliefs were certainly no longer to be taken seriously among modern men and women.

And yet, once Pagans emerged into the public eye after England's anti-Witchcraft laws were repealed, our numbers grew steadily. The original public figures associated with its emergence, such as Gerald Gardner, Doreen Valiente and Alex Sanders, have passed away, but the traditions they helped establish have continued to grow and elaborate. Along the way new traditions have risen, sharing broad similarities but focusing on the Sacred from different perspectives.

The term 'NeoPaganism' differentiates us from Pagan traditions with unbroken roots to traditional and often pre-Christian cultures. As with our Pagan predecessors, we exist in enormous and, for some, confusing abundance. The first NeoPagan groups to become public grew from the teachings of Gerald Gardner, and are loosely grouped under the term 'British Traditional Wicca'. These include Gardnerian, King Stone, Alexandrian and some other traditions of practice. Some other people claim their practice also derives from traditional covens predating the abolition of England's anti-Witchcraft laws. Despite their claims, some are obviously of recent origin, perhaps very recent; others deserve to be taken much more seriously as genuine links to much earlier origins.

Reconstructionist traditions have also arisen, in which practitioners attempt to revive old and usually European Pagan religions that died out over years of religious oppression. Within the NeoPagan community the three best known are Ásatru, or Norse reconstructionism, Celtic reconstructionism, and Druidic groups. But there are many others. In 1979 the talented Witch and teacher Starhawk published her book *The Spiral Dance*, rooted in the Feri tradition as passed on by Victor Anderson, thereby initiating the Reclaiming Tradition and its offshoots, one of the most important modern traditions. NROOGD, or the 'New Reformed Orthodox Order of the Golden Dawn', grew from a folklore class and chose its name with tongue firmly in cheek. It has since grown into a creative and powerful Wiccan tradition centred in Western North America. Finally, 'Eclectic Wicca' perhaps has the most practitioners, drawing inspiration from many sources and often being learned by people studying the many 'Wicca 101' books that have been published over the past twenty years. My list is illustrative only. There are many more groups.

How many of us are there? It is hard to tell. Most groups meet very quietly. Some people are serious practitioners; others come to public Sabbats, and do little more. Counting NeoPagans and herding cats are probably enterprises of similar difficulty. The Graduate Center of the City University of New York conducted a survey of American religious identification.[1] From 1990 to 2001 they reported that religious identification by American adults dropped from 90 per cent to 81 per cent. During this time the number who identified themselves as Wiccans rose from 8,000 to 134,000. Those identifying themselves as Druids rose from negligible to 33,000, and generic 'Pagans' were unreported in 1990 but numbered 140,000 in 2001. This all adds up to 307,000. Unlike the US, the Canadian census asks about citizens' religious identities. In 2001 Stats Canada reported that there were 21,080 Wiccans alone, a 281 per cent increase since 1991. If US proportions are similar, there were 197,429 Wiccans, not to mention other Pagans.[2] In short, according to these studies we are a minority, but hardly a negligible one, and certainly a rapidly growing one.

My own experience supports this general picture, as the size of the oldest NeoPagan festivals and gatherings has grown to several thousand and the numbers of such gatherings are increasing rapidly, particularly 'Pagan Pride Day' events. I think it is significant that large numbers of young people are attending them.

As we have grown in both numbers and experience, we have

increasingly made the acquaintance of older Pagan traditions rooted in non-Western practices such as Santeria, Voudon and Candomble from the African Diaspora, and traditional Native Americans here in North America. I understand similar contacts have been made with aboriginal peoples in other lands such as Australia. In these cases relations have sometimes been very friendly, sometimes suspicious – as might be expected given past European treatment of these peoples and the practices most important to them. But it seems to me that increasingly our relationships are becoming friendly ones.

When I taught at Whitman College in eastern Washington state, Naxi people from south-western China arrived for a year's residence as part of Whitman's creative East Asian programme. One was a young Naxi priest who was attempting to strengthen the tattered spiritual traditions of his people, which had been dealt a serious blow during Mao Tse-Tung's 'Cultural Revolution'. I invited them to a 'healing circle' I had established while there, thinking they might appreciate the opportunity to see practices more similar to their own than anything else they were likely to encounter while visiting America.

At the end of the session, the priest told the professor of Anthropology responsible for inviting them, 'There is shamanism in America!' He saw the resemblance, and he liked it.

But even as we and older Pagan traditions see our similarities, we are also something new. NeoPaganism is perhaps the first theistic religion not oriented around a specific teacher to evolve within the context of Western modernity. We have no prophet, guru or other spiritual authority. Of NeoPagans known to me personally, some are PhDs not only in the social sciences, but also in medicine and chemistry. Others are highly skilled innovators in the computer industry. Still others are herbalists, midwives, musicians and even successful electoral politicians. In fact, we probably work in every field. Far from being primitives (a misleading term in any case), Pagans Neo and otherwise can be found in virtually every kind of society.

Our ubiquity raises the question of what we believe. And in terms of this volume, how does it compare with the dominant Christian beliefs of the contemporary West? That is the purpose of this small volume: to give you, the reader, whatever your beliefs, a sense of the commonalities and differences between Christianity and NeoPaganism.

My contributions will reflect the kind of Pagan I am: a Gardnerian Wiccan. As an initiated Gardnerian Elder I am regarded as competent to teach and pass on my tradition. But I am not regarded by other traditions as competent to teach and pass on their beliefs and practices. So my words here reflect my British Traditional orientation.

Yet if you interpret me as suggesting there is something intrinsically superior to Gardnerian or even British Traditional Wicca compared to other NeoPagan traditions, you will miss my point completely. I nearly ended up within another tradition, and the events that made me a Gardnerian had nothing to do with the superiority of one tradition over the other. But I am far more competent to write from a British Traditional perspective than from any other, and that, rather than any judgment of comparative worth, is why I often do so.

The Sacred permeates this world, and many are the ways to honour, harmonize with, and grow closer to it. I am blessed to have my path, and others are no less blessed to have theirs. I pray you are similarly blessed in whatever way you follow.

Philip Johnson

Welcome to this dialogue between me and Gus diZerega about Christian and Pagan pathways. Back in 1999 I wrote an article that suggested Christians should make a conscientious effort to understand Pagans and to enter into dialogue.[3] Meanwhile around the same time Gus began his own probing comparisons of Pagan and Christian perspectives.[4] We wrote quite independently of each other but we both recognized the need for Christians and Pagans to *listen to* each other rather than just *talking about* one another. In *Beyond the Burning Times* Gus and I have finally encountered each other, and we have also been joined by Don Frew and Lainie Petersen as conversation partners. We invite you to listen in and hopefully you will then want to carry on conversations among your Christian and Pagan friends.

Beyond the Burning Times represents a small but much needed step towards improving relations between Christians and Pagans, because historically there have been some ghastly episodes. The story is long and quite variegated. The earliest Christians lived as a religious minority in the 'pagan' Roman empire and were subjected to imperial discrimination, persecution and martyrdom. As Christians were marginalized and ostracized, they found it was both valuable and necessary to occasionally open up literary dialogues on Pagan views.[5]

Eventually Christianity was legitimated as a religion and from the fifth century onwards the persecution receded. Over the subsequent centuries Pagan peoples in different geographical contexts were converted to Christianity. These conversions sometimes brought blessings but in other contexts Pagans were treated disgracefully.[6]

The 'Burning Times' is an expression that refers to the grim and horrible events that occurred from time to time in the late Medieval, Renaissance and Post-Reformation eras when Christians persecuted Witches in Europe and North America.[7] The Witch trials loom large among many ignominious and shameful deeds done in the name of Jesus Christ by Roman Catholics and Protestants. Although we cannot alter the past, we can surely be repentant about what happened, just as King Josiah asked forgiveness for the serious spiritual neglect and oversights of his ancestors.[8] Today many Christians and Pagans retain deep heartfelt suspicions about one another and some nasty and misleading folk stories still circulate that readily fuel appalling social panics.[9]

Beyond the Burning Times signifies that Gus and I are acutely aware of these problems and that we want to move beyond the ignorance that nourishes bigotry and distrust. We are trying hard to understand specific aspects of each other's spiritual journey, practices and beliefs in an atmosphere of mutual respect. We are striving to generate better understanding of Christian and Pagan views about spirituality, the Divine, the natural world, human beings and spiritual authority.

When it comes to our respective experiences of Christianity and Paganism, we are on opposite sides of the planet: Gus lives in the United States of America and I live in Australia. Although both cultures can be characterized as young frontier nations, the role and influence of Christianity on the history of each nation varies enormously, and there are also considerable differences in social attitudes towards the expression of religious beliefs in the public square. Hopefully we have overcome the cultural divide and not talked past one another.

So *Beyond the Burning Times* constitutes a brief dialogue that breaks the ice and opens up discussion on these important topics. Each topic deserves to be explored in much more detail and space limitations have also meant that many other subjects were omitted. Hopefully other Christians and Pagans will take matters further in future discussions. The basic aim of the dialogue is to increase understanding between the two spiritual communities and to clear away potential misconceptions that either side may unwittingly be prone to.

Over recent decades some Christians have collaborated with sceptics and atheists in worthwhile literary debates on God's existence and Jesus' resurrection.[10] However, *Beyond the Burning Times* was not written along the lines of a polemical debate. It is not an exercise in defensive Christian apologetics where the spiritual teachings, practices, historical claims and logicality of Pagan thought are critically compared with the Bible and church creeds.[11] While there are occasions when critical evaluations of major religious ideas and practices are surely warranted, the present dialogue is not dedicated to that sort of task.

This book does *not* issue a call for Christians and Pagans to downplay significant differences in belief. There are some very clear and profound differences in their beliefs and practices. Although a few may misconstrue *Beyond the Burning Times* and imagine that we are trying to mix and match Christian and Pagan beliefs, that is *not* what this book is about. Others whose imaginations are preoccupied with the eccentric divinatory practice of interpreting current events as a grand apocalyptic conspiracy may *wrongly* insinuate that it is part of a devious plot to lure unsuspecting Christians into interfaith worship.[12] This dialogue does not have any such aim in mind and, frankly, conspiratorial claims reveal a lot more about the critics' paranoia than they do about the subject matter.

Several years ago the late Eric Sharpe was my lecturer in the study of religion at university and he made these apt remarks about religious dialogue:

> *The best dialogue is one in which those old-fashioned virtues of courtesy and mutual respect are allowed to have the upper hand of what our culture seems to be best at: points-scoring and vilifying the opposition. I can think of no better way to conclude here than with a biblical word; the most frequently broken of the ten commandments is not the one about not committing adultery or stealing, but the one that follows it: 'You shall not bear false witness against your neighbour.' For the ultimate limitation on dialogue is that one must not bear false witness, either in your neighbour's hearing or more especially behind his or her back.*[13]

I pray that this dialogue helps us all to better understand one another's spiritual lifestyles and beliefs, and that the Spirit of Jesus shines through my words.

CHAPTER 1
The Nature of Spirituality

Gus diZerega

'Spirituality' concerns our personal relation to the Sacred. 'Religion' describes what constitutes the beliefs and practices of a spiritual community. Religions are social. Of course, my personal spirituality will be shaped by my religion and my religion has been and is continually shaped by the spirituality of its members, sometimes in opposition to those supposedly exercising ultimate authority over its tenets. In some religions this lack of fit can become a source of internal crisis, leading to a concern with rooting out heresy. In Pagan religions these problems are largely absent, and the reason for this lies in the character of Pagan spirituality.

What is Pagan spirituality? It is very different from that which dominates within the religious traditions with which most modern Westerners are familiar, whether as members themselves or as a part of their cultural heritage. Since around 500 CE Western civilization has been profoundly shaped by Christianity, and to a lesser extent the other 'religions of the book', meaning religions characterized by adherence to a sacred text, written down for humans to read, ponder and learn from. The Pagan religions preceding this time were for the most part not so characterized, though sacred and inspired writings did exist. Late Classical Pagans often regarded the *Hermetica* and *Hymns of Orpheus* as divinely inspired.[1] Many people, myself included, consider Hindus to be Pagans, and they possess an extensive sacred literature. Even so, as a rule this literature plays a different role from sacred scriptures within the Abrahamic traditions.

This lack of text-centredness is equally true for today's NeoPagan religions. In fact, NeoPagans share common defining characteristics with Pagan religions in general, differing primarily in that we are not contemporary representatives of unbroken traditions many thousands of years old. Rather, NeoPaganism constitutes a re-emergence of Pagan spirituality within modern cultures where Pagan practices have been largely extirpated, often violently, for over a thousand years. Pre-Christian Celtic, Classical or other European forms of Pagan practice died out in the sense that no strong unbroken lineage survives. The re-emergence of Pagan spirituality within the modern West is inspired first by people experiencing the reality of our Gods, and second by what is known of our ancestors, as well as what we know of contemporary Pagan traditions that have managed to stay in close connection with their roots because their encounter with repressive monotheism was more recent and fleeting. Among these traditions are many Native American practices, Santeria, Umbanda, Candomble and Voudon from the African Diaspora, shamanism in its various forms, Hinduism, and other less visible traditions. There is also intriguing evidence that some European Pagan traditions may have survived into modern times in a vestigial sense, and in the case of Lithuanian Romuva, more than vestigially.[2]

Sometimes the resulting NeoPagan practices appear syncretistic, but syncretism is not as controversial within a Pagan context as it is within a scriptural one. I shall explore this issue at some depth when we get to the question of spiritual authority, but here simply observe that integrating other insights into one's tradition is far less controversial if Spirit is conceived as being everywhere, and potentially approachable everywhere, rather than far distant from us. Even so, in its most fruitful forms religious syncretism involves much more than simple spiritual mix-and-match.

In addition, cultures where NeoPaganism has emerged have generally embraced science as our most reliable means for learning about the material world. While there were earlier precursors particularly in the Renaissance, modern science emerged during the Enlightenment after the devastation of the Thirty Years' War. Many people saw science as a way to find reliable knowledge without having to rely on religious texts with their divergent and seemingly unbridgeable interpretations.[3]

Science's enormous success has guaranteed a complex relationship between it and religion ever since. The relationship of science to religion is once again very controversial from both sides. But, as we will see, a Pagan perspective on these matters differs from those within the Abrahamic traditions. Paradoxically, NeoPaganism brings traditions that in a broad sense predate scriptural religions by thousands of years into cultures that are among the world's most modern and secular.

Practice Before Belief

Pagan spirituality is primarily a spirituality of practice, not belief. I do not mean to say we Pagans do not believe in our practice or our Gods. We do. But there is no single authorized or universally accepted doctrinal tradition even within a single Pagan spiritual tradition. People who have worked together for years may well have, indeed probably do have, different individual interpretations as to what they are doing and what it means in the bigger scheme of things.

Certainly that has been my experience. I am a Gardnerian Wiccan.[4] This name comes from Gerald Gardner, the founder of our tradition, who took our practice public after England finally repealed its anti-Witchcraft laws in 1951.[5] Gardnerian Wicca has the deserved reputation within NeoPagan circles of being the most conservative and most resistant to innovation. But our conservatism focuses on ritual practice, not textual interpretation. Even so, as Gardnerian Wicca has gone worldwide, variations in our practices have developed, with the most ritually 'liberal' groups being found in England, where our tradition arose. In the United States, 'California line' Gardnerians are the most liberal, which probably does not surprise anyone.

A Gardnerian coven of which I was long a member consisted of people who practised well together, but who had very different interpretations as to what they experienced. Sometimes we discussed our varying interpretations, but our differences, the stuff of schism in Abrahamic theology, caused scarcely a ripple within our group. No one questioned anyone's right to be a Gardnerian Wiccan because his or her view of the Gods differed from someone else's. Gardner himself observed that his original teachers' views were in accord with the late Classical writer Sallustius.[6] But far from these writings being considered 'scriptural', most Wiccans have little idea what they say. They haven't read Sallustius, and usually not even Gardner. This lack of knowledge has little if any impact on the spiritual validity of Wiccan ritual, though it can influence how well Wiccans understand their own tradition historically and philosophically.

One of Gerald Gardner's original High Priestesses, and arguably the most important in creating Gardnerian Witchcraft, is the late Doreen Valiente. In *Drawing Down the Moon* Adler asked her what makes someone a valid Witch. Valiente replied, 'If someone is *genuinely* devoted to the Old gods and the magic of nature, in my eyes they're valid, especially if they can use the witch powers. In other words, it isn't what people know, it's what they are.'[7]

Consequently, a certain risk accompanies my trying to write down and describe what 'Pagan spirituality' really is. What is most important to us as Pagans is not written down, nor really can it be, or at least it cannot be done adequately. A Wiccan *Book of Shadows* is not considered a divine revelation. A '*BOS*' is more like a spiritual 'cookbook' and any Witch who keeps one will often add new 'recipes' once they are found to reliably bring them into better connection with the Sacred or to be useful for some other purpose. Even many of our defining practices, such as our Sabbats, can still vary over time, as people receive new inspirations, or as circumstances impose changes which, once tried, are later deemed worth doing for their own sake. For example, increasingly Australian and New Zealand Witches are switching the underlying meaning of specific Sabbats around because they are based on seasonal and solar cycles that are different there from in the northern hemisphere.

To an outsider this fluid diversity can appear undisciplined and sloppy, hardly up to the standards of traditions claiming immutable texts and possessing thousands of written volumes describing what these texts really mean. That is how it first appeared to me when I was new to our practice. But my judgment then and that of those who share it now are mistaken. This approach prematurely evaluates one religious tradition by the standards of another. Before any such judgment can be fairly made, both traditions of belief and traditions of practice need to be understood on their own terms, as their practitioners see them.

Pagan spirituality was humankind's dominant spiritual practice for most of human history. If we include Hinduism and Chinese folk religion as essentially Pagan, its practitioners still comprise about 25 per cent of the world's population – not including Christians and others who also practise Paganism, as is common in Brazil. However, in the West, Paganism is a minor religion and little known.

As the practice of Pagan spirituality grows in the modern world, and if we as Pagans are to interact fruitfully with people drawn to Spirit within other paths, it is important we try and communicate in terms as familiar to others as possible. My first effort to do this was in *Pagans and Christians: The Personal Spiritual Experience*. It was successful enough that I have been asked to co-author this volume with Philip Johnson, in which we address certain fundamental issues of spirituality, issues both perennial and very contemporary.

But before I go further, I must emphasize, and emphasize strongly, that what follows is one Pagan's interpretation. If another sees things differently, that does not necessarily mean he or she is more or less correct than I. How this can be without reducing our views to simple relativism I must set aside for a while. But rest assured, I will return to it in Chapter 5.

A Pagan's Practice

Perhaps a way for us to begin is to describe my own personal practice, how I integrate Pagan spirituality into my own day-to-day existence. Once I have done this, I will explore in greater depth what spirituality is within a Pagan perspective. My personal description is purely illustrative. Different Pagans will practise differently, which need not mean one of us sets a better example than another.

When I first awaken I go to my altar, light a candle and incense, and give thanks, first to the Source of All, for love, for this beautiful world, for my friends, family and loved ones, for those I would love if I knew them better, for the fascinating work I have been privileged to do, and for the other blessings in my life. Among these I include thanks for the likely blessings I do not (yet) experience as such, for I have long since learned that what I want and what I need are often different. I then thank the Goddess as She has manifested most powerfully for me – My Lady of Forests and Fields, as I call Her – for Her blessings and the path She opened for me. Next is Lord Cernnunos. I thank Him for His blessings as well, and then other spiritual beings with whom I have worked and from whom I have learned. Time and pre-coffee focus permitting, I conclude by meditating or doing other spiritual or psychic exercises.

Before eating breakfast I give thanks to All That Is for this world and My Lady for Her abundance and to the spirits of all I consume, plant and animal alike. I usually do the same before my other meals, silently if I am with others. If I am at home or alone, I generally take a small portion of food and put it in a relatively undisturbed area outside, to share with the spirits of the place before sitting down to eat.

Less often, and in the company of others, I celebrate the full moon and sometimes other lunar phases, seeing in them symbols for the great rhythms and powers of life on earth. We call these celebrations 'Esbats'. Eight times a year we gather, often with guests in larger more public places, to celebrate our 'Sabbats'. Four are geared to the solar cycles of solstices and equinoxes, four others to the agricultural cycles typical of northern temperate climates. As with the phases of the moon, we see these cyclical times as symbols for the basic rhythms of embodied existence. As individuals each one of us generally sees ourself, and life as a whole, as immersed within a cycle of birth, growth, decay, death and rebirth.

More irregularly, I ask spirits whom I have encountered for help in conducting physical and psychological healings. I studied with shamans, and one in particular, for many years. In my own way I have sought to act in harmony with their commitment to healing and serving their community. This practice of mine is not Wiccan, for Wiccan healings generally take place through the efforts of the coven as a whole. But it is NeoPagan. Sometimes this work is a big part of my life, sometimes a small one. Usually, but not always, the people I seek to help say they have benefited. I do not charge for this work. My capacity is a gift, and I use it accordingly.

As opportunities arise, I also teach the basics of Pagan ritual and practice. But we do not proselytize, and we do not believe a person need be spiritually impoverished, let alone 'lost', if they do not have the same religion as we do. If they are interested I also help people learn healing practices that work with the spirit world in assisting others.

What I am describing are spiritual practices because through them I seek to bring myself into better relationships with everything around me, physical and spiritual alike, and to better my relationship with the all-encompassing reality that includes and transcends us all. And what is all around us? From a Pagan perspective the world is a vital and living place. Our relationships include not only one another as humans and the most obviously encompassing dimension of reality; they also include a world of Spirit, including spirits of nature and spirits of those who have gone before.

I have described one form of Pagan spirituality, one I have practised for over twenty years. After so many years almost everything I do is influenced, sometimes subtly, sometimes powerfully, by my spiritual involvement – not that I ever perfectly exemplify complete harmony, but I believe I fall less far from that ideal than I once did. On the surface and to some degree in its inner meaning, Pagan practice differs from the spiritual practices of Christians, Buddhists or practitioners of other non-Pagan religions. More superficially it differs from many other Pagan practices because Paganism is overwhelmingly diverse. Yet when examined more closely, differences among Pagans are usually only matters of form and emphasis. In a general way the underlying meaning among these many traditions remains remarkably similar.[8]

Pagan Spirituality

Spirituality is how we relate to the ultimate context of our being. From a Pagan perspective this context has two dimensions. First, this ultimate context is differentiated into many spiritual forces and powers, some manifesting physically and some not. Second, in most Pagan traditions including my own, what exists is seen as encompassed within a great unity. Both these dimensions of Spirit are part of Pagan spirituality, yet they are very different.

At their best, humankind's religions reflect the different ways we, as individuals immersed in our cultures and times, have related to this ultimate context. Our spirituality is what provides the most inclusive and important source of value for us, the source within which all things ultimately find their meaning. Because this context dwarfs us, and vastly exceeds our powers of comprehension, and because we are all creatures of our time and place, it is small wonder we differ in the forms and to some degree the content of our spirituality. No human practice can fully grasp the super-human. Hence the plurality of forms by which Pagans come into relationship with 'all our relations'. This Native American term gives us a key insight into Pagan spirituality: we are members of a community encompassing the More-Than-Human, rather than just-the-human. Further, *all* physical members of this community have a spiritual dimension.

But what do we mean by 'Spirit'?

As constitutive of spirituality, 'Spirit' refers to a dimension of innerness and depth to the world. This dimension is foundational to the world's ultimate nature, and integral to what is of greatest value. By 'ultimate' I mean that which is most complete, most inclusive, the fullest context within which everything else takes its appropriate place. In addition, Spirit is or can be open to us. It is not completely transcendent. There is no huge gap between us.

Someone might ask me, 'Why don't you just use the word "God" to refer to this ultimate context?' In casual speech I sometimes do. But for a book such as this, a book seeking to facilitate clear understanding between different spiritual traditions, the differences between what I mean when using that word and what is commonly associated with the term 'God' are great enough that I have chosen to avoid it. Understanding why takes us a good step further in understanding Pagan spirituality. Even so, I will defer a lengthy discussion of Pagans and God until Chapter 2. For now I simply assert that Pagans do not believe in a single Creator God with an individual personality, and a set of plans for humankind. Many of us, myself included, are monists – we believe there is an ultimate unity and source – but we are not monotheists. Deities have individuality, the One does not.

Reflect back on what I described as my Pagan spiritual practice. Both the ultimate Source of All and our most appropriate relationship to It, *and* our being members of a vast community play a central role in this practice. Christianity in general, and American Protestantism in particular, often focuses on the individual's relationship to God, with all else fundamentally devalued by comparison. This follows logically enough from belief in a universal fall and a need for individual salvation. The communal dimension of life therefore receives lesser status, if it receives any status at all.

For the most part this orientation is not true of Pagan religion. Excepting only certain late-Classical views in which physical existence was thought to be pretty problematic (largely because for so many it was oppressive), Pagan spirituality has honoured Spirit as it manifests throughout the world.[9] Thus, Pagan spirituality emphasizes relating to the sacredness in *all* things. We generally think doing less is disrespectful and even self-centred.

Everything is permeated by Spirit because no fundamental distinction exists between the world of Spirit and the mundane world. This common distinction lies instead with what *we* bring to our experience. It is our own importation.

When we are focused in a narrow, self-regarding way, treating others – humans or otherwise – as means or impediments, or as irrelevant to our ends, we live within the realm of the mundane. Indeed, a good definition of the mundane is that dimension of life concerned with narrowly conceived contexts to the denial of wider ones. We can eat, wash, make love, and work in either a mundane or a spiritual way. The same holds true for what are on the surface our spiritual devotions. It all depends on our mindfulness of the context of our actions.

Spirituality decentres the self as my locus of value in the world. If my religion makes me feel more important, better than or superior to others, to that extent my self has *not* been decentred. My world still revolves around me in the narrow sense of that term. And while I may be devoutly religious, like the Pharisee who prayed 'God, I thank Thee that I am not like other men – extortionists, unjust, adulterers, or even as this tax collector', Jesus taught that 'everyone who exalts himself will be humbled, and he who humbles himself will be exalted' (Luke 18:10–14). Jesus' teachings here are in harmony with many Pagan traditions which emphasize that humility is one of the most appropriate human attitudes.

Self-centredness is a deep immersion within the mundane. As the context of our involvement widens and deepens, we encompass more of Spirit, and as we do, our perception of intrinsic value also widens and deepens. Spiritual growth is characterized by the mundane playing a diminishing role in our lives, and a growing attention to the Sacred, the most encompassing context of all.

We can accomplish this goal in two ways, only one of which I will explore explicitly. First, we can ever more deeply explore the spiritual reality focused on by our own spiritual path. I hope what I write in this volume will help Pagans and Christians (and anyone else reading these words) appreciate the spiritual depths possible within Pagan practice. The second, which I will not discuss much, but which this book in its entirety exemplifies, is appreciating the many faces of Spirit, for that which is more than any of us can possibly encompass shines out to us in a multitude of ways. At one time the first sufficed for almost everyone. But in today's pluralistic world this second has become increasingly important as well.

Practising Spirituality

In so far as we seek more clearly and completely to embody and live values that expand our sphere of care and concern, we can be said to be acting spiritually. We *incorporate* the mundane into the spiritual rather than rejecting it as an impediment. Here I believe is an important point: spirituality refers to how we relate to the Sacred as it manifests in *our* world, but not to the totality of the Sacred itself. That remains beyond our understanding. We are a part of this totality and so can never get outside it to observe it. Correctly perceived, Spirit is everywhere. We, however, are not.

Given that we *cannot* put the full experience of Spirit adequately into words, all formal theological systems are suspect when their tenets go much beyond acting as a finger pointing to the moon. The finger is not the moon, but when properly attended, it directs our gaze there. It is illuminated by the moonlight towards which it points. If we become engrossed in looking at the finger, studying the whorls on the surface of the skin, the shape of its knuckles and the condition of the nail, we can get so caught up in ever more subtle and accurate descriptions of that which is pointing that we never see the moon. Fingers can be beautiful, but we need to keep them in perspective. In the absence of moonlight we can neither see nor appreciate their beauty. The same holds true for theological systems, which are intellectual and institutional fingers pointing towards the Sacred.

From this perspective our actions and their motivations are of greater importance than our particular theology. There are many pointing fingers. Spirit is everywhere, and because each finger starts from a particular vantage, it is confusing to try to deduce the nature of the Sacred simply by studying a variety of fingers.

These considerations explain why most, though certainly not all, Pagans emphasize a common practice over common doctrine. This Pagan perspective is also even present in the Bible (Luke 10:25–37; Matthew 25:31–45) but historically in Abrahamic contexts it has taken a back seat to doctrinal interpretation and concern with orthodoxy. Pagan religions tend in the other direction.

Spirituality and the Spirit World

There is another dimension to spirituality as practised by Pagans, one that is far less likely to be read sympathetically by my Christian readers. My first discussion of Pagan spirituality linked it with similar beliefs within many other spiritual traditions, including the mystical traditions in Christianity, Islam and Judaism. But obviously there are many differences between these religions' concrete spiritual practices and Paganism. I can love the writings of Meister Eckhart, St Francis or Rumi, but my world of spiritual practice is very different from theirs, for its roots carry us back not to Palestine several thousand years ago, but back tens, maybe hundreds of thousands of years, to the dawn of humanity. People then lived in a world they found animated by various powers with whom they could relate.[10] As a rule, contemporary Christianity either denies their existence, or considers them 'fallen'. We know they exist and do not consider them fallen.

There is no evidence that at one time Pagans or their forebears worshipped a single deity and, afterwards, fell into spiritual confusion, worshipping many lesser beings. Many of the arguments that at their core either traditional Native American or Chinese religion had a concept of a single God are based on mistranslations.[11] With the coming of literacy and opportunities for deeper study and practice, some Pagan philosophers acknowledged a unitive or monist Source, but this Source is not a personality. The Roman NeoPlatonist Plotinus called this Source the One; British Traditional Wiccans such as myself label It the Dryghton. But, and this point is important, while the One does not Itself have a personality, each personality is contained and cherished within it. In my experience, it is not impersonal.

Spirits

Pagan spirituality as well as its religious practices *focuses* on relating to the spiritual as it manifests through concrete forces and beings within the world. We view, and many of us experience, the world as enspirited, that is, that spirits, forces and 'energies' exist within the world independently of us. We experience them as independent entities, with whom we can sometimes enter into relationship. The most generic term for these phenomena is 'spirits'. More than most religious traditions, Pagans deal with the world of Spirit as it manifests in and through spirits. As a rule, the most powerful of these entities are called 'Gods' and Paganism is accordingly polytheistic. I believe Pagan traditions inherited and have further built on an appreciation of these realities, as well as knowledge of how to contact them, from their original roots in shamanic practices.

Many practitioners of the Abrahamic traditions also see our world as inspirited, nor are all these spirits 'bad' or 'fallen'. In *Pagans and Christians* I referred to Rabbi Zalman Schachter's description of angels, suggesting his description was in harmony with a Pagan sensibility.[12] Many years ago I remember reading an account written by a late Roman Pagan to a Christian in which he argued, in essence, 'You call them angels, we call them Gods. Is it really worth fighting over?' I have never been able to find the quotation again, but it accurately describes Pagan Gods not as creators of the universe, but rather as powers and forces with their own independent and conscious reality immersed within a context that is bigger than they are.

The difference is that for the most part we do not see these 'angels' or Gods as occupying levels of authority in some celestial monarchy. They are all manifestations of the One, just as we are. We are never truly alone, not only because we all exist within the One, but also because more or less individuated forms of awareness are everywhere. But spirits, like we ourselves, are also immersed within a context that is greater than they are.

Some of these spirits are apparently akin to our own spirit and energy selves, dimensions of who we are that seemingly can leave our physical body or are not closely attached to it. They are described in reports of astral projection and near death experiences (NDEs). The important point is that other beings in the world also possess these spirit selves. In my own experience this appears true of both animals and plants.

There is also the 'spirit of place' about which I shall say much more in the chapter on Nature. This dimension includes inspirited dimensions of the material world in all its forms. Suffice it to say here that having spirit does not seem necessarily connected to having a biological metabolism, even for physical things such as a mountain, an ocean, earth or fire. I have also experienced these phenomena as entities. For me, they are not simply a theoretical category.

In addition, there appear to be forces existing quite independently of any body. This is also from my own experience. Some seem to be impersonal forces or 'energies'. Others appear individualized. Some I have seen, others I have felt. I suspect there are also many I have neither seen nor felt. Pagan religions worldwide recognize the existence of such forces and regard them as natural parts of existence.

Living in harmony with 'all our relations' is a common theme in most Pagan traditions. *All* our relations are manifestations of Spirit in its most inclusive sense, and therefore *all* merit respect: other animate beings, such as plants and animals, disincarnate spirits, and those of basic material and more subtle forces. It is as appropriate to give thanks to the broccoli as to the meat, and to both as to That from which we and they all came. In a sense, much of Pagan spirituality consists of good manners.

Of course we can and do frequently fall out of harmony, a fall largely attributable to our own ignorance of how to live in proper relationship with the rest of the world. This kind of ignorance is not doctrinal or theological; it is essentially relational and practical. I think this kind of ignorance is the Pagan equivalent of sin. We are always ignorant of important things, and so we will always tend to fall out of harmony, but there are degrees of ignorance and disharmony into which we can fall. From this perspective what Abrahamic traditions term evil constitute the deepest levels of disharmony and ignorance.

Like a member of an orchestra who has lost the beat or of a dance troupe who has confused a step, under conditions of disharmony our task is to regain our place in this world, to re-establish our harmony. Pagan ritual is first and foremost a way to remind us of this all-embracing rhythm, and secondly, a means by which we may again come into better accord with it. I believe this is part of the reason why for us practice counts for more than dogma.

An alternative image for grasping this point is of a gigantic multidimensional tapestry, of which each of us constitutes a thread. We can contribute to the beauty of the overall pattern, or we can fail to do so. If we fail, the pattern will adjust in order ultimately to include our own errors within its beauty, for its pattern is far greater than any strand. But it is better for us and for those around us if we minimize the need for such alterations.

These images of music, dance and art are rough approximations. Even so, I believe they are less misleading than a more detached and abstract description. They incorporate more than our mental understanding, calling on us to experience our bodies and physical senses as a part of the Sacred.

I hope these words give you a sense of Pagan spirituality. For us, or at least for a great many of us, our spirituality refers to our relatedness to and immersion within ultimate contexts. This context is not simple facticity. It is not describable by reference only to surfaces, however beautiful those surfaces may be. There is an innerness to All That Is. Ultimately our universe is, in Martin Buber's sense, a Thou, not an It.[13] All Thous have innerness, and all innerness, even our own, ultimately ends in mystery.

Philip Johnson

I want to thank Gus for presenting a sketch of his spiritual practices, giving us a glimpse into the diversity of Pagan spiritual ways, and for his observations about spirituality. I would like to start with a few glimpses into what I do. Life is ultimately about a continuous pilgrimage of being open to God's presence and love and then being open to others. I cannot hide from God, who is continuously present, and it is futile to pretend that I can make God go away. The closeness and constancy of God, who willingly offers love to me, puts me in a position where I must come to terms with both the One who cares for me and with my responses.

This is a relationship in which God chooses to be close to me and sometimes that is welcome, but at other times I feel very uncomfortable. This has a lot to do both with what God discloses and with me crossing numinous thresholds that require me honestly to face up to who I am. It is one thing to tacitly acknowledge God is the centre of all things and entirely another to live in that reality. I find it is difficult to be theocentric when it is so much easier to be egocentric. Like John the Baptist in the Gospel of John, I must embrace the reality that I must become less self-centred and allow Jesus Christ to be at the centre of my life. The risks involved in this spiritual relationship are reciprocal in that God is being vulnerable while I am often reluctant to do likewise. Can I relinquish control over my life, be vulnerable and open, and trust God in all aspects and circumstances?

My relationship with God involves tangible emotions such as trust and love as well as intangible values, commitments, wisdom and beliefs that take me through all of life's cycles. So my spiritual life involves growth and discovery as well as the relinquishing of dysfunctional attitudes and habits. It is not privatized or confined to a formal celebration once a week in a building. It is much more about being immersed in a way of living that is centred in an intimate relationship with the Spirit of God. It is personal but it also connects with other people and intermediary creatures of the unseen spiritual realm, as well as extending to other sentient life on Earth.

Life has many rollercoaster experiences that test my spiritual mettle and contribute to my formation as a person. In recent months I have experienced repeated episodes of involuntary and interrupted sleep. It is largely triggered by external sounds that wake me up. After a short slumber I am suddenly awake and often it can take a few hours before I drift back into sleep. I do make use of the recommended techniques for re-entering a drowsy state but they are not always effective. A lack of proper sleep over successive evenings is not a space one desires to be in. When these episodes happen I feel dazed and miserable and the only thing that makes any sense is the desperate desire to fall asleep. Things do seem very different in the middle of the night when the house is unlit and the outside darkness is slightly dispersed by the kerbside fluorescent lights. Late night television shows are often mind-numbing but sometimes nudge me into slumber.

When I am awake at these times I am aware that God is present but I admit I am not enthusiastic about late-night praying! However, I have times when my reluctance gives way and I enter into reflection and prayer. I cannot fathom what is happening and have no idea what I may learn from all of this. Perhaps I have to live with some mystery and paradox as I try to recover proper and healthy patterns of sleep. Unlike the biblical characters Joseph, Samuel, Daniel and Paul, my night reveries have not involved prophetic visions or dazzling appearances of God.

This all sounds rather grumpy and is not what I regard as my usual experience. I am generally more inclined to a sunnier outlook seasoned with the comical. The proverbial 'dark night of the soul' is not something that I readily identify with in my life's experiences. So let me briefly describe a more normal routine. Most days begin with a chorus of natural 'alarm clocks'. First there is the rough-throated chirping of a honey-eating bird that feeds off a Grevillea tree outside the bedroom window. This is soon followed by the plaintive meows and deep purrs of our two Manx cats. They often sit on the window-sill waiting for the bird to appear, no doubt contemplating it as breakfast-on-legs (but we never let them catch birds). Then they deliberately part the curtains so that for a moment sunlight is cast across my face. They sit on either side of the pillow purring in my ear. This is their 'wake-up' call for breakfast.

The stirring of the cats always prompts Arwen, our rough collie dog, to begin whimpering. She whimpers to let us know that the cats need to be attended to. It is comforting to know that she is watchful and in her own way makes some communication. Sometimes the cats rub themselves against her long fur to ensure that she persists with her whimpers. That becomes the signal for Nelson, our Border collie dog, to jump onto the bed and roll around on his back.

Neither my wife Ruth nor I begrudge the wake-up call because we love our furry friends. Others probably think of us as a pair of sentimental 'animal-loving nutters' but we don't care how we are regarded. The natural world matters to us greatly because we believe we must act responsibly and compassionately in tending to the animals and plants. So we take our role very seriously, even when the cats and dogs cause us both to lose sleep!

As we prepare their food and our breakfast we hear the noise from the fruit market next door as fresh produce is being unloaded off a truck. I switch on the television for the early news telecasts. Sometimes it is the tail-end of America's NBC, or one of our local networks has just begun its news broadcast. The screen flashes with images of crimes, distant wars, accidents, some shocking natural disaster, the latest inane gossip about celebrities, and the outrageous antics of local and international politicians. I absorb what I can from these filtered morsels of news because I will need time later in the day to probe, reflect and act on those things that matter.

Spiritual Exercises

Now attending to our companion animals might seem like a great distraction from spiritual practices but God loves the animals. So in the kitchen we are all in the presence of the Creator. Of course there comes the time for me to properly focus my attention on God. There are various spiritual exercises that I do alone, and others that I do with my wife, relatives and friends.

When it is not inclement, that early morning flurry sometimes leads me into the backyard to the pebbles, sandy soil, grass, shrubs and trees. I take the time to centre my thoughts and senses to recognize God's presence. I am in the garden listening. I am in what is called a 'thin place' – a transition zone where two different zones converge, like the place where land and sea meet. Here it is the transition from a dwelling into the biosphere. In this 'thin place' the perceived gap between the physical and spiritual can disappear.

The hum of the morning traffic does not intrude on these moments. I am here to express love for God and for others, and to receive love from God. I pray in silence as my thoughts coalesce into a dialogue with God. I am reverential and grateful for the gift of life. I bring into that silent speech the wonder I have for God. After a while I then converse about those I know and love and give thanks for the privilege of our relationships. They have needs for nourishment, healing and wisdom. The injustices and woes of the wider world then come into focus: the needs of the poor, the sick and the refugee are pleaded, followed by the plight of wildlife, agricultural and domesticated animals, and the polluted biosphere. Here I sometimes call to mind the Hebraic Psalms. Some of those Psalms are centred in praise, and others raise complaints about gross injustices. Those Psalms of 'complaint' indicate that it is okay to be mad at God!

Much of my day involves working from home, so I can set aside different times of the day for spiritual devotions. They also happen in the grounds of the college campus where I sometimes teach classes on various spiritual topics. At other times we gather at someone's home or in a park. Then there are occasions when rites are performed in a church building. Beyond these overt and familiar exercises there are other kinds of spiritual activities that my wife and I participate in. For us every facet of life, action and thought involves the Sacred and we are priests acting before God in whatever we do here on Earth. So we are not just being spiritual when we pray or meditate on God's revelation. We see our Jesus-centred spirituality in a wider context where acts and rites of worship encompass everything in life.

I grew up in a Christian family but chose this faith as my own when I was 9 years old. So I have been a pilgrim on a journey for about 38 years. I feel passionate about my spiritual life and am fascinated by the figure of Jesus. Sometimes I feel greatly frustrated by what takes place in Christian institutions, particularly when the character, example and message of Jesus are sidelined. I feel similar annoyances about social and political injustices and once again my outrage is imperfectly inspired by Jesus.

As a young adult my curiosity about faith led me into an informal but extensive time of questioning what I had grown up with. I understood that my spiritual practices and beliefs would have no authenticity to them unless I had the courage to live by them. If this faith was about an integrated way of living then I needed to probe, question and reflect. Although I had a strong intellectual focus on critical matters, it was not to the exclusion of other equally significant aspects of spirituality. For seven years I worked through courses in two degrees covering theology, religious studies, Islamic studies and new religious movements. I was challenged repeatedly by these courses as I had to ask myself about the integrity and practicality of my faith. I also had to examine my attitudes and preconceptions about people of other faiths. All of the challenges I confronted in formal study remain with me today as I seek renewal and growth as a follower of Jesus' way.

Gus has mentioned that there is a modern way of conceptualizing life that divides things into the categories of sacred and secular. Just like Gus I reject it as implausible and reductionist. I find the sacred/secular category an artificial construct that hinders us from seeing and valuing a holistic or integrated way of living.

Spiritual but not Religious

Robert Fuller notes that for many people today the word 'spirituality' seems to be used as an antonym to religion and is captured in the sentiment, 'I am spiritual but not religious.'[14] The contrasts are acute as religion is perceived as formal and institutional, dogmatic, bound up in inflexible rules and codified beliefs, whereas spirituality seems to involve the freedom to explore and experiment, is highly experiential and non-dogmatic, and is frequently expressed in a wide range of human contexts. At a deeper and subtler level spirituality correlates to a way of living and Gus has already drawn our attention to this important point.

There are devout religious practitioners who seem to be incredulous about the wedge that is driven between spirituality and religion. In their understanding how could one be religious and not also be authentically spiritual? In long-established spiritual traditions the place of community and the importance of accountability loom large and these elements can stand in some tension with the modern Western emphasis on the importance of the free individual. When individuals appear to be living according to a spiritual pathway of their own creation, with little evidence that they are forming relationships in a network or community and with no apparent concern for ethical action, then understandably suspicions are aroused that their do-it-yourself religion may be superficial. In popular culture it is easy to pinpoint a few faddish activities and trinkets that purport to be spiritual and understandably these things provoke criticism. I share those sensitivities and here I do not hesitate to include in this category some Christian bookstores that remind me of an emporium rather than a place where I might find an enriching book filled with the wise thoughts and experiences of others.

Of course, one can be inflexibly religious to the point that authentic spirituality shrivels up. Jesus' critical retorts to members of the religious establishment of his day remind us that well-meaning religious people can lose the plot.[15] What Jesus said still has great application for our time. It would not hurt if some Christians could realize just how close they come at times to resembling Jesus' opponents!

There is a great danger on the part of devout religious people of mischaracterizing the genuine yearnings of those who are looking for meaning and personal renewal. I believe that one should listen first to what people are saying about themselves and their experiences and how they relate all of this to being spiritual. It is only by listening first and then carefully reflecting that we can minimize rash and unfair judgments. The fact that people are looking for spiritual renewal and perhaps do not include our spiritual communities on their list of places to investigate might say more about us than it does about the seekers!

We are living in a period of rapid cultural change when the inherited fabric of Western understandings about life and the cosmos no longer makes sense to most people. People are disenchanted with the institutions, beliefs and patterns for living that have come down to us in modern times. There is acute critical sensitivity about unhelpful dualistic views that divide matter from spirit, humans from nature, males from females and Westerners from other cultures. This ethos undervalues our capacity for a 'feeling intellect' that includes the intuitive, the relational and the numinous.

There is a plethora of academic and pop texts describing, classifying and analysing the contours of this cultural change. Although many of these texts contain interesting insights that excite academics, such as what is globalization, consumer culture, postmodernity, Generations X and Y, re-enchanting the world and so forth, I think that these abstract matters are of little immediate concern to most people. So I do not propose to discuss in any detail the various facets of today's broad new spiritualities since other capable writers have already undertaken that descriptive and analytic task.[16]

The main point is that there is much serious questioning of the institutions, beliefs and lifestyles that characterized the modern era. Many people do not merely feel disenchanted with various aspects of contemporary life but they also feel stirred into pursuing a deeply personal quest for meaning and belonging. The starting points for this quest are quite broad and the spectrum of ideas is diverse, but the words 'spiritual' and 'spirituality' are strongly connected to them. What many people see as an integral part of spirituality encompasses the everyday practical things of life found in both their personal and professional pursuits: health, education, work, recreation, decision-making and relationships. For some this ardent quest has a lot to do with using spiritual disciplines that give a strong sense of identity, values, wisdom and empowerment to live. For others it is focused on exploring and embracing mystery, myth and mystical experiences as an integral part of life's journey. In still other instances it entails a rediscovery of traditional faith, and there are those who reassert the traditional but do so in volatile, confrontational and reactionary ways. Everyone faces the challenge of coming to terms with different aspects of cultural change, particularly when elements of it surface in those areas of life that matter most. Lots of people intuit that they need to develop a spiritual life in order to cope, to grow and to become the best possible person that they can be.

There is a spectrum of attitudes among Christians about the processes of cultural change that spans from welcoming and critically relishing many aspects of it to seeming quite threatened by it. One common thread that ties the spectrum of attitudes together seems to be that of discernment, but even this entails different emphases. I won't dwell too much on these matters in this chapter but I will summarize two kinds of discernment-based responses.

Those Christians who are enthusiastic about cultural change identify with their non-Christian peers about the shortcomings of the modern era. They also discern that some aspects of modern church life mirror many of the defects of the modern era: dualist thinking; consumerism; excessive reliance on cognition at the expense of mystery, imagination and intuition; abstract belief and absent *mythos* (i.e. 'story'); beliefs disconnected from personal consistency and integrity; and the production-line of predictability, calculability, control and conformity replicated in church hierarchies and assemblies.[17] How these kinds of Christians are grappling with the implications of that discernment is the subject of much current discussion. Some seem to focus on the possibilities of reinventing church while others think the matter is less complicated than that. The latter feel it is more about recovering from the past some valuable insights and disciplines that will lead to a healthy spiritual renewal.

Other parts of the Christian community emphasize a form of discernment that is concerned with pinpointing spiritual compromises and being alert to things that can cripple authentic spiritual life and belief. Much of the emphasis centres on questions about ethical practice and truthful beliefs and how we might be hindered by things that are at odds with divine revelation. These Christians invite the whole church to reflect on some serious and valid points: Are we prepared to admit that not everything that people call 'spiritual' is necessarily good or life-enhancing? Are we able to identify that which is 'untruth' especially in light of the teachings of Jesus?

Both kinds of discernment have their place and an over-emphasis on one to the exclusion of the other will only produce stunted spiritual outcomes. What I like to point Christians to, using insights from both forms of discernment, are the following questions: Are we willing to admit that we are spiritually stale, in need of renewal and prepared to become agents of change? Are we ethically embodying and expressing spiritual truth that unequivocally refers to the divine revelation in the person, life, actions and teachings of Jesus? Have modern Christians created some bad spiritual debts that have long accrued due to our neglect of truth and our forgetfulness to live truthfully? Can we discern that the processes of cultural change cry out for Christians to repay those accrued spiritual debts? Put another way, are there forgotten truths embedded within the Bible and the Christian tradition that God's Spirit is prompting us to rediscover?

Spirituality as a Technical Word

In Christianity the words 'spirit' and 'spiritual' are very familiar due to their usage in the Bible. There is also an emphasis found in many biblical texts concerning the spiritual person in contrast to those whose priorities in life manifest an absence of spiritual vitality. However, the word 'spirituality' does not appear in the Greek or Hebrew vocabulary of the books of the Bible. The expression 'Christian spirituality' began its life in French Catholic thought and from the nineteenth century onwards found its way into wider usage among Protestants and Eastern Orthodox believers. In each church context spirituality refers to different aspects of the spiritual life as understood in specific traditions.[18] So the word is attached to groups or movements when one speaks about Greek Orthodox, Dominican, Benedictine, Lutheran, Puritan and Evangelical spirituality.[19]

Each church movement has had a set of theological assumptions about the nature and goal of the spiritual life, and each tradition has been worked out in particular historical settings. So to take one quick example, in Medieval European monasteries there was an emphasis on the vision of God and attaining perfection. The spiritual disciplines associated with it (vows, prayers, chants, sacraments, meditations etc.) were geared towards pursuing perfection on the part of those who had dedicated themselves to a monastic order. The assumptions behind that understanding of perfection were very different from those later expressed by Martin Luther in the sixteenth century.

Although the word 'spirituality' has had various lexical and theological meanings in past contexts, today the word is used by some Christians in ways that lack precise definition or even clear points of reference. Some Christians who contemplate reinventing the church today like to cherry-pick bits and pieces from Medieval practices.

While this cherry-picking produces some interesting outcomes, a few do so without any deep awareness of the theological assumptions and historical circumstances undergirding these practices. However, those oversights on the part of a few do not prevent us from gaining a clear, healthy understanding about the vital and practical elements that make up Christian spirituality in today's world.

Christian Spirituality

God is at the centre of Christian spirituality. All things on Earth belong in a unified and harmonious web of interdependent relationships with each other and most importantly in relationship with God. Christian spirituality is theocentric. As I will discuss in later chapters, all Christians are meant to be agents of blessing to other people and to the whole biosphere. So our spirituality is expressed in all facets of life as a liturgy before God and on behalf of others.

Christians place much emphasis on worship but the sacral ceremonies that are celebrated in church buildings do not constitute the sum total of a Christian's spiritual life. Christian spirituality is very much concerned with an integrated way of living that is expressed in emotional, physical, intellectual, ethical and relational ways. If you wish, worship is about choosing a theocentric lifestyle. In the modern era much emphasis has been placed on various intellectual and cognitive elements of Christianity. The impulses of today's cultural change suggest that Western Christians have over-emphasized these cognitive aspects. That imbalance is not in keeping with the gospel's affirmation that we are to love God with all our heart, mind, soul and strength, and also to love our neighbours.[20]

A major forgotten truth is that all the business of life is encompassed by spirituality. People from biblical times would be puzzled by our modern sacred/secular divide. Many biblical stories relate how individuals and families both enjoyed their spirituality and also grappled with spiritual struggles in their everyday affairs. One Christian catechism reminds us that our chief priority is to *both* worship *and* enjoy God. It is easily forgotten that the enjoyment of life is celebrated in the wisdom books of the Bible.[21] There are aphorisms, poems and practical observations about love, food, wine, sex, friendship, work, possessions, beauty, pleasure and happiness. All of these things are clearly included under the canopy of spirituality. In his many letters Paul the apostle wrote a lot about the practicalities of life: family relationships, resolving conflict, dealing with responsibilities and disappointments, illness, food, sex, and attitudes to work and rest. The spiritual person whose life is anchored in God is one who is also concerned with the ordinary things of life.

The gospels indicate that Jesus sanctified the ordinary everyday things of life. When Jesus spoke of the kingdom of God he saw this as the ultimate reality breaking into the everyday things of life: family relationships, friendship, relating to neighbours, helping the needy, paying taxes and so on. Jesus also made the connection between spiritual meaning and purpose in all kinds of life settings including wedding parties, banquets, festivals, children's playtimes, funerals and fishing. Christian spirituality is energized by God's Spirit who empowers us to live in the everyday world. At the heart of this is the prospect of finding personal renewal and exploring who we might become in partnership with God.

God is understood to be both transcendent and immanent, which is a paradox that we cannot fathom. What we come to understand, however, is that God is not identical with the cosmos (hence transcendent), but also that God is not a remote being who is uninvolved in the Earth (hence immanent). God's immanent presence is found everywhere, which is something that is made clear from the opening pages of the Bible. As God's presence is everywhere, one can encounter God anywhere, anytime. This has amazing ramifications for Christian spiritual disciplines of prayer, guidance and meditation: they can operate in a forest, in a garden, on the beach, at sea, inside a house, at the work station, or even on a space shuttle.

Christians maintain that some elements of God's nature are knowable, while other elements are unknowable, and in Christian spirituality there is much room for cognition, mystery and paradox being held in tension and balance. This is very apparent from the Bible verse that says 'beyond all question, the mystery of godliness is great'.[22] God is a personal being with three centres of personhood expressed in what Christians refer to as the Trinity. The relationships between these three centres of personhood indicate that loving social-communal relationships abound within the mystery of God's being. As the next chapter is specifically concerned with talking about God, I will not go into any more detail here. The basic point to note is that Christian spirituality is theocentric, and Christian spiritual practice is empowered by God's Spirit birthing in us the power to live and be renewed.

Christian spirituality is also open to experiencing the extraordinary invisible spiritual realm and encountering intermediary spirit beings. Quite a few biblical episodes describe how various people are enchanted by what they feel, see and hear in an unseen realm. Individuals experience altered states of consciousness in visions, dreams and what seem to be out-of-body activities. They encounter extraordinary beings, witness strange and stupefying events, and speak in symbolic and mystical terms about messages that they received. Each one who undergoes these other-worldly experiences is powerfully transformed and returns to our mundane realm with completely new attitudes about life. Some obvious examples include women such as Hagar, and men such as Joseph, Isaiah, Ezekiel and Daniel. These people had night-visions and dreams, or encountered angelic creatures, and received oracles about events or words of comfort and strength.[23]

Other remarkable experiences of the numinous are seen in Moses' encounter at the burning bush, Ezekiel's mysterious journey between Earth and heaven, Philip the evangelist's mystical transport from Gaza to Azotus, Paul's 'third heaven' experience, and John's visions on Patmos.[24] One sage aspect of the biblical texts that report these remarkable experiences is the prompt they give the reader to discern what is valuable and truthful, and to be alert to what will harm and divert us from connecting with God. Sometimes today's Christians need reminding that what happened in biblical times can also happen today. While I cannot include myself in the exalted company of the biblical characters, I can attest to angelic encounters in my own life.[25]

Christian spirituality is a two-sided coin. One side consists of beliefs while the other side consists of experiences. When one side of the coin outweighs the other then Christians can easily lose touch with an integrated, balanced and holistic spiritual life. A spirituality that consists only of cognitive beliefs and no experience is arid and dysfunctional. Similarly, a spirituality consisting of a cluster of subjective experiences that remain unreflected on will merely produce spiritual candyfloss.

For Christians the experience of God is centred in following Jesus and this requires that all things are expressed relationally and in a safe community. The need for ethical accountability looms large in the tapestry that makes up the spiritual life. In that framework we can explore who we are and who we might become in partnership with God and in relationship with other pilgrims. Our reflections and experiences need that point of connection to guard against drifting into a harmful and unbalanced spiritual life. Also, by constantly referring our experiences and beliefs back to the teachings of Jesus, the apostles and prophets, we have another form of accountability and a way of checking that we are not going off-track spiritually. One other resource we can fruitfully draw on is the accumulated wisdom of the Christian community down the centuries. A proper and healthy Christian spirituality consists of *both* beliefs *and* experiences that are theocentric and that are integrated into the very fabric of our daily life.

CHAPTER 2
The Divine

Gus diZerega

Before proceeding more deeply into Pagan conceptions of divinity, I want to criticize the common image of the supreme Source of everything as a personality – not to rebut monotheistic religion as a valid spiritual path, but to suggest that the most common ways of conceiving its deity make little sense, spiritually, logically or empirically. I believe there is a core insight of great value in the monotheistic intuition, but it has been lost by many who claim today to be monotheists. Ironically, many Pagans, myself included, will argue that the normal conception of God in our society is not monistic enough!

In the United States 'God' frequently refers to a completely transcendent being, separate from the Earth and everything within it. Due to some primordial or perhaps always occurring lapse, in a vital way we are alienated from God, living in a world cut off from the sacred. From this perspective we, and often everything around us, are *radically* separated from God, hence our need for salvation from without. This concept of 'God' implies the existence of that which is *not* God.

Most popular Christian characterizations of God also describe him as having a personality and gender. He is able to be pleased, patient, annoyed, angered and jealous. He tests people to ascertain their sincerity and the depth of their faith, and so on. His is supposed to be a perfect personality: perfectly just, perfectly jealous, perfectly angry, perfectly loving, and so on.

From a Pagan perspective this popular conception describes *a* God. As a description of what is spiritually most inclusive and fundamental it seems truncated and incomplete. For example, any personality is unavoidably partial. Particular personality traits can exist to varying degrees, and if we consider the personalities around us, it is hard to grasp what we might mean in describing a 'perfect' personality before which all others pale. What we call a 'personality' only carries meaning because it exists in the context of other personalities distinct from it. How, for example, can anything be jealous without there being at least one other entity?

In addition, for the term 'male' to make sense, 'female' must be implied. Gendered words only make sense in relation to one another. We cannot call an amoeba 'male' or 'female'. It is sexless, and reproduces from division. An organism either is self-contained, like an amoeba, or its gender implies the existence of at least one other gender. Some organisms have more than two. A paramecium has eight.

This same point holds if we say instead that the term 'male' refers to certain psychological rather than physical characteristics that we associate with maleness rather than those we associate with femaleness. This alternative either takes us back to gender, confronting the problem I described above, or it creates a duality in which only one side of two traits is 'perfect' but the 'perfect' male characteristics necessarily imply other imperfect 'female' characteristics.

Is 'mothering' a sign of imperfection such that a perfect being does not ever 'mother'? And how can a perfect being who lacks the feminine trait of mothering depend on others with that trait for his creation to exist? It means that the creation was initially and necessarily imperfect: a strange limitation on a supposedly omnipotent being. In fact there is plenty of feminine imagery of God in the Bible, suggesting to me that even within the Bible a purely male image of the supreme source is inadequate to its task.[1]

The biblical God can be viewed in ultimately non-gendered terms, but historically and popularly God is not so viewed. My target here is not the perceptive understanding of some, but the unreflective understanding of many, ministers included, who would substitute a part for the whole. Doing so gets in the way of their grasping what we as Pagans often believe.

Pantheism and Panentheism

The conception of Highest that fits much Pagan belief, and my own experience, includes *all* characteristics. *Everything* is a part of what is Highest. It is therefore misleading to use *any* limiting term to describe the Ultimate, and God as a 'personality' seems a limiting term. For many of us, squeezing the Source of All into the image of a human being is the opposite of humility.

From a Pagan perspective, what is most inclusive cannot be adequately encompassed by what is popularly meant by the term 'God', because this term usually excludes the natural world. For some people, this claim raises the question whether Pagans are pantheists: that divinity is equated with Nature. The question is ultimately unanswerable because we have no clear agreement on what 'pan' (all) refers to in 'pantheism'. If it means that we worship the physical world, few who call themselves Pagans are pantheists.

But if the term 'pantheist' includes honouring a sense of deep unity and awareness within the surface multiplicity of Nature, while *focusing* our spiritual attention on spiritual multiplicity rather than its inner unity, the term would fit many of us – myself included. In practice, the term 'panentheism' better avoids confusion because it implies that the Sacred is both immanent in the physical world and also in some sense transcendent to it. 'Panentheism' preserves divine immanence while protecting against reductionism and recognizing transcendence. While the term is encountered in liberal Christian theology, panentheism has roots back to NeoPlatonism, and perhaps even earlier to Heraclitus.[2]

The Mystical Experience

Throughout the written history of human spirituality, people have described what is commonly called the mystical experience. Those who report having had this experience describe it as revealing to them – indeed as immersing them within and as part of – the ultimate ground of all being. In its most complete sense the person reports that their sense of self disappears into what has no distinctions.

Classical Pagans and Christians, Hindus and Buddhists, Muslims and Jews, and others have all reported such experiences.[3] They also universally report that theirs is an experience of perfection in which even what we usually and reasonably term evil is located within a redemptive context. This experience is obviously transitory, or no one would ever emerge to try to describe it.

The most complete form of this experience includes the sense that the individual ego disappears. In less complete experiences, such as has happened to me, the sense of self to some degree remains, but its boundaries become indistinct. I and everything else are part of something that transcends us all, and in which we find ultimate value. *These descriptions suggest there is both unity and diversity within the very structure of existence as human beings experience it.* When some people go beyond this they describe a complete but temporary annihilation of their self, entering into a state without differentiation, a divine 'Nothingness'. These kinds of broad descriptions appear to be cross-cultural. But for people *as human beings* these experiences always illuminate both differentiation and unity.

There is no contradiction at all between this kind of unitive mysticism and polytheism. In fact, it is a dominant element of philosophy in Pagan civilizations. Not only is it a fundamental dimension of Classical Pagan NeoPlatonism, it is also recognized as Brahma in Hindu thought and practice, in Chinese Daoism, and in many other contexts. Eastern Orthodox Christianity also recognizes this dimension of the Highest. However, in the Catholic and Protestant West it has played a lesser role, and has often been questioned for its undermining of the tenet that a vast gulf separates God from us.[4]

On the other hand, particular descriptions of this experience often differ in their details, leading to an argument among theologians and philosophers about whether the mystical experience offers an unmediated encounter with the Ground of All, or whether the historical, cultural and psychological factors that shape our minds and understanding always filter and interpret the experience, so that we never have a direct encounter with the Highest.[5] I sympathize with both perspectives. In my own case, insofar as my experience was pre-theoretical, and I was simply immersed within it, my interpretative filters and mental filing cabinets appeared to me to have been swept away, although some sense of myself as observer remained. But, when I began to think about my experience, even while within its midst, I began standing back, separating myself, observing and interpreting what was happening. In so doing I could not help but use my cultural context to try to grasp what was happening.[6]

A universal point made by those reporting mystical experiences is that language cannot do them justice. Certainly that was the case with me. This caution is not taken seriously enough by those who have not experienced such events in their lives. People reporting personal encounters with All That Is to those in their own place and time believe they cannot really communicate what happened. Words are merely pointers to what is beyond words. How much more must this be true for us when reading people who wrote from within very different cultures from ours? To lay so much weight on differences in verbal descriptions is risky. I think many of the differences in detail among reports arise from this second stage of the experience, when we begin 'trying to understand' what happened.

Regardless of whether our personal encounter with the Most Fundamental is socially, historically and psychologically mediated or not, as soon as we begin describing it to others, we must rely on our language, culture and personal knowledge to describe our experience.

It is hardly surprising that we do not get universal agreement. On the other hand, we do get a great deal of verbal overlap. Themes of perfect love, peace and compassion, and the redemption of everything, repeatedly show themselves.

People who did not have these experiences have these reports mediated to them twice, first by the person who had the experience and second by the cultural, linguistic and historical context that influences which words that person picks to describe his or her experience to us. Yet even so, these basic themes of love, redemption, perfection, peace and compassion appear and reappear.

Monism and Monotheism

If their practice is traditional, every English Traditional coven at one point or other in their gathering makes use of the following blessing:

In the name of Dryghton,
the ancient providence,
which was from the beginning,
and is for eternity,
male and female,
the original source of all things;
all-knowing, all-pervading, all-powerful, changeless, eternal.
In the name of the Lady of the Moon,
and the Lord of Death and Resurrection;
in the name of the Mighty Ones of the Four Quarters,
the Kings of the Elements,
bless this place, and this time and they who are with us.

This blessing succinctly recapitulates the basic principles of late Classical NeoPlatonism whose primary philosopher, Plotinus, contributed so much to the development of Christian theology.[7] To borrow from Don Frew's discussion of this issue, the Dryghton is the monistic One. The Goddess and the God are from the dimension of mind, and are eternal. The Mighty Ones are the daimons, from the realm of soul, and are ultimately temporal. The elemental kings are from the realm of matter, and are also temporal.[8]

Historically, Pagan philosophy has tended to be monist. This observation also holds true of Pagan thought in its Hindu and Chinese forms. When we get to tribal forms of Pagan spirituality, in which no community of thinkers has arisen to investigate and develop insights had by different people, the evidence is less clear, as we would expect. But certainly as it has developed historically, Pagan conceptions of the Divine in its ultimate form have been monist, but not monotheistic.

Making Sense of Polytheism

What, then, is polytheism? What does it mean to believe in a multiplicity of deities? Some Pagans argue their deities are the same or nearly so as other Pagan deities under a different name. This is an old Pagan view, going at least as far back as Apuleius' claims about Isis in *The Golden Ass*.[9] But a great deal rests on what we mean by 'same'. Careful scrutiny shows that one Pagan pantheon does not translate without remainder into another. Deities within one culture are often different from those within another, and it is difficult or impossible to argue that they are simply the same entities with different names.

For example, the Orixas (Orishas) of Brazilian Candomble and Cuban Santeria in many ways resemble the Greek and Roman Gods. In all these cases, stories and myths abound of their sometimes not so harmonious relations with one another, along with other similarities. To take a good example, in Candomble and Santeria Oxum (Oshun) is the Orixa of feminine beauty and sexuality and in many ways seems remarkably close to the Roman Goddess Venus and the Greek Goddess Aphrodite. Venus was sexually connected to Mars, as Aphrodite was to Ares. But the Orixas are *not* the Greek or Roman deities in different cultural garb. While a God of war, Mars was also a God of spring and other more pacific qualities. Ares was more narrowly associated with battle. Oxum is not as strongly connected to Ogum, the Orixa of war and iron work, and while Oxum is associated with fresh flowing water, Aphrodite is connected with the sea.

In addition, the powers and attributes of Pagan deities change over time. Hekate was once a relatively minor Goddess in the Greek and Roman world, although important in Thrace. Over time Her powers grew until She was recognized as the Goddess of philosophy and Witchcraft, among other things. Even so, in different places Her powers are described differently.[10]

In short, there is no unambiguous correspondence from one deity to another, or even in the relations between major divine qualities, or a deity's power and characteristics over time. Some Wiccans argue that the female Orixas or Classical Venus and Aphrodite are aspects of our Goddess, and the male deities are aspects of our God. But this effort simply returns us to Apuleius' problem regarding Isis. We can safely presume that many a Classical devotee of Hekate would not consider Her an aspect of Isis. This effort at categorization would also not impress followers of Santeria or Candomble.

Yet in some sense Isis does refer to more than the personal Goddess to whom Apuleius was devoted. She, like the Wiccan Goddess as I have experienced Her, was also considered the Goddess of Nature. And there have been many other ways of acknowledging the power and reality of the Earth as feminine, from Europe, China and the Americas.

This divine variety has convinced many secularists that all deities are simply cultural constructs, none with any reality beyond their followers' imaginations. Radical secularists apply this argument to the Christian deity as well as to the others. At first glance this secularist debunking seems well taken. But, and here is the rub, it only makes sense to people who have never *experienced* the actual presence of a deity. Encountering a deity changes a life. It certainly did mine.

Many Pagan traditions, including Traditional Wicca, are *based* on personal encounters with their deities. In what we term 'drawing down the moon', the Goddess can and often does enter into the body of the High Priestess. Less often, the God is drawn down into the body of the High Priest. Sometimes they enter into an onlooker. At other times they manifest to participants as powerful presences. That is what happened to me.

In my own experience the Goddess is far more than a poetic metaphor or a cultural construct. She is quite real, beautifully and wonderfully so. She is also quite individual. To refer to another deity whom I have encountered, She is not the Celtic Goddess Brhide. As I have sometimes encountered these deities, they partake of a reality that I experience as 'more real' than my day-to-day world. I am not sure how to describe this beyond saying that the world 'presents' itself to me in my day-to-day awareness, and in these experiences the 'presentation' is far stronger.

All committed secularists can do is impute something pathological or irrational to such experiences. Because they have not had our experiences, they assume there is something wrong with us. Ironically Socrates, the person who initiated the West's 2,500-year exploration of rationality, repeatedly spoke of his reliance upon a deity or spirit to warn him of errors as he led his life. Indeed, this entity is responsible for his becoming Athens' 'gadfly' with its transformative impact on the West.[11] To many Pagans Socrates' example does not appear unfamiliar.

At the same time Pagan deities appear wedded to particular contexts, not in the sense that they do not cross over into other traditions (some do), but that we do not often (if ever) see the same deity independently discovered/encountered in very different cultures unless in the most general terms, such as Mother Earth.

How might we make sense of this?

Images of Divinity: Transcendence within Immanence

This divine variety and complexity is enough to drive to distraction anyone who loves everything to be neatly categorized in its place. This is especially the case if they think of divinity in terms of a political hierarchy with God as king, a kind of heavenly bureaucracy.

There is another way of viewing the Gods.

I want to suggest a way of understanding that honours the experiences of people in the midst of their different spiritual practices, recognizes the reality of the Sacred, and appreciates that we live within a universe that is most appropriately conceived of in terms of Thou rather than It. And at the same time this is a perspective that honours modern science, not in the sense that it claims to be scientific, but that it involves no leaps of faith to deny what science has found to be reliable knowledge.

I do not argue my proposed explanation is the Absolute Truth. We are, after all, discussing the super-human. My suggestion relies on an apparent similarity between different phenomena to shed light from one to the other. I believe it captures a part of the truth better than any other model I have encountered, and relies on concepts that are proving themselves increasingly important in the sciences – concepts that change what we mean by the term 'hierarchy'. But the super-human is, by definition and experience, beyond the power of the merely human to grasp. I simply offer one more finger pointing at the moon.

When considered as a whole, Pagan religions *decentre* spiritual reality, rather like spirituality decentres the self. *There are many religions and no point at which they all converge*. This is because the One is everywhere. So spiritual reality is not hierarchical in the most taken-for-granted sense of the term.

What conceptions might fit such a pluralistic spiritual reality? Like those before us, we are thrown back on our experience and the metaphors available to us to try to make it sensible to others who have not had such experiences. But unlike the peoples of several thousand years ago, when the defining metaphors for most contemporary religions were developed, we live in a world without many kings or strict and unquestioned status hierarchies. Not only that, we are also aware of the serious abuses so often committed by those claiming superior status.

We moderns also have a sense of what might be termed *distributed authority* as an alternative to hierarchy. In modern democracies, to a substantial if still limited degree the people as a whole are the ultimate political power, but 'the people' are distributed throughout society. Other modern institutions such as the market economy, science, language and the World Wide Web also develop impressive structure and differentiation without any single authority needing to be in charge. These processes shape and order themselves 'spontaneously' in the sense that the ultimate pattern that emerges is unplanned. Science, the market economy and much else now demonstrate to us that impressive order can arise in the absence of a central authority or directing hand.[12]

The argument that follows relies on the modern metaphor of a net or web, but interestingly this modern metaphor echoes the ancient Hindu one of Indra's net, in which every jewel within it mirrors all the others. Often this image is taken to point to the nondual character of ultimate reality, for everything is mirrored in everything else. Without in any sense denying this aspect of the metaphor, I want instead to focus on the jewels themselves. Each jewel reflects the whole, *and is an individual expression as well*. Each reflects from a *different* place within the net.

If we grant with many mystics, as I do, that love and compassion are among the most basic elements of the Divine, at least as soon as we are able to describe it, only by manifesting in wondrous individuality can the maximum opportunities for practising and exploring love and compassion be attained. Love cherishes particularity. Divine love cherishes all particularity. The more the particularity, the richer the field of love. Transcendence exists in and through immanence; indeed it must, to manifest what is fundamental to it within the world of matter. In the final analysis transcendence and immanence cannot be clearly separated. To perceive transcendence one must already be separate from it: in other words, one must be an immanent expression of that which when viewed from afar appears as transcendence. Transcendence versus immanence is a false dichotomy.

Deities might be thought of as the most important nodes in that maxi-dimensional divine web. From this perspective divine or human individuality is a focal point of multiple relationships. The richer the relationships, the richer and more multifaceted the individuality. Deities can therefore partake of many of the same qualities within one another, and be involved in many of the same relationships, and still be distinct. The same is true for us, but less so.

As this web is aware, alive and made up of us all, deities themselves are not static. They can reach out to us, as we can reach out to them, and in the connection perhaps both are changed. Individuality is genuine, but partial. Oxum and Venus and Aphrodite share elements of this web, and so are connected; and they also each partake of different elements, and so are individual.

This may appear very fuzzy headed, but a central teaching of Jesus makes a similar point. As is related in Matthew 25 verses 31–45:

> *When the Son of Man comes in his glory, and… all the nations will be gathered before him, and he will separate people one from another as a shepherd separates the sheep from the goats… the king will say to those at his right hand, 'Come, you that are blessed by my Father, inherit the kingdom prepared for you from the foundation of the world; for I was hungry and you gave me food, I was thirsty and you gave me something to drink, I was a stranger and you welcomed me, I was naked and you gave me clothing, I was sick and you took care of me, I was in prison and you visited me.' Then the righteous will answer him, 'Lord, when was it that we saw you hungry and gave you food…' the king will answer them, 'Truly I tell you, just as you did it to one of the least of my brethren, you did it to me.' … [And to those he rejects for not acting in this manner] 'Truly I tell you, just as you did not do it to one of the least of these, you did not do it to me.'*

I know of no reasonable way of interpreting this passage that does not recognize that Jesus, or some vital dimension of Jesus, is immanent in everyone. Yet there is no suggestion that those who hunger or thirst or are alone or ill or in prison are not also individuals. If from a Christian perspective this is true for relationships between human beings and the Son of God, my Pagan interpretation of polytheism is hardly a stretch. The divine king metaphor is as obsolete in matters of theology as it is in matters of politics. Whatever clarity it once had has been irrevocably muddied by the passage of time and human abuses of authority.

Our world brings forth extraordinary variety, creativity, and beauty, each in its own way a manifestation of the Sacred. Different peoples have lived within this abundance, and in their spiritual practices each has tailored their conception of the Divine from out of their encounter with the Sacred within their time and place. And Spirit responds. Because the Sacred is literally everywhere, there is no place from which we begin that cannot lead us to the Divine. No place.

Darkness and Shadow: the Problem of Evil

Any discussion of the Divine inevitably confronts the problem of evil. But how we think about evil reflects how we think about the Divine. For example, if the world is a divinely created artefact, and the artificer is omnipotent, omniscient and good, evil can only exist for one of two reasons. First, it is a necessary contributor to a greater good, and so ultimately is not evil. Second, there was a rebellion or fall from accord with this creation, although the Creator might still be able to bring about a greater good as a result. Western monotheisms in general come down heavily on the second option.

Pagans reject this view. How then might we treat the issue? If the ultimate reality is good, why is there so much suffering? Especially, why is there so much apparently unwarranted suffering? If everything is an expression of the Sacred, how come we have smallpox, war, serial killers, tapeworms, sociopaths, tsunamis, rape, earthquakes and so very much more?

Throughout the history of Pagan spirituality a number of interpretations of this most basic of problems have been tried. Some NeoPlatonists conceived of the One as perfect, and as its 'emanations' spread further from their source the proportion of perfection was reduced, enabling error and suffering to manifest. Some suggest that reincarnation enables us to explain why bad things happen to apparently good people. Others suggest that ultimately evil is illusory, and that misfortunes often turn out to have been benefits, once they have been thoroughly digested. Regarding these and similar explanations, I have two observations. First, they make at least as much sense to me (and usually much more sense) than arguments that there was a primordial rebellion, with the rebel afterwards seeking to undo the goodness of the original creation. Second, I have never encountered an argument that clearly stands out as superior against all other possibilities. We are each of us immersed within a world far more vast and great than we are, and our knowledge of it is comparatively tiny. Any explanation of evil should be tendered with humility and tentativeness.

Nevertheless, we must confront it, because it is such an obvious part of daily life. I discussed this issue at some length in *Pagans and Christians*, and here I will give only some highlights of my argument.[13] So far I have encountered no reason to change it.

First, evil must be disaggregated. Sometimes there seems to be an attitude that holds that any misfortune is a sign of a deep metaphysical problem or lack. This is childish. A great many people like challenges of various kinds, and I am among them. Challenges would not be genuine if there was no way we could make errors. So I want to distinguish examples of evil from simple misfortune and its attendant suffering.

At a minimum we can separate three kinds of possibilities. First, there is the suffering caused by error and accident, and it can be considerable. The young son of friends of mine drowned while playing near a river. His parents' attention wandered briefly, and he was gone. How can things like this happen in a good world?

Second, death and suffering is caused by natural phenomena, from earthquakes and tsunamis to parasites and disease. These are a part of the world we inhabit, and they cause enormous suffering. How might they be squared with a good world?

Third is genuine malice, a desire to hurt others, or use them cruelly without regard for their own feelings. It can be the hot malice of rage, or the cold malice of the heartless, but in either case how can it exist if the foundation of everything is love and compassion?

With respect to the suffering caused by error and accident, I think my earlier remarks concerning challenges cover most cases. But I want to add something more. For various reasons we are not a particularly loving or wise species. We have enormous potential, but even with respect to something so obviously wrong to us today as slavery, it took thousands of years for most to acknowledge it as wrong. Aristotle, one of the most insightful people in Western history, defended slavery. He did so because even then it had its critics, though their words have not survived.[14] It took another 2,200 years, and the invention of machinery, for those critics to prevail. Too often we allow pride and love of power to override care and compassion.

Loss gets through to some people, to crack open their hearts. All too often it takes our own suffering, or the suffering of someone we care about, to open our hearts to the full depth of human experience. That opening can be extremely, shatteringly painful. In retrospect, sometimes it had to be.

But what of the little boy who drowned? What did *he* do to merit such an untimely passing? For me as a Pagan, here is where something that comes closest to what Christians often call 'faith' enters in. I know as much as I know anything that the Source of All is characterized by perfect love. I know for similar reasons that the high Gods are similarly characterized. I also know that they exist, and powerfully exist. Based on my experiences, I simply cannot take seriously that the being who was this little boy has ceased to exist. My 'faith' is based on encounters with the Sacred, not promises in a text. It is more akin to faith in a trusted friend than faith in faith. It is rational because it is based on my own experience.

What then of the second kind of 'evil' – the death and suffering rooted in the natural world? Let us make one point before going further. We will die. Every one of us. This is not a design flaw. Fundamental to Wiccan practice is our honouring and recognizing the ultimate *appropriateness* of the power of death. I would be dishonest if I denied that I fear some of the ways in which I might die. But dying? Of that I have no fear at all. In fact, I'm rather curious about it.

Our Earth and all on it manifest the same divine source as we do. As physical beings we need to take in energy. Apparently this process first started with bacteria. But when one being came to be able to consume another, taking energy from it rather than the sun or the heat of the Earth, life exploded in variety and complexity. Predation and death was the source of this development, for those forms that became more competent at survival flourished. Others did not.

As complexity developed, minds became more differentiated in their awareness, and in time ethical behaviour was possible. Acting with care and compassion became possible in the physical realm. In my understanding, what is happening is a slow expansion and development of divine characteristics into ever new forms of existence. There is no general fall. Instead there is growth and development. My favourite metaphor is that physical bodies are like radio or television sets that, depending on their capacities, can 'tune in' to and manifest greater depths of awareness.

Charles Darwin described how an ethic based on sympathy – on empathetic awareness – was a natural outgrowth of evolutionary development once beings as mentally complex as humans had arisen.[15] Darwin thought that once we truly understood evolution we would expand our ethics to encompass the rest of the world, rather than – as his critics and some who claim to be his followers argue –

that our caricature of the physical world as a heartless place would erode human ethics. I agree with him.

These remarks bring us to the question of malice.

Malice is *always* rooted in error. We tend to be self-centred beings, and when someone does something to injure us, or that has the unintended consequence of injuring us, we often take it personally. We then frequently attribute bad motives to the other. If we give in to our anger or resentment, we lash out to 'get even' or show we cannot be taken advantage of. If we have misunderstood our target's actions (and who among us has not at some point done just this?), he or she may well think of *our* aggressive actions against him or her as unprovoked maliciousness. If they then react in anger or self-defence against us, a vicious spiral can develop in which people who initially had nothing against one another become enemies.

This is just one way of several in which malice can come into existence from sources who themselves are not malicious, just ignorant. And once in existence, malice can feed upon itself. We need no Satan, we can do it all by ourselves; and I suspect each of us is aware of times when just what I have described has happened.

Anger, resentment and the like are emotions. We generate them, based on our beliefs. Emotional energy has power. If the world of spirits is at all akin to the world of physical beings, some spirits will have developed ways to feed off emotional energy. Those that are attracted to negative emotional energy will have developed skills at generating it. And thus Pagans have no problem acknowledging the existence of negative spirit forces. I have encountered them myself, and some are very dangerous. But they require no demonic creator any more than does malice within physical beings.

A good world of fallible beings is quite capable of generating enormous malice. We need only look around ourselves to see that this is true. Blaming others such as Satan for it seems to me to be passing the buck. Malice is our creation, and it is we who have the capacity to clean it up. I will discuss this later in Chapter 4.

Philip Johnson

Humans have a remarkable capacity for contemplating the Divine that is evident across all cultures from the distant past to the present day. Most people seem to have deep and mysterious yearnings for God and, as one biblical writer puts it, God has put eternity into everyone's heart.[16] The same thought was expressed centuries afterwards by Augustine of Hippo when he wrote, 'You have made us for yourself, O God, and our hearts are restless till they rest in you.'[17]

Our common yearning for God finds an echo in the pioneering neurotheological studies of Andrew Newberg (*Why God won't go away*) and Dean Hamer (*The God Gene*).[18] I do not propose to digress here by surveying this new research except to note that there seem to be some neurological, biological and chemical indicators that suggest humans are hardwired for spirituality. If the evidence rings true it complements what believers have long affirmed, namely that we have 'eternity' woven into our hearts – and into our genes and brains.

Gus indicates that there are many different representations of the Divine found in human understandings of polytheism, pantheism and monotheism. These understandings of the Divine are built around very different metaphysical and theological assumptions and revelatory claims. Although Pagans and Christians are open to the reality of the Divine, both pathways have arrived at considerably different conclusions about the nature, character and attributes of God. The great challenge before us is discovering if we can all let God be God. Moses' encounter at the burning bush led him to remove his sandals when he realized he was standing on 'holy ground'.[19] We all need to slip off our sandals and start pondering where we stand in relationship to God.

God, Language, Gender

God is a personal and relational being who is infinite, uncreated, eternal and self-sufficient. God's sufficiency means that God does not depend on anything or need the creation in order to be, but he has freely chosen to create the cosmos. The wonder of the cosmos often prompts us to express awe and appreciation, and understandably many of us want to connect with God in the natural realm. We can sense God's presence across the Earth and through the hints we find in nature we are wooed into deep communion with God, which is at the heart of the meaning of life. What we must not trick ourselves into when sensing the Divine around us is conflating the natural world into God's being. Heaven and Earth are filled with God's presence but neither heaven nor Earth is God.

Theologians have long emphasized that religious language is analogical, and some feel that poetry provides a helpful avenue for theological expression.[20] Analogical language is used to refer to things that are similar but that are neither identical with nor completely different from God. A further distinction is that some analogies are metaphysical while others are metaphorical. So statements such as 'God is love' and 'God is good' are metaphysical analogies that refer to intrinsic or essential truth. On the metaphorical side are statements such as 'the eyes of God' and 'the hand of God'. These kinds of statements are poetic and anthropomorphic and are not to be taken literally.[21] The Bible uses a variety of images, similes and metaphors when referring to God, some of which are personal and anthropomorphic, while impersonal metaphors are also used when describing God as a refuge, rock, fire, pillar and light.

Much Christian God-talk uses terms such as 'he', 'him' and 'father' with the latter word being a title not a gender-based name. This vocabulary is often misunderstood by people who are alienated from Christianity. Mary Daly asserts that 'God is male'.[22] It is certainly the case that the people who wrote the books of the Bible lived in either the Levant or Greco-Roman cultures where patriarchy was the norm. Yet even though they were living in patriarchal contexts the biblical writers were quite clear that God does not have any sexual characteristics: 'For I am God and not man'.[23] The biblical understanding is that sexuality is confined to the structures of the creation whereas God's being is identified as wholly independent and distinct from the creation. Daly is incorrect in saying that God is male.

Unlike many of their ancient near-eastern neighbours the Israelites refused to make carved or physical representations of God. This activity was prohibited in the Ten Commandments, which guarded against directing worship to a carved artefact but also restrained them from visually representing God as male or female or as being identical with the creation.[24] In neighbouring cultures there were plenty of cultic gods and goddesses, but these were patriarchal societies using masculine images of sex projected into systems of worship that perpetuated a male–female dualism. These images of deity were unsuitable for Israel's consciousness about God, who is beyond gender. They were also unsuitable given the creation narratives' egalitarian imperative about the unity of women and men imaging God's unity and oneness. To take up a male or female deity involved breaking that imaged spiritual unity in favour of gender-based power games. At various times the Israelites lapsed into following their neighbours' cults but those dualist practices did not bring harmony with one another and the Earth. The prophets repeatedly called the nation to abandon all dualist gender-based cults and recover their spiritual poise in relationship with God.[25]

Today we have heightened sensitivities concerning patriarchy, but if we were living thousands of years ago we would not have questioned it. It is nigh on impossible for most people to enter imaginatively and empathically into the times in which others lived. We bring our own prejudices to bear when examining the past. I find it very challenging to be critically reflexive about how I understand the past, other cultures and people of other faiths. What I feel often happens is that people talk at cross-purposes by debating the negative impressions that the past makes on our minds. When that occurs we may not grasp what it was like to live in a previous epoch but instead end up ruminating over impressions we have formed which have been shaped by contemporary disenchantment. When we grumble about the oversights of earlier eras we may need reminding that in years to come others will be deploring our blind-spots.

It is easily forgotten that in the Bible there are feminine and maternal similes. These images are not of a goddess but they reflect the biblical affirmations that God is tender, gentle, nurturing and loving. Isaiah recites God's words of comfort and consolation to the people of Israel in which God is likened to a mother who nurses and comforts her children.[26] God gasps, pants and cries out like a woman in childbirth when speaking to the Israelites about their hope for restoration as a people from exile.[27] Again, God 'carried' the people of Israel from conception to birth and on to their maturity.[28] The imagery of a midwife delivering a baby and breast-feeding is evoked by the Psalmist when referring to God's intimate care.[29] Birth imagery of the womb is used in referring to God bringing forth ice and frost in the Earth.[30] Jesus likens God's care for the creation and for basic human needs to that of a seamstress clothing us in fine linen.[31] The wisdom of God in creating the world is imaged as a co-worker and is personified as a woman.[32]

Other maternal images are drawn from the natural world. For example, God's tender support is depicted as an eagle hovering over her nest and as young birds sheltering underneath protective wings.[33] Jesus parallels this when he weeps over the city of Jerusalem and likened his concern to that of a mother hen gathering in her chicks.[34] Another image is found in the final message from Hosea when God appeals to Israel to repent. Fresh blessings are offered as God says, 'I will be like the dew to Israel', and 'I am like a green pine tree, your fruitfulness comes from me.'[35] These images from nature point to refreshment and new growth, but God is not identified as being identical with the stuff that makes up the Earth.

In the Old Testament different names for God are used to convey a particular quality or attribute. In most instances God reveals the personal name when interacting with particular characters, but there is one striking instance when a name is conferred by a woman. The woman servant Hagar is the only person reported in the Bible to have ever conferred a name on God.[36] That may seem an incidental point but it should not be down-played, particularly when it is remembered that Hagar lived in an abusive patriarchal household where she was humiliated, maltreated and ostracized.

Another maternal image is drawn out in Genesis from one of the names used for God, *El Shaddai*. This name is cognate with the Hebraic word *shad*, meaning 'breast'. It is interesting to note that Martin Luther, the 'father' of the Protestant Reformation, remarked on this linguistic point in his commentary on Genesis. Luther saw maternal images implied in the very divine name and he stated, 'God depicts Himself to us, as it were, in the form of a woman and mother.'[37] Luther, however, did not pray to God as mother. Other Christian figures who have spoken of the motherhood of God include: John Chrysostom, Gregory of Nyssa, Venerable Bede, Thomas Aquinas, Bonaventure, Bernard of Clairvaux, Hildegard of Bingen and St Anselm. These images however do not mean that God has a specific gender.[38]

The Mystery of God

At the heart of the biblical revelation is the mystery of God: 'Beyond all question, the mystery of godliness is great.'[39] Various biblical stories show people encountering God in ways that impart a strong sense of reverence, awe and mystery that boggle our finite minds. Isaiah receives a staggering vision of God's holiness in the Jewish temple.[40] In a similar vein, when telling of his experience of God's glory, the prophet Ezekiel expresses this through very mysterious pictorial images of strange looking creatures with many eyes enveloped in wheels within wheels.[41]

The notion of mystery is also important in the writings of Paul the apostle. Sometimes he associates the word 'mystery' with divine revelation.[42] Paul holds that there is a divine mystery that is synonymous with the good news about Jesus, but it is no longer 'mysterious' because of divine revelation.[43] Yet Paul also conveys the idea that there are things about God that are hidden from us and are beyond our comprehension or that transcend our present experiences of reality.[44] Paul likened our present vision to that of peering through a darkened glass in contrast to our being 'face to face' with God in the future.[45]

Theologians have long insisted that there are elements of God that are both knowable and unknowable. In very broad brushstrokes the theologies associated with Roman Catholics and Protestants have generally been characterized by a strong emphasis on affirmative propositions about the knowable things of God, while the theologies of Eastern Orthodoxy emphasize the unknowable or ineffable things of God.[46] Both approaches recognize the place of mystery and paradox alongside that of the cognitive.

Another major aspect concerns the understanding of God as Trinity. This is an unfathomable mystery about God's oneness and unity that has exercised the best efforts of great thinkers, but which defies our capacity to comprehend or fully analyse it. Without going into detail, the concept of the Trinity encompasses God's nature, character and attributes as a personal being. In the oneness of God's being there are three centres of personhood. These centres of personhood do not constitute three different deities, modes or dimensions. Each centre of personhood relates to the other two in a unified reciprocal relationship expressing *agape* (love). This understanding of God in Triunity enables us to dimly glimpse a perfect interrelationship of persons in dynamic fellowship and love. The Triunity of God directs us away from static Deist understandings of a lone remote being, and likewise from pantheistic ideas that see God and the whole cosmos as one and the same thing. Deist and pantheist perspectives cannot be reconciled with a theology which affirms that God's being is transcendent and has intrinsic attributes of personhood, such as expressing love, self-consciousness, creativity and social relatedness.[47]

Images of Transcendence and Immanence

Gus has drawn attention to monarchical images in past cultures that referred to deity, and pointed to their misuse in harmful hierarchies and their inadequacy as metaphors today. In the case of the Christian church there is a considerable legacy of viewing God from monarchic and hierarchical standpoints. There are numerous monarchic biblical images and understandably theologians have drawn on them along with various other images of transcendence found in the Bible. The church has sometimes represented God to other people in terms of the abuse of power while neglecting or under-emphasizing many of the Bible's relational images of partnership and vulnerability. Monarchical and hierarchical imagery flourished as the church's structures grew. For example, Pseudo-Dionysius the Areopagite proposed a detailed and exaggerated hierarchy of angels that correlated to emerging ecclesiastical hierarchies of his day. Lamentably, violent imagery of a conquering deity went hand-in-glove with the conflicts of later eras involving the Crusades, the Conquistadores and colonialism. This imagery has unhelpfully reinforced a very negative impression of an autocratic, unpleasant God.

There are many biblical statements about both the transcendence and immanence of God, and this is a paradox that we cannot fully fathom. What we understand from the Bible is that God is the Creator and is not to be regarded as identical with the cosmos (hence God is transcendent in being). The Bible from its opening pages also upholds that God is not a remote being uninvolved in the Earth but is continuously present everywhere (hence God is relationally immanent). The Christian understanding consists of a 'both/and' not an 'either/or' concerning God's transcendence and immanence. When one aspect is emphasized to the detriment of the other then we are left with a distorted picture of God.

I suggest that the recent cultural turn to immanence represents in part a protest at the church for neglecting this aspect of biblical truth. It may be regarded metaphorically as a heavily accruing unpaid theological debt that must be redressed rather urgently. The Pagan emphasis on the immanence of deity easily triggers important critical theological responses. However, I wonder if we could also see this as a cultural signifier to a church that has over-emphasized transcendence and de-emphasized immanence? The solution is not to concentrate on immanence and downplay transcendence but rather to recalibrate theology and the spiritual life so that we once again have a balanced 'both/and' portrait.

A recovery of a biblical understanding of immanence in our time would be spiritually valuable for many reasons. One is that it could assist us in deepening our appreciation for the work of God's *Pneuma* (Spirit) in the creation (which I will refer to again in the next chapter). When divine immanence is kept in focus it can also act as a restraint on any tendency to move towards a distorted view of divine transcendence. This latter point was something that B. B. Warfield (1851–1921) sagely observed:

> *It would not be easy to overestimate the importance of the early emergence of this doctrine of the immanent Spirit of God, side by side with the high doctrine of the transcendence of God which pervades the Old Testament. Whatever tendency the emphasis on the transcendence of God might engender towards Deistic conceptions would be corrected at once by such teaching as to the immanent Spirit.*[48]

Warfield was evidently concerned that conservative Protestants were very much in danger of losing their grip on God's immanence. God's relationship with the Earth and his participation in the lives of all creatures needs to be brought back into balance. Warfield affirmed the Spirit's continuing work and presence in the world:

> *The Spirit of God thus appears from the outset of the Old Testament as the principle of the very existence and persistence of all things, and as the source and originating cause of all movement and order and life. God's thought and will and word take effect in the world, because God is not only over the world, thinking and willing and commanding, but also in the world, as the principle of all activity.*[49]

Biblical statements about relational immanence abound in the Old Testament in connection with God's *Pneuma*. The creation story opens with God's Spirit hovering over chaotic waters as life on Earth begins.[50] This thought is carried forward in other passages in which God's *Pneuma* is described as the fountain of all life and where the heavens are garnished by the Spirit.[51] The continuing presence of God throughout the creation is affirmed in Psalm 139 where God's Spirit sustains, maintains and renews the soil, and the life of all creatures. Other passages attest that God's *Pneuma* imparts the breath of life and sustains it in humans, and God sends forth the Spirit in creating all life.[52]

The interconnectedness of all life is a thought sustained by Paul the apostle in his understanding of all things being held together by Christ.[53] It also comes through in Paul's thinking about the redemption of the whole Earth, and points to his acceptance of the continuous presence of God's Spirit throughout the creation.[54] Paul happily affirmed immanence when he quoted the Greek philosopher Epimenides, saying that God 'is not far from each one of us' because it is in God that 'we live and move and have our being'.[55] As I mentioned in the previous chapter, humans can encounter God anywhere because of his relational immanence. In other parts of the New Testament the immanent Spirit of God is also understood to be the One who stirs us into participating in a relationship with God and others. The Spirit of God is interested in forming, nurturing and sustaining individuals in communal relationships that image what Jesus taught about God's new community.[56]

A major argument in the Bible is that Jesus holds a unique relationship with God and offers the clearest revelation and representation of God's character. In Jesus' life and actions we are shown that God chose to become a vulnerable baby, dependent on adults for love, care and nurture. While the Gospels indicate that Jesus is a descendant of King David, there are no images of regal grandeur in the Christmas manger. In his adult life Jesus declines the efforts of those who seek an immediate coronation ceremony in order to start armed rebellion against imperial Rome.[57] Instead Jesus refers to his kingship in terms of humility and powerlessness.[58] In effect Jesus reframed the monarchic images altogether as symbolized by the servant–king.

When Jesus was born God's immanence was portrayed through his life-story, yet at the same time God's immanent Spirit remained present throughout all the world. As a child Jesus is represented as God who is present with us in powerlessness and vulnerability. His relational vulnerability is further expressed in the deep bonds of interpersonal friendships which Jesus has with women and men alike. He has human experiences of relationships involving peace, joy, trust and love, but also pain, sorrow, deprivation and betrayal. So instead of images of a seemingly inaccessible, remote and unpleasant God we are introduced to One who is open to us, is understanding and lives alongside us.

Panentheism

Gus has drawn attention to panentheism as a way of integrating other conceptions of God that keeps immanence in focus. Some theologians such as John Cobb, Charles Hartshorne and Matthew Fox advocate panentheism, but the critical discourses on this subject between Christians indicate a critical divide on several theological and philosophical points. Chief among these is that it defines God and the Earth as mutually necessary: God depends on the organic processes of the universe to grow and change just as much as the processes require God. Another concern is that its understanding of human sin is inadequate. The problem ensues when trying to make sense of God's incarnation in Christ, and the healing effect wrought on the whole world in redemption. If the world and humans do not need redemption then the incarnation and the gift of the Spirit make no sense. Panentheism's conception of the Divine over-emphasizes interrelatedness and fails to do justice to the self-identity of persons participating in the process.[59]

Gus refers to the passage in Matthew's Gospel in which Jesus was received, welcomed and blessed by hospitable people when he had physical needs for food, shelter and clothing. A few points of clarification are needed. The first point is that Jesus expects his followers to emulate what others have done to him: welcome and bless the stranger, the refugee and the needy. These actions that Jesus spoke about reflect the early Hebraic traditions concerning care, shelter and food for the stranger, the refugee and the poor.[60]

The second is that such acts of blessing correspond to the creation story's imperative of being an agent of blessing, particularly towards other humans, because all are made in God's image. We are, as Paul the apostle puts it, to do everything as unto Christ.[61] Our response to those in need then is given a parallel: just as we have welcomed Jesus to our tables so too we must welcome the stranger who is loved by Christ and made in God's image and likeness. In effect, what we do to others and image to them is ultimately what we offer back to Christ. The third point is that in Lutheran theology the resurrected Christ's bodily presence is understood to be found everywhere so that Luther sensed Christ as 'substantially present everywhere, in and through all creatures, in all their parts and places' including 'the most insignificant leaf of a tree'.[62] For Luther, this was an expression of God's relational immanence in the world, and not monism.

Darkness and Evil

Christians feel the acute tension in reconciling suffering and evil with the image of an all-loving and all-powerful God. If God is benevolent and powerful then why are evil and suffering permitted? The Bible starts with a story that displays harmonious relationships between God, the Earth and humans. The biblical stories carry forward the point that all things are held together in a unified interconnected web of relationships. There is a divinely blessed creation and humans are invited into a partnership that reflects what God does in blessing all sentient life. As the known characteristics of God point to love and goodness (and there is no evil in God's nature), they become the prime point of reference for any human behaviour. Other parts of the Bible uphold this same point when referring to the ideal king who serves others in humble, wise and equitable ways.[63] Jesus is shown as the clearest representation of this divine love and humble way of life in which power is found in weakness and vulnerability. The central positive motif for humanity is one of peaceful humility and gracious service exercised in love.

This idyllic picture of a universal web of harmonious relationships is subsequently characterized as fractured and alienated. Human relations begin shifting away from interdependence and mutual trust. A much more serious fracture occurs as humans withdraw from intimacy and transparency with God. Human autonomy displaces the prior harmony and unity, and a ripple effect spreads so that all relationships with animals and the biosphere are likewise frustrated and broken. Oppressive and abusive social hierarchies subsequently emerge as human self-centredness repeatedly leads to malicious and disastrous activities.

Gus has stated why he does not accept the Christian notion of a human fall into sin, but he clearly acknowledges that humans are a very malicious and selfish species. Genesis pinpoints self-centredness as one important aspect of the complex human condition of sin that comes into focus in broken relationships. It seems to me that these biblical stories give a fairly realistic snap-shot of the human condition. They portray the effects of dark behaviour once decisions have been made to withdraw from unity and interdependency. They show people who want to avoid taking responsibility for their decisions by deflecting attention onto others but the biblical stories make it plain that they are held responsible for their own actions. Similarly, while some Christians exaggerate the role of demons and imply some sort of buck-passing for evil, they do so in dualist ways that are clearly in conflict with what is taught in the Bible and in classical theology.

There is a tendency among some Christians to refer to sin in terms of bad behaviour that is summed up in a shallow list of 'thou shalt not's. However, the Bible offers a broader understanding. It recognizes that sin is individual, social and institutional, and many biblical stories depict people who, because of the actions of other persons, become marginalized and helpless victims. Yet sin involves more than just an individual being morally and spiritually corrupt. At its deepest level the Bible shows that all relationships have broken down so that the entire creation suffers. The offer of a relationship between God and humans entails vulnerability and risk, especially since we were not created as automata. As God offers us love, we can either reciprocate or spurn it altogether; similarly, our decision-making and the consequences of our actions are woven together. So in any reflections on evil and suffering the possibility that humans might reject God looms large.[64]

The wisdom literature of the Bible also questions the naïve understanding that good people prosper and calamities only befall bad individuals. The dialogues between Job and his friends, and the internal dialogue of the 'teacher' in Ecclesiastes, restate these familiar ideas about the presumed moral order and retribution. However, as these dialogues run their course it is shown that very often the 'wicked' seem to prosper while the 'righteous' suffer, and that often suffering remains a mystery to those experiencing it. A rigid and naïve understanding of calamities is rejected as an inadequate understanding of evil and suffering.[65]

In the central biblical drama we are shown how, through Jesus, God experiences grief, suffering and pain, and in crucifixion is rendered physically helpless. This disturbing imagery enables us to begin coming to grips with evil because at the heart of the Jesus story are images of a shattered God who shares our experiences of trauma, weakness, betrayal and vulnerability. We are invited through the story to discover that Jesus understands and accepts people in all their faults and failings, while enabling us to overcome our brokenness and move forward in life. The imagery of a new birth invites us to look to the possibilities of who we might become through the transforming power of God's Spirit. I find that the divine images represented through Jesus make sense of the experience of personal renewal and help me to find spiritual power through the Spirit to take life's journey in partnership with God. [66]

CHAPTER 3

Nature

Gus diZerega

I walk outside in the depths of winter here in New York's North Country, the land where the North Woods begin. The coldest days turn my moustache white with breath-frost and my glasses are quickly covered in ice. Summer's leaves have long since fallen from the maples and birch, their branches now bare, seemingly devoid of life. But if I look with care, I see each tree surrounded by its own aura of energy, manifesting its presence within the land well beyond its reaching trunk. I have taught many people to see this field, yet our culture 'knows' phenomena such as this do not and cannot exist. So few look, and those who do look and see normally choose to keep quiet about it. Often that is wise.

Those of us who see these energies of the land know that, like the trees, our own boundaries extend beyond our skins, interacting and intermeshing with other fields from other bodies. No one is truly disconnected. We live immersed within a field of relations, physical, mental, emotional, energetic and spiritual.

This sensibility is deeply at odds with that prevailing within the secular and monotheistic West. The mundane world of separate objects is the world of the lonely and isolated. It is a world we all live within to some degree. But too many of us live within it all the time. For them, Nature has been desanctified and turned into an object. This outcome has been the joint product of both modern religion and modern secularism. It is also an intellectual, moral and spiritual error.

If we can see that our own boundaries do not end at the limits of our physical bodies, but extend outwards, blending and intersecting with everything else, we know our sense of isolation from the world and from other people, however strong it can be, is ultimately illusory. Our challenge becomes how to connect with greater awareness to these manifold kinds of relation. Here is where Pagan spiritual practices offer something of enormous value to modern men and women. We do not have a monopoly on these practices. For example, Vipassana meditation retreats are also a powerful means to make these connections. But many of these practices were developed by Pagan peoples and are in particular harmony with a Pagan worldview.

Years of spiritual practice have convinced me that the natural world is deeply sentient. Mighty trees and ephemeral flowers have their own presence, and when appropriately approached they can and sometimes do respond to humans. In my experience the same also holds true for the rolling Pacific, as it crashes against the Californian coast, and a Cascade volcano mantled in ice and snow, with a heart of fire.

In keeping with their shamanic roots, Pagan religions generally – and Wicca certainly among them – emphasize the Sacred as it manifests in and through Nature. In the sharpest possible contrast with the dominant secular and monotheistic worldviews, we view Nature as a direct living manifestation of the Divine. Nature is neither a creation nor the brute result of insensate natural forces. The material world is a world of sense, of awareness and of value, and it is all three to its very core. We forget this to our loss and to our peril.

Some accounts of Pagan religions such as Wicca say we 'worship Nature'. This is not quite right, at least given what the words 'nature' and 'worship' mean in most contexts. We respect, honour, serve and love the Sacred as it manifests *in and through* Nature. Nature is sacred, but the Sacred transcends what we usually think of as 'nature'. To keep my meaning clear, when I capitalize Nature I refer to the natural world and its elements as subjects. In Martin Buber's insightful term, they all constitute, both individually and together, a 'Thou'.[1] When I do not capitalize the word, I refer to nature in the usual secular sense, as well as that of many monotheists, where nature is simply an object, a thing or a collection of things. If there is a divine Creator, and the world is Its artefact, divinity rests in the Creator, not the creation. In Martin Buber's sense, this mentality treats nature as an 'It'.

For Wiccans and most other Pagans, Nature is both a manifestation of the Sacred and our principal teacher for growing into greater harmony with the Sacred in all dimensions of our lives. Some religions possess sacred texts. Nature is our sacred text. A printed text is in many ways a passive repository of knowledge from elsewhere. Nature is anything but passive, and the knowledge that we gain in relationship with Nature comes to us unmediated by the understandings and limitations of a human scribe. A text can only be interpreted based on *our* understanding. Nature can interact with us.[2]

This of course does not mean that interpreting Nature-derived knowledge as it relates to us is always easy. We can misunderstand the meaning of the Sacred in Nature, particularly if we do not attend carefully or our hearts are not open. But this is a problem faced within any spiritual tradition, certainly including those that rely on printed texts as the repository of their wisdom. Some thousands of years after their creation, people still find multiple incompatible meanings of sacred texts, and among Jews and particularly Christians and Muslims, cases of people killing one another over differences in interpretation comprise important elements of their histories.

Nature is Aware

In this context, contemporary Pagans are in harmony with the religious experience of most human beings throughout our species' history. For the historical Pagan religions evolved from the shamanic practices of tribal peoples before the rise of agriculture, constituting an unbroken tradition leading back into the Pleistocene epoch.[3] For example, the Greek Goddess Artemis quite possibly was once a bear spirit.[4] The practices of the ancient Greeks, so rightfully admired for their honouring of the power of reason, were also rooted in these primordial traditions, practices secular moderns term 'irrational'.[5] Moderns largely ignore the implications that Classical Antiquity's greatest thinkers, such as Plato and Aristotle, were *also* practising Pagans and initiates of traditions such as the Eleusinian Mysteries.

For thousands of years, trance and dance, song and poetry, ritual and art, isolation and ordeal all served to break through the boundaries of people's mundane concerns, opening them up to wider and deeper contexts of existence. By contrast, our contemporary world prides itself on its focused thought, and on distancing ourselves emotionally from what we seek to know, so we may know it 'objectively'. But when we *focus* our attention we also *narrow* our awareness. Some things are clarified, even magnified; others, like those auras around trees, are cast into the background or even disappear from our conscious awareness.

Wisdom knows when to focus and when to have that wider awareness, and wisdom can only come from repeatedly experiencing both. Few have the time or take the time to do so today. It cannot be taught from a book.

The modern ideal of impersonal knowledge has brought us great blessings. I would be the last to deny it, as I type these words into my computer, my vision aided by my bifocals. But it is one thing to say that impersonal standards for knowing can be useful; it is another to say that they are all that constitute valid knowing.

We *cannot* really know subjects by impersonal means. If we treat them as objects, we will never take their subjectivity seriously. We may not even notice it. If I treat you as an object, subject to my observation and attempts at control, you will be unlikely to reach out to me. I have demonstrated rudeness and self-centredness: hardly an invitation for a relationship. Of course, for certain purposes I can legitimately distance myself even from loved ones, as, for example, when they ask me how they did in a performance or on a job. In such cases they *may* want 'objective' information. But my distancing is immersed within and constrained by a broader context of care and relationship. It is the subordinate partner.

We know this from our relations with other human beings. We will never know them if we treat them as objects, though as many corporations and politicians and all sociopaths demonstrate, we can learn to manipulate them. But we do not know them. A purely 'objective' description of someone you love leaves out what is most important: their interior.

It is the same with Nature.

It is not that we do not have intimations of this truth in our daily lives. Today many people vaguely intuit this dimension of the natural world as having interiority, a presence, when they say they are going into 'God's country' or that getting out into nature helps them to find 'peace' or 'put things into perspective'. Even though modern Westerners lack both a vocabulary for and in many cases even an awareness of the possibility that Nature is sentient, we intuit and feel the presences that pervade the natural world, the field of awareness into which we enter as we leave mundane social fields for natural ones. We can then begin to feel the field created by those interacting auras of trees and rocks and water and deer. As our minds gradually quieten we become more attuned to these presences, finding peace, rejuvenation and healing.[6]

The mind that does not relax becomes bored because it sees only surfaces, and compared to a football or a city street, the surfaces of Nature are usually very placid. It can take some people weeks to get through their boredom and begin noticing what is happening around them. In the modern world many do not have that time, and even many who do never see why they should take it.

If directed towards the world around us, spiritual practices can facilitate our re-connecting with the greater and deeper world around us of which we have lost sight. If a person seriously develops his or her spiritual practice within a Pagan context, he or she increasingly *experiences* Nature as a field of awareness, and individual elements within Nature also begin to have their own distinct presence, a presence that is more than simply being an object. As I described from my own encounters, we discover that trees and flowers and even an ocean or a mountain can respond to our presence. That discovery is unforgettable. Nothing again is ever the same.

From a Pagan perspective, our society's failure to realize this truth is akin to its being a culture of sociopaths. Sociopaths have an inability to recognize the interiority of others. They fail to empathize with other human beings. They constitute the most extreme expression of what I see as a vast cultural failing on the part of the modern world: a closing off of awareness of the interiority of existence. The many who are not so wounded as to become sociopaths still usually fail to see it in the other-than-human world. But they feel their emptiness.

Knowing that Nature is aware, and a manifestation of the Sacred, we use it as a primary source for both learning about and celebrating the sacredness of existence. Its very otherness from the human world helps us to broaden our appreciation of the sacredness in all things. Nature helps get us away from our preoccupation with our own hopes, fears and wants, placing them in that broader context that opens us up to Spirit. And She is beautiful.

Nature is often subtle. An attentive person can tell much from a person's demeanour – the twitch of an eye or the way they hold their shoulders, leaning forward or sitting back during a conversation. Nature most often communicates the same way, and requires similar levels of experience and attention if She is to be heard well. But on rare occasions, She can be anything but subtle. Hers is a rich world, a sentient world, a world to which most moderns have become both deaf and blind.

Sacred Sexuality

The Wiccan ritual year is based on Nature because nature is the context within which Spirit manifests most directly to us. The more deeply we enter into these practices, often the more directly we enter into relationship with the More-Than-Human as it manifests within the world. There are two basic dimensions of sacred embodiment that taken together describe our practices: sexuality and cycles.

Sexuality is basic to Nature. Beyond single cells, life depends on sexuality. If human life is good, so must be what it depends on, not just evolutionarily, but from one generation to the next. And in contrast to those who ignorantly repeat the claim that the natural purpose for human sexuality is simply procreation, it is clear to all with sense to see and a heart to love that it is also for fostering intimacy, closeness, care and pleasure – with or without issue.

The sacredness of sexuality is as basic to our practice as it is to Nature. On every Traditional Wiccan altar stands a chalice, symbolizing the female, and near it lies an athame, or ritual knife, symbolizing the male. Every Esbat incorporates a symbolic Great Rite, an act of symbolic intercourse when the athame is dipped into the chalice, High Priestess and High Priest saying, 'As the athame is to the male, so the cup is to the female. And conjoined they bring blessedness.'[7]

I will defer more discussion of sacred sexuality until our final chapter. Sorry! (But please do not skip ahead.)

Sacred Cycles

Nature is characterized by recurring cycles: the seasons, phases of the moon, growing and shrinking populations, good and bad years, and the growth and decline of every physical life. Nature is also characterized by circles, be they the turning of the night sky, the travel of the sun, the shape of our and other planets, and the horizon as it stretches out away from us into the four directions. Circles are a fitting way of representing recurring cycles, and our Wheel of the Year captures both these recurring patterns in a single image.

The cycles that we perceive around us teach us something fundamental about the Sacred: that change is fundamental to reality. Some of the ancient Pagans, and Christians after them, made a serious error in equating the Highest with what was unchanging, based on the mistake of thinking of the stars and planets as more perfect than the Earth, and of death and decay as evidence of something amiss in the world. I believe this error was rooted in their being from urban agricultural cultures.[8] The error assumes change is a corrective to a deficiency rather than a necessity so that every dimension of the perfect can shine forth, because all cannot shine forth simultaneously.

Consider a sunset. Think of the most beautiful one you have ever witnessed. That sunset was continually changing. At every moment the sun fell lower towards the horizon, painting the sky and clouds with shifting colours. You were transfixed by the beauty before you. But each moment of beauty was followed by another, perhaps equally beautiful, but different. The sunset is *all* these moments. Change is essential to it. And sunsets are among the most beautiful sights on Earth.

The same is true for a life. There is a beauty and goodness in childhood that must pass if we are to experience the beauty and goodness of young adulthood. The same holds true at every stage of a life. Now I am on the downhill side of my life. The things that engrossed me when I was in my twenties or thirties no longer possess the same allure. Other things do. But they are rooted in those younger years and would not be what they are had I not lived my life of years ago.

Is one phase in a cycle more or less imperfect than another? That question misses the point. Each is potentially perfect in its own way. And each contains the seeds for what comes next, as with the sunset. If toddlers never grew older, but remained toddlers, there would be something sad about their daily discoveries, discoveries that could never accumulate into growth, but would presumably continually be forgotten and relearned. For many of us, much of the charm of a toddler lies in watching it discover and grow in awareness. And for a toddler, a great deal of pleasure comes from that same exploring and learning process.

The stages of a life cannot come together simultaneously except, perhaps, in the richness of memory. A good life has a richness of memories, but change is central to it.

The Wheel of the Year

Our Sabbats and Esbats are organized around either natural solar and lunar cycles or around the agricultural and grazing seasons of north-western Europe. As such, they reflect universal Pagan insights as well as the spirit of the Place where our particular practice first arose. Both Sabbats and Esbats honour the Wheel of the Year that symbolizes the cycle of birth, maturation, decline, death and ultimate rebirth that most NeoPagans seek to honour as a sacred rhythm. In short, *every* dimension of life is sacred in its own way, and is to be honoured, again in its own way.

Witches' Sabbats are celebrated eight times a year.[9] Four of the dates are established by solar cycles: the Winter and Summer Solstices and the Spring and Fall equinoxes. Here the symbolism of birth, growth, maturity, decline and death is explicit, and is followed again by the same cycle in the year to come. In the northern hemisphere where I live, the Winter Solstice, or Yule, as the longest night of the year, marks the death and rebirth of the sun. The Spring equinox, often called Ostara, honours the time when days and nights are equal, but the momentum of the year is towards greater light. The Summer Solstice, called Midsummer or, less often, Litha, celebrates the longest day, when the vitality of earthly life reaches its peak. The Fall equinox, or Mabon, is the time of final harvest followed by decline, a pattern that will continue until Winter Solstice, when the great pattern repeats itself.

Intertwined within these universal solar celebrations are the four 'Great Sabbats' linked to Celtic farming and grazing cycles. Imbolc (pronounced 'im-OLk') or Brigit (after the Celtic Goddess Brhide) is traditionally celebrated on or around February 2. Imbolc is a fire festival, though in keeping with the time the fires are small, a mere promise of the coming warmth.

Beltane or May Day occurs during the height of Spring in many regions. The May Pole, the May Queen, and the shenanigans and bonfires that take place on May Eve all honour and celebrate the powers of life abundant, beautiful and lusty. When I lived in areas where it was possible to do so, I would be up well before dawn to watch the Morris Dancers 'dance the sun up' at sunrise. The day would continue with more public celebrations, for among Wiccans this Sabbat is the one most often celebrated with the general public.

Three months later comes Lammas, or Lughnasadh (LOO-na-sah), celebrating the beginning of harvest. The emphasis is on the coming abundance of the harvest, the richness of the Earth, and the blessings of the soil. But every harvest involves a cutting short of life, and this sacrificial dimension is also present, a bittersweet reminder that life is never to be taken for granted.

Three more months bring the second of the greatest Wiccan Sabbats, Samhain (SAOW-win), popularly known as Halloween. As Beltane honours the energy of life, Samhain honours that of death. The harvest is over, or nearly so. Our altars are decked with pictures and mementoes of our ancestors and loved ones who have passed on. Their spirits are invited to join us if they will for a nighttime feast. To an outsider Samhain might appear morbid or scary, but it is far from that; yet it most certainly does not have the playful exuberance of Beltane. For with death comes a final parting from this life and entry into mystery. Each of us makes that passage on our own, and while we believe those united in love will meet again, it will not be in this life.

The Wheel of the Year begins with Samhain, then proceeds to

Yule, Imbolc, Ostara, Beltane, Midsummer, Lammas and Mabon. These eight Sabbats provide an ongoing reminder of life's cycles and an opportunity to meditate on the essential stages of embodied existence. Existence being good, we consider each stage, including Samhain, as ultimately good. But we have no books or texts that make this case. It is through the celebrations and the changes in awareness that they bring about, both during and afterwards, that our primary sources of instruction lie.

The Mythology of the Sabbats

Different NeoPagan traditions celebrate these cycles with somewhat different mythologies, and sometimes several combined together, all rooted in the same broad context of meaning I have outlined above. For some there is an alternating reign by the Oak King during the summer and the Holly King during the winter. For others, the Goddess gives up Her primacy during the winter months, only to take it up again later, as the sun returns and life revives. For others, the Goddess is reborn. Taken as attempts to explain literally what is happening, these stories appear to be naïve romanticism. But that is a misunderstanding.

While even in Pagan times myths were sometimes (mis)understood as literal truths, a more accurate understanding treats them as a kind of sacred poetry.[10] They point to levels of meaning *in* the world that could not be made as clearly by more discursive or philosophical accounts. In particular, they point to the fact that the world and everything in it is aware. Conscious. In a more than trivial sense, alive. That we do not normally experience this truth reflects more on ourselves than on the world.

Second, myth appeals to the same part of our mind that responds to music, beauty and a sense that life is filled with meaning, rather than, as Shakespeare put it in *Macbeth*:

> *Life's but a walking shadow, a poor player*
> *That struts and frets his hour upon the stage*
> *And then is heard no more: it is a tale*
> *Told by an idiot, full of sound and fury,*
> *Signifying nothing.*
> *Macbeth, Act V, Scene 5*

A mythic view would never have this sentiment. Tragedy? Yes.

Suffering? Often in abundance. But meaningless? Never. Life *is* meaning, and as everything is alive, so everything is filled with meaning. Myth captures that. And so, myth teaches us the meaning *in* the world, not the meaning *of* the world. The modern world is the poorer for having lost this sense of reality. I believe Shakespeare knew this, which is why it is Macbeth, with his love of power and ego, and his ultimate failure, who utters these lines.

As a consequence, our Sabbats help each of us to understand our continued participation in life cycles carrying many levels of meaning. Our own lives deepen as we penetrate to more fundamental layers of this meaning, a journey which is often not pleasant, but always worth it when we finally reach a place where we can pause, look back and see how far we've come. As such it is fitting that we prefer celebrating Beltane over Samhain, that Midsummer brings far more merriment than Mabon. As physical beings we want to live and flourish abundantly. But as I wrote in *Pagans and Christians*, 'we are also beings of Spirit, and our flourishing is of little moment if it does not ultimately deepen our awareness, our love and our wisdom. For when our time comes that is what we will take with us, our life's true and final harvest.'[11]

The Esbats

While our Sabbats are frequently open to the public, our Esbats almost never are. Wiccan covens are working groups, with all the potential stresses and strains any working group undergoes. Whereas Sabbats are almost always primarily celebratory, Esbats, or lunar celebrations, usually mix work with celebration. What kind of work? Perhaps a member has returned from an operation in the hospital and has asked us to help the healing process. Perhaps someone is undergoing a personal crisis or seeking a job or wants to help a relative or friend in need. The possible kinds of work are as endless as the problems of human life, and a well-functioning coven provides not only emotional support, it can also seek to actively assist at the level of spirit in helping to improve a member's situation. While these efforts do not always bear visible fruits, they do so often enough that we find them worth our while. And even when there is nothing visible happening, we cannot tell the bigger picture of which we are only a part.

Such a group needs unity of purpose, enormous trust and, for our society anyway, a great deal of openness. Strangers can disrupt this environment. So Esbats are almost always closed to outsiders.

But at their root our Full Moon Esbats, the most frequent kind, replicate the symbolism of Midsummer, but in a lunar context. We also meet on a new or horned moon, but less often, and only because the symbolism is more in keeping with the work we are gathering to perform. Nature's cycles pervade every aspect of the Craft.

In some of the Wiccan traditions most closely connected to Gardnerian Craft, the Goddess is invoked to be present not only in the circle, but within the High Priestess, as a Sacred Possession. (Less often, and usually only on some Sabbats, we men get a similar honour with the God.) This kind of direct encounter with deity is the greatest mystery in the Craft, a mystery not because it is secret (I've just mentioned it, and I am hardly the first) but because no description can do the experience justice.

Ecology

Every religion focuses on some dimensions of the Sacred more than others. This is to be expected, as we are all limited beings, and the Sacred far surpasses us in every sense. We are immersed within it, but we can only look in one direction at a time. Like any other religion, Wiccans focus on certain dimensions more than others, even if we, like many others, do not deny that there is more to the Sacred than we explicitly attend to.

Because natural cycles and the contrast of female and male are our major symbols for the Sacred, we emphasize the value of material life not as objects to consume but as manifestations of what is more than we. We live in a world of subjects, where the trees, clouds, rocks and water all have a presence: all have an inner dimension that removes them forever from being simply objects whose only value comes from their utility to ourselves.

Someone might ask, if rocks and trees and the ocean are subjects, Buber's 'Thous', how can you justify using them? The way to clarity here comes from examining friendship. You and I have friends. Our friends are useful to us. Indeed, being without friends is in my view one of the most unfortunate fates that can befall anyone. But if someone is only useful to us, we are not their friends. The usefulness of friendship lies within a wider and deeper context of care and respect. Even love.

For us, there is nothing amiss with using Nature and Her elements. What *is* amiss is using them thoughtlessly and without respect or care. In this regard we differ little from the wisest of other

Pagan cultures, particularly hunting and gathering ones, in which the abundance of the natural world was appreciated as a gift that would continue to be given only when treated well. Native peoples on the Pacific north-west harvested hundreds of millions of salmon over thousands of years, yet when Lewis and Clark explored the west for the new American government the runs were abundant beyond anything they had ever witnessed.[12]

Within 100 years of the first Euro-American harvests of Pacific salmon the species had become extinct in many places where it had once flourished, and only maintained healthy populations in a small fraction of its original territory. Some people argued that the reason the indigenous peoples of the north Pacific coast had failed to destroy their salmon runs was because they lacked the technology. But we know this was false. They most definitely possessed the technology. What they did not possess was the greed unmodified by any ethical restraint. The Yurok, Salish and other tribes immersed their salmon fishing within a larger sacred ethical context, and so preserved their runs for millennia.[13]

What the modern world did to salmon it is now doing to the oceans.[14]

Life and Death

Nature exists through the cycle of life and death. Death in itself can serve great goods. Were there never any carnivores on our planet, life would likely have never evolved beyond being blue green algae. It is not death as such that is a moral or spiritual problem. It is the kind of death.

One of my greatest perplexities about the connection between belief and practice in our society is its utter denial of death. It may seem that, for secular people, fear of death makes sense because they believe that afterwards there is nothingness. If they love life they reasonably enough fear leaving it. But I know self-proclaimed atheists who do not seem afraid of death, and who are grateful for life.

Yet within monotheistic communities fear of death seems quite strong. In fact, in my experience in the United States it seems greater among traditional believers than nonbelievers. Yet their beliefs tell them that Paradise awaits after leaving this vale of tears. I truly do not understand this.

Wiccans honour death not as superior to life but as part of life. As I grew older and those close to me began to pass on, I wondered whether my reaction would be in keeping with my beliefs, or demonstrate the same apparent gap between word and deed that so characterizes our society. When loved ones died, I grieved, but the reason for my grief was not that they were gone forever, but that I had lost (most) contact with them for the rest of my life, and that there were opportunities for experience, love and beauty that they would now be denied in this world. My grief acknowledged and honoured their importance to me and the suffering they had undergone in their lives. And appropriately so.

But I had no feeling that death was unfair, that a tragedy had unfolded. Of course from our perspective death can come inopportunely, and tragedies do happen. This is particularly true when the young die. But the tragedy is more in the timing than in the ultimate outcome. Death itself is no tragedy.

Think of that sunset again. It is beautiful, and always changing, until night falls. Night has its own beauty, of course, but my point here is that we do not normally see the end of the day as anything but a part of the cycle of life, a part that helps us not only to enjoy the sunset, but also to value the day itself rather than simply assuming it will go on forever. Furthermore, the sun is not gone; it is gone from sight, which is quite another thing.

Days are better because they end, and sunsets are more beautiful because they are constantly changing, approaching a time when the sun will disappear.

If Nature teaches us to see even the passing of physical life as a part of the beauty and sacredness that surrounds us, Nature is a very great teacher indeed. A good death, like a good life, is one appropriate to its circumstances. From a Pagan perspective, this means it acknowledges and honours the great patterns within which it is immersed, and the love that ultimately supports all things.

The mundane, where we spend so much of our time, is ultimately the realm of the lonely. Its pain is healed through love, which is how the mundane reaches out and touches the Sacred. And in the process it learns that within constant change there is one thing that can truly last.

Philip Johnson

The first pages of the Bible affirm that the natural world is precious to God and is divinely blessed. Throughout the Bible pictorial images are often used to describe the relationship between God and the

Earth. God is portrayed as a loving, wise carer who patiently creates, nurtures and sustains life. God's delight is in the seas, land, trees, fish, birds and animals, and human beings, with all things pronounced good and blessed. The songs and poems of the Psalms depict the whole of nature rejoicing.[15] Isaiah the prophet uses similes to describe mountains and forests singing and trees clapping their hands.[16] The creation is also shown to be the work of divine wisdom.[17] God is found at the centre of all things, being present everywhere and imparting blessings, but the Creator and creation are clearly not synonymous.

It seems to be a forgotten truth that the Bible presents the creation as a priceless gift in which all the plants, animals, Earth and people are intended to flourish harmoniously. Walter Brueggemann sums this up by saying that 'the central vision of world history in the Bible is that all creation is one, every creature in community with every other, living in harmony and security toward the joy and well-being of every other creature'.[18] Humans are meant to be agents of blessing and to express that through relationships and by the moral choices we make.

As the biblical stories unfold, those harmonious relationships are described as being broken. This is repeatedly illustrated by humans showing contempt for the One who made all things, and disrespecting other sentient life. The same dysfunctional behaviour is obvious in our time when we are confronted by the consequences of human decisions that damage the natural environs. While the moral burden to care for the natural world rests with all people, Western Christians should be facing up to the consequences of their own consumerist lifestyles. So I appreciate Gus's comments concerning the desanctification of the Earth and how Pagans respond to Nature. There are some obvious points of difference between Pagans and Christians but there are also areas of mutual concern.

Mixed Christian Legacy

Today there are many earnest people, including Christians, who are responding to the complex problems of cleaning up waste and taking responsibility for damaged eco-systems. Pagans in particular are to be commended for their valuable efforts in exploring countercultural ways of living, using renewable non-polluting energy, and for their political activism on ecology. As human sensitivities to ecological degradation have widened over the past 40 years a negative judgment has been persistently made about Christianity. The same point is repeated by secular scientists, ecological ethicists and animal rights campaigners: Christians hold to a dualist view of humans separated from nature, promote an arrogant speciesist view that the Earth exists solely for people, and believe that the Bible mandates exploiting the Earth.[19]

There is undeniable evidence of anthropocentric and negative attitudes towards the Earth among Christians. In past eras some Christians were influenced by NeoPlatonic dualist views that devalued the natural world and regarded God as remote from the Earth.[20] Thomas à Kempis partly reflected this in his sentiment that 'every time I go into creation, I withdraw from God'.[21] It must be admitted that dualist ideas about matter and spirit have led some Christians to lead distorted lives by concluding that the Earth, human creativity and culture, sexuality and the physical body are corrupt and loathsome.

Scholastic theologians in late Medieval times regarded the Earth as an instrument solely for serving human needs. Some evangelicals today believe that the Earth is ultimately doomed, and that as Christians will go to heaven, what happens to the creation is not very important. The modern era also reveals appalling examples of English clergy who sponsored fox-hunts, bull-baiting and cock-fighting. Dutch Calvinists in South Africa decimated the quagga species; Protestant industrial entrepreneurs have polluted the Earth with their factories and mines; and Christians were among those who caused the extinction of the passenger pigeon.[22] The lifestyles of many modern-day Christians follow the patterns of consumerism that contribute to ecological harm. Clearly, heartfelt repentance is warranted, values and attitudes must change, and Christians must accept that our spiritual credibility and integrity has been undermined by following deviant beliefs and acting unwisely.

This disturbing portrait can become exaggerated when other Christian views are ignored. The church existed for some 1,500 years before the Industrial Revolution gave us the technological means to generate waste on a worldwide scale. The early church affirmed the creation over against Gnostic beliefs that regarded the material world as a spiritual prison. The ancient liturgies commemorated Christ's life in feasts and rites that also celebrated all sentient life. In the Eastern Orthodox tradition the feast of Epiphany includes the prayer of the great blessing of waters, which says 'with four seasons thou hast crowned the circuit of the year', and in which the sun, moon and stars give praise.[23] The Eucharistic prayers invariably started by including all creation in Christ's sacramental work.[24] Liturgy offered a structure for participating in seasonal rites that have their roots in the Old Testament festivals. For example, the annual harvest festivals and the development of the tithe barn were modelled on the biblical Feast of Tabernacles. These spiritual observances made much sense to people living in an agrarian society.

In monastic spirituality the creation was viewed as a precious gift and their contemplative meditations centred on God's creative work. Their theology reflected biblical ideas about God's presence in creation and people acting as trustees who care for the Earth. The monasteries used sustainable methods of agriculture.[25] The later Dominican and Franciscan orders were opposed to land sales for personal profit and money-lending involving interest, but in an era of cultural change they became a minority voice protesting against exploitative practices in the market economies.[26]

St Basil in the fourth century prayed a lament over ruthless human cruelty shown to the creation and included animals as 'brothers' in our common fellowship. St Isaac the Syrian was a vegetarian in the Nestorian Church who wrote about the charitable heart of those who pray for birds, reptiles, animals and the whole creation.[27] Similar sentiments are evident in the lives of Gregory of Nyssa, Catherine of Siena, Hildegard of Bingen, St Bonaventure, Francis of Assisi, Julian of Norwich and St John of the Cross.

John Wesley's theology of animals and the creation was expressed in the many hymns he composed, in his vegetarian lifestyle, and in the written encouragement he gave to William Wilberforce to campaign against animal cruelty. Arthur Broome and William Wilberforce co-founded the RSPCA as a specific Christian response to animal cruelty in England.[28] The Cadbury family that established the famous English chocolate company were Quakers who developed a holistic model for working in environmentally healthy settings. The Cadburys created the village of Bournville where clean air, fresh water and beautiful gardens were essential elements to both the factory and homes for their staff. John Cadbury also campaigned against animal cruelty.[29]

The novelist C. S. Lewis opposed vivisection and several of his fictional works reflect a Christian romantic theology of creation.[30] John Klotz, Francis Schaeffer, and Loren Wilkinson were among the earliest contemporary North American evangelical voices to speak out on ecology and theology.[31] Christian relief agencies such as Tearfund have been assisting local communities from developing nations in practising sustainable agriculture and in campaigning for fair trade. Recently, the Eastern Orthodox 'Green Patriarch' Bartholomew I and Pope Benedict XVI have published theological declarations about stewardship of the Earth, while various Christian organizations are now involved in repairing local eco-systems and in lobbyist campaigns.[32]

A Common Human Problem

I believe that the misuse of the Earth reflects a fundamental problem in human behaviour. In pre-industrial times some regional cultures acted unwisely. The First Nation people across the south-western Pacific altered the flora and fauna centuries before encountering Europeans.[33] The Polynesians of Easter Island caused the extinction of all animals and the settlement collapsed.[34] The twelfth-century settlement at Angkor, Cambodia, eventually collapsed having exhausted its natural resources.[35] The Fertile Crescent spanning from Egypt's Nile River across to the Euphrates River and the Persian Gulf was home to various empires: Assyrian, Babylonian, Egyptian and Sumerian. Each empire reverenced the seasons and geographical sites with fertility deities. Various political, military, social and economic factors contributed to their collapse but all were interlocked with their use of dubious irrigation practices, and the way they deforested and over-harvested the land, causing deserts to expand.[36]

Human activity affected the ecology of the British Isles in the Mesolithic, Neolithic and Bronze Ages, and the Iron Age Celts cleared large areas of forest in England particularly in the Midlands.[37] In the pre-Christian Roman empire the natural environs were linked to the presence of spiritual powers and deities. When no monotheistic faith held sway the Romans witnessed the extinction of the lion in Europe, and brought about the end of the hippopotamus and the elephant in North Africa. Much of that was caused by an enormous trade across Europe and North Africa in wild animals that were captured for gladiatorial jousts with human contestants of both sexes.[38] The Romans also deforested the North African coast and, according to the first-century satirist Lucius Seneca, the very air of Rome reeked of soot and foul vapours.[39]

Our modern era, however, has primarily operated from a belief about controlling nature for human gain that developed out of many different ideas. Some ideas were opposed to Christianity while others were reshaped into theological views. It would take a book to discuss the details, but the modern mindset about exploiting the natural world owes much to: the rise of Deist views of a remote God and the social decline of European churches; the exaltation of human reason over intuition in the Age of Reason; the centrality of the individual as expressed in the Reformation and Renaissance humanism; the emergence of mechanistic models of the universe that reduced nature to an object of analysis; a modern speciesist view that zoologically typecasts some creatures as puny and therefore of lesser value; the colonial exploitation of under-developed nations; the Industrial Revolution and the global expansion of capitalism; the ascendancy of the secular nation-state; and the advent of atheistic communist societies in Eastern Europe in which eco-systems such as the Caspian Sea were ruined.[40]

The modern attitude displaced the older guardianship view held by the church. However, although many non-Christians have come to understand the Bible and Christianity in a negative fashion, as I noted earlier very few will have reached this outlook by any extensive study of theology. With a few exceptions, such an outlook is more likely to have been conveyed to them by those Christians who interpret the Bible in ways that foster a negative attitude towards creation. Scottish theologian John Drane believes it can be shown that Christians who reflect such attitudes do so as people whose values have been primarily shaped by ideas that are at odds with the Bible.[41]

Relationships: God, Humans, Nature

One of the central themes of the Bible is that God is the Creator who has brought the entire cosmos into existence. As we came to understand in the previous chapter, God is transcendent, which indicates that God and the creation are not identical. We also discovered that God is immanent, which means that God's Spirit is continually present throughout the entire creation, nurturing and sustaining all things. The biblical concept of creation is centred in dynamic relationships: God relates directly with the Earth and animals, and likewise with humans. The other significant feature concerns the relationship between humans, the Earth and animals.

I agree with John Drane that a helpful way to start appreciating the biblical concept of creation is to consider the stories it tells.[42] The opening pages of the Bible tell ancient stories that draw us into questions and themes we find perennially intriguing. Precisely because those early pages tell stories, they invite the discerning reader to reflect on the questions implicit in the plot-line: Who am I anyway and who might I become? How can I find my place in the cosmos? Where do I find the divine source of all life? What makes us, females and males alike, so interesting and different and yet at times so frustrating to fathom? How should we relate to the soil, rivers, seas, plants, birds and animals? Why is it that the cosmos appears to have some purpose and ought to be harmonious and yet is so messed up?

The initial story invites us to consider an idyllic place that we would love to inhabit. It is a beautiful sanctuary, teeming with all kinds of living creatures and wonderful plants, with a pleasant and hospitable climate. All life forms are brimming with potential. The people living there are the direct opposite of the 'tenants from hell' because they live in transparent harmony with one another and take responsibility to care for everything. They are open to the Creator's presence and enjoy an intimate relationship of deep spirituality that is expressed reciprocally. The Creator's presence is felt in their lives but also fills the entire place in a harmonious loving and unbroken connection. They have been invited into the 'garden' as co-workers with the Creator to wisely bring this place to the fulfilment of its divinely appointed potential.[43]

As the plot unfolds the humans begin to consider other possibilities that divert their attention from the three-way relationship of Creator, humans and the Earth. Perhaps they can do a better job by becoming independent of God rather than remaining in an interdependent context of relationships. They opt for being self-reliant and become over-confident about what they can do. As they choose to go their own way everything quickly becomes distorted and ripped asunder. First, they lose their honesty and open transparency with each other and a blame-game begins. Second, they are ashamed to be in any intimate relationship with God. Third, their harmonious relationship with soil, water, plants and animals is broken and immediate harm is done to the delicate ecology of the place they are living in.[44] Fourth, sibling rivalry erupts out of jealousy and leads to murder.[45] The shattering effect of this behaviour spreads out like a ripple on the surface of a pond and soon the self-assurance of humans seems boundless, but as each episode in the plot unfolds more misery and frustration occurs.[46] So, in a primordial setting, spiritual and ecological harmony is depicted as becoming fractured. It is accompanied by the message that 'human self-sufficiency, self-confidence, and self-indulgence lead to disaster'.[47]

After reading the biblical stories, it is possible to identify some important elements that have direct bearing on how Christians are supposed to behave towards and think about the Earth. Drane suggests there are four primary elements: (a) We are to be God-centred; (b) People have specific value, which has ramifications for the way both the Earth and humans are treated; (c) We are morally accountable; and (d) The Christ-story is central as it points to God's blessing on the Earth, and reveals the mutuality of divine, human and environmental relationships. These elements form a framework for theological reflection on the biblical stories and particularly those passages about the role and status of humans.[48]

Theological Reflections

The theocentric focus of the Bible provides an important base from which Christian attitudes towards the Earth can be evaluated. The prophets exposed corruption in ancient Israel's monarchy and the nation at large by protesting how far they had deviated from God's concern for equity and justice and abused the land.[49] This sort of soul-searching, if applied today, could shock us into realizing how far we deviate from God's intended way. Referring back to the theocentric message of Jesus, the apostles and prophets provides an excellent starting point from which Christians can be effectively challenged.

The broad plot-line of Genesis presupposes a web of unified relationships involving God, humans, animals and the biosphere. The creation stories contradict dualist theologies that divorce humans from the rest of the natural world. In these stories humans are very much a part of the natural world and do not exist in isolation from it. This is expressed at the start of Genesis when humans are described as being made from the dust of the Earth.[50]

Although the relationship between humans and animals is not one of equality in status, both belong in the natural realm. Adam's relationship with the animals does involve some conferred responsibilities of caring for them because he names them. This act of naming points to humans having relationships with animals with implied duties of responsibility. A popular assumption is that the act of naming the animals signifies Adam's power and control over them. This thought is often misconstrued as conferring *carte blanche* on humans to do as they please. However, that line of thinking is undermined by two important points. The first point is that in the Bible the act of naming does not necessarily correlate to humans having power at all. The servant woman Hagar gives a personal name to God but the text does not imply that she had power over God.[51]

The second point concerns the statements about humans having dominion and being created in God's image and likeness. How we understand these statements will have direct implications on how we think and act. A helpful way to understand the meaning of dominion in the Genesis text is by first examining how it is used in other biblical texts. When the word is used elsewhere in the Bible it refers to authority conferred on and exercised by a benevolent monarch. The ideal portrait is of one whose status was first among equals in the community. The one holding the royal office was to express spiritual devotion to God by acting wisely in equitable, merciful and caring ways.[52] The biblical texts frequently point to the failings of Israel's monarchs to act in this way.

Adam's dominion can be best understood as a parallel to the way in which the ideal monarch was meant to act. The tasks that he has to perform involve service and are undertaken in the very presence of God. The terms that are used for work or cultivating the soil in the creation story correlate to the term that is used for worship elsewhere in the Bible. So the humans who work in the garden do so in what constitutes a liturgical or priestly role. William Dumbrell observes that 'dominion is the service which takes its motivation from the ultimate human relationship with the Lord God on behalf of whom dominion is exercised'.[53]

The other critical phrase that is used refers to humans being made in God's image and likeness. Much learned discussion has ensued over what this means because the creation story does not present a specific definition. The consensus is that humans are God's representatives, so they are to care in the same way that God does by being equitable, merciful and loving.[54] In other words, humans must image the loving and gracious characteristics of God towards the rest of the creation.[55] In light of these details it is possible to understand that human dominion involves a serious moral trust, which carries with it the further thought that we are accountable to God for our actions.

The covenant with Noah reiterates that all other sentient life is valuable to God.[56] It is further illustrated in the Hebraic laws concerning the Jubilee year, Sabbath rest for all creatures and for the soil, and in other passages that forbid cruelty to animals.[57] Isaiah also envisaged a future utopian age with a renewed creation that encompasses animals, humans and the biosphere.[58] All these themes are expressed in biblical images of the whole world resembling a healthy household.[59]

A deeper theological understanding is nurtured from the biblical witness to God's presence in the world. Psalm 139 shows the Spirit of God as the source of all life, who is in the world continuously sustaining, maintaining and renewing the Earth.[60] The immanence of God also opens up the possibility of personally encountering the Divine anywhere on the Earth, and this is what various biblical characters experience in deserts, on mountains and at sea. The apostle Paul understood the interrelatedness of all things when he wrote that the creation is frustrated by humanity's fall and waits for complete liberation.[61] As Paul understood Christ to be the Creator his writings present a Christocentric outlook on the positive worth of the creation.[62] The incarnation of God in Christ centres on the life experiences of Jesus as both a vulnerable child and an adult who is very much a part of the world that he cares for. Christ's redemptive work is not just about human beings but involves the entire creation, and the future-oriented biblical vision sees the whole creation fulfilled and renewed.[63] So a theology that represents God as uninvolved and remote from the Earth or that devalues creation is very much at odds with the major biblical themes of creation, incarnation and redemption.

Life and Death

The books of the Bible include stories, songs, poems, aphorisms and reflections that point to a holistic way of living in relationship with God, one another and the world. They present realistic portraits of individuals and families undergoing experiences of birth and death, love and hate, joy and sorrow, ecstasy and pain, success and failure, forgiveness and rejection. Humans are portrayed as having God-given capacities that are blessed but at the same time, due to our broken relationship with God, our entire being is now spiritually harmed. This understanding of humans is kept continuously in view, as is the possibility of renewal and the invitation from God to discover a better way. The natural world is upheld as precious to God but it is also understood as suffering from broken connections. In this regard the biblical texts do not draw romanticized or sentimental portraits of nature, such as those that we are more familiar with from some poetry.

The ordinary things of life are quite integral to the spiritual messages presented by the biblical writers. The Song of Songs is entirely devoted to celebrating the love and sexual passion of a woman and a man. The wisdom literature conveys many practical observations about coping with life through the cyclic rhythms of birth, growth and death experienced under the sun, moon and seasons.[64] Paul the apostle had a theology of the routines of life from which he wrote about the ups and downs of relationships, resolving conflict, dealing with responsibilities, disappointments, illness, attitudes to work and rest, food and sexuality.

Aside from Jesus, all other characters who appear in the Bible have serious flaws and struggle to become better persons. Very often they are people who confront tremendous hindrances, grapple with failure, and find spiritual depth in the midst of frailties, difficulties and suffering. The Gospels show Jesus experiencing two fundamental processes of life: being born as a child and coming to the end of things in death. During his childhood Jesus was exposed to parental love and nurture, becoming a refugee due to political death threats, experiencing conflict with siblings, and learning about creativity and labour. As an adult he gained a reputation for enjoying food and drink, which some of his critics pointed to in order to discredit him.[65] He spent time alone with God in the desert, on mountains and in gardens, and carried out much of his teaching in open spaces. So Jesus experienced a wide range of the ordinary things of human life and sanctified them.

In light of these things many Christians over the centuries have been inspired to express their creative spirituality in art, literature, poem and song.[66] For some Christians, such as Ephrem the Syrian (306–373) and Charles Williams (1886–1945), poetry has been a very important way of 'doing theology'.[67] Alongside the theologizing about the enigma of pain and suffering, some Christians have contemplated the intrinsic human capacity for pleasure and joy as experienced within the natural world. This emphasis on joy was a particular preoccupation in the writings of C. S. Lewis, J. R. R. Tolkien and Charles Williams.[68]

Some years ago I worked in a context where I administered deceased estates and interviewed people who gave instructions for their last will and testament to be drafted. On occasions I met people on their death-beds. I later interacted with beneficiaries who were left gifts in the person's will. These encounters gave me brief glimpses into a range of attitudes that different people hold about death. After someone's death I likewise saw those who were in grief and also those who were impatient about having to wait for the money from the estate. I have faced personal bereavement before and it is looming ahead for me in the lives of those I am closest to. I sometimes meditate on this thought: at the end, knowing the kind of life I have had and holding to belief in Christ, would I regret having ever lived? For me the answer is 'no' and my reasons for this are wrapped up in the life and message of Jesus, which is the subject of another chapter.

CHAPTER 4

Humans and the Divine

Gus diZerega

Religion focuses on strengthening, repairing and maintaining appropriate human relations with the Sacred. Because the Sacred is everywhere, there are many ways in which we can do this. Humankind has developed polytheistic, monotheistic and, in Buddhism, even nontheistic religions, with doctrinal, experiential and revelatory foundations, focusing on different levels of individual and community participation. The world's greatest religions often exhibit many of these dimensions within their frameworks. But however great their number, they have relatively few abstract values in common. Perhaps the most basic of these values is *mindfulness*: remembering the greater context within which we live, a context that is the ultimate source of value and goodness. All situate the mundane ego within a context far bigger than it.

From this insight arises a focus on living in *harmony* with this great context. Falling out of harmony is a major source of suffering and misfortune. So religions develop ways for repairing, re-establishing and preserving our personal and communal harmony with this sacred context.

This context, we have seen, is nearly universally described as the Good, the True and the Beautiful, or in some similar terms. In so far as we exemplify some of the qualities of this source, we manifest greater peacefulness, loving-kindness, charity, compassion, love and the like. These words differ from tradition to tradition, but too much can be made of this seeming diversity. The words do not contradict one another. Their values can easily co-exist. In addition, they are used to describe what those who have experienced this source universally say cannot be adequately put into words.

Let me give a very mundane example to illustrate this point. In English the word for a chilli pepper's spiciness is 'hot'. But in German it is 'scharf'. In English we translate 'scharf' as 'sharp'. Germans say 'Das Messer ist scharf': 'The knife is sharp.' When I discuss these words with bilingual German friends they say 'scharf' makes more sense to them than 'hot' to describe a chilli pepper's spiciness. For the life of me 'hot' makes more sense. I can only conclude the word we learn to describe an experience to some degree shapes our perception of the experience. It brings some aspects to the foreground at the cost of relegating others to a lesser status, or perhaps even invisibility. The taste of a pepper is actually neither hot nor sharp. These words *point* to the experience but do not faithfully describe it, only aspects of it. However, once we learn the aspect most emphasized, the other dimensions can fade from our awareness.

If we cannot agree across cultures on the word used to describe how chilli peppers taste, small wonder we have difficulties describing the nature of the Ultimate across cultures. But it is significant that the words we use in this latter task are all in greater mutual harmony than are the words 'sharp' and 'hot'. That there is a diversity of religions within the world, with some variation in the values they hold dearest, is not necessarily evidence that a hierarchy of access to divine truth exists between them, distinguishing better from worse religious traditions. (That religious practices can go awry *within* any tradition is another matter, to which I will return when we discuss religious authority.)

Agreement on just how we should relate to the Divine has proven impossible to reach within *all* the world's greatest religions. Even those claiming the clarity of revealed texts have divided many times. In fact, division has proven a fundamental characteristic of any particular religion. What does this mean? Does diversity challenge or support a religious outlook?

For Pagans it supports it. Pagan religions have diversified enormously. Given that they long predate other religions, usually by thousands of years, it would be strange were this not so. But from their beginning to the present time, certain themes characterize them collectively as 'Pagan'. To make a list, they are:

1. Panentheism
2. Animism – the world is alive
3. Polytheism
4. The eternal present – we emphasize the cyclical and mythic over the linear and historical
5. No principle of ultimate evil
6. Religious pluralism
7. Emphasis on harmony
8. Greater emphasis on experience than faith or others' revelations[1]

While panentheism as an explicit dimension of Pagan spirituality had to await the arrival of literate urban cultures, the other traits can be traced back as far as we can go in human history.

Shamanism

Paganism's earliest roots are shamanic. Some people within a hunting and gathering group were called out by Spirit to learn more, and so assist their fellow tribe members in regaining and maintaining harmony both individually and as a community. Those we broadly identify as shamans appeared in many forms depending on the characteristics of the land and the histories of the people. Because the word itself was first devised to describe shamanism as practised among the Turkic-Tungus people of Siberia, a great deal of ink has been spilled over who is or is not a shaman. I think we can safely set most of this controversy aside.

When we look at hunting and gathering peoples, we find little in the way of institutionalized religious hierarchy or any elaborate division of labour. In other words, practising a religion is not the same as having a spirituality. For hunting and gathering peoples, spirituality will often colour every dimension of their lives; however, in our sense of the term, they will not be practising a religion. Alternatively, they are so immersed within their religion that it is ultimately indistinguishable from their way of life. While some beings and places may be more sacred than others, there is no place or being that is completely secular in the modern sense.[2]

Because people remain in obvious and immediate dependence on their environment, they generally emphasize living in harmony and restoring the damage done by disharmony. Healing illnesses and divination are two universal practices shamans have excelled at, both of which are important to peoples living where challenging environments make small the margins of error. Both emphasize bringing people and community into greater harmony with their world. Shamans depended on spirits to give them healing and other information, so they developed many ways wherein they could listen to and cultivate the spirits of the land. While shamans could specialize, in all cases their knowledge was passed down individually, through close association with apprentices and often through years of instruction.

In the process shamans discovered and developed the basic spiritual practices that typify Pagan practices in general: dance, ritual, song, isolation, ordeal, entheogens (psychoactive plant substances) and trance are among them. They have been handed down now for uncountable generations and remain important today. All are means by which we can take leave of our mundane concerns, the better to interact with and learn from the Sacred.

From an Abrahamic perspective, trance, in which one is in direct contact with spirits who can also work through the person, is probably the most controversial and least understood practice. At the same time it is central to many traditions, including my own.[3] In practice, trance apparently exists along a continuum, from a condition in which the person is largely the tool of the spirit and often remembers little if anything of what happened while in that state (usually termed a 'medium'), into explicit conscious cooperation between spirit and person (more typical of shamans). I write 'apparently' because I have only experienced the second. Shamanic journeys to the upper and lower worlds are less common outside hunting and gathering cultures. In trance we open ourselves up in as intimate a way as a human being can to the more-than-human world of Spirit. Many techniques have been developed to facilitate entry into this state and assist those already there.

In its purest form shamanism is probably always practised by only a few. Its demands are too great, its call of service to the community too strong and consuming, to attract many. Even within traditional societies people who became shamans often did so against their will. Substantial as they are, its benefits do not come cheaply, and many people would prefer not to pay the price. On the other hand, as Jordan Paper among others notes, in societies with strong shamanic traditions, virtually everyone would partake of shamanic abilities to some degree or other.[4]

Even so, shamanism is very much with us today, and not only among the dwindling number of hunting and gathering peoples. In the modern West, and even more so in modern Asia and Latin America, people are still called to this path, a path of healing and service to others. While many of their more immediately practical tasks have been taken over by modern medicine, and organized religions have increasingly served the function of maintaining appropriate individual and community relations with the Sacred, apparently there still remains a need for shamans. Perhaps it is they who, more than anyone else, keep open the possibility that even moderns can re-establish connection with the other-than-human world.

In my opinion, the debt humanity owes them is without measure.

PaleoPaganism

I believe it was with the rise of agricultural civilization that, along with its benefits, a deep divide began to emerge between daily life and the Sacred.[5] Greek and Roman Paganism as well as that of traditional China, India, Mesopotamia, agricultural Africa and the settled cultures of MesoAmerica were no longer shamanic, although shamanic elements remained within their practice. I believe the earlier emphasis on being in harmony with the place was increasingly challenged by the need of agricultural societies to control and manipulate Nature. By Hellenistic times harmony was increasingly replaced by concern with a fickle Fate.[6]

As societies grew in complexity, wealth and numbers, organized associations arose, and priests and priestesses became increasingly differentiated into separate groups, sometimes by inheritance, sometimes through political appointment, sometimes by 'calling'. In different ways they were responsible for helping their communities stay in harmony with their spiritual environment. With these developments came both the advantages and disadvantages of religious practices being administered by large organizations.

In other words, practising a religion is not the same as having a spirituality. The two overlap, but as concepts and as frames of mind neither fits entirely within the other. In William Irwin Thompson's words, at its inception religion is 'the form spirituality takes in civilization'.[7]

In addition, the world of spirit connection appears to have become more diverse. In settled agricultural communities the ancestors became increasingly important. As the human world became more divorced from that of Nature, the animal and elemental powers apparently began taking on more anthropomorphic visages.[8]

In some cases these PaleoPagan traditions have survived relatively unscathed into the present day. Chinese and Korean popular religion, Hinduism, Shinto and the practices of some agricultural tribal peoples in Africa would all be situated here. Except for Native Americans and, I understand, some of the aboriginal peoples of Australia and the Maoris of New Zealand, these traditions have been largely invisible within the English-speaking West. However, as immigration brings people who follow these practices to culturally European shores, and a modicum of justice begins to be administered to the original inhabitants, this is beginning to change.

One fascinating development is taking place in Lithuania and Latvia. With the collapse of Communism, Baltic Pagans are seeking to revive their own relatively recently suppressed tradition. Lithuania was the last Pagan state in Europe, surviving into the fourteenth century before succumbing to invasion by the Teutonic Knights. The last sacred groves in Lithuania were cut down by Christian authorities in the late seventeenth century.[9]

NeoPaganism

Contemporary NeoPaganism marks a rediscovery by moderns of the spiritual insights and practices that characterized most of human society throughout most of our history as a species. But it is a rediscovery by people who, for better and for worse, are coming from a culture that has rejected and largely forgotten much of what earlier Pagan cultures took for granted. I take this as largely for the worse. We are *relearning* much of what has been lost to our society for millennia.

But our Gods, the Earth and other Pagan peoples have taught us. When I look at the development of Pagan practice since 1984, when the Goddess first made Herself known to me, I am astounded at how much we have grown not only in numbers, but also in understanding of our own tradition. We have learned from teachers in other Pagan traditions, such as Santeria, Umbanda and different Native American peoples. We have also learned as our elders have increasingly become true elders, people with many decades of practice behind them, and a modicum of hard-won wisdom. I became qualified to teach in terms of my formal status after a few years' involvement, but it took me almost twenty years to feel genuinely qualified.

We have come a fair way since one beautiful and vibrant tradition emerged from a 1960s folklore class at UC Berkeley when, after performing an imagined re-creation of the Eleusinian Mysteries as their class project, some students asked others, 'Did you feel what I felt?' And the reply was, 'Yes!'[10]

At the same time our society is radically different compared not only to Greece and Rome, but also to contemporary Pagan cultures with relatively intact roots. With the advent of agriculture, increasingly the powers of nature became not a source of the gifts of the land, but a whimsical threat to the farmer's labours. Large concentrations of people without modern hygiene were repeatedly devastated by plague and other sickness on a scale far beyond the capacity of traditional healers to heal. Poverty was the lot of most, lorded over by autocrats and aristocrats of various sorts, who often used religious terminology to justify their privileges. In societies such as those it was very easy to see embodied existence as problematic, and salvation or enlightenment and removal from the wheel of existence as desirable outcomes. It is only rather recently that the death rate in cities has been lower than their birth rate and the poor have been a minority group in much of the world.

For most of us in the West today Nature is a source of renewal. Her threats come from our not listening. More and more people farm because they want to, not because the alternative is starvation. In a curious way, we are more open to a hunting and gathering perception of Nature as home than previous agriculturally based civilizations have been – though even in Greece and Rome prosperous urban dwellers often had idealized views of life in Nature.

Furthermore, we are far less hierarchical than earlier settled cultures, Pagan and Christian alike. Equality under the law, democracy and relative prosperity have undermined relations of domination either as appropriate for humans or as convincing metaphors for our relation to the Divine. Ironically, here too we share more with hunting and gathering cultures than with their agricultural descendants.[11]

NeoPaganism both reflects these aspects of modern culture and is able to address the ills and needs of modern life. It is not unique in this capacity, but its strengths here are major ones. At a time when we as a culture and as individuals have become increasingly alienated from the world that is our home, within which we dwell, Pagan religion teaches us how to be at home again. We are too clever and too shallow to be able to rely on our 'self-interest' alone to live in this world. Our mundane self has too narrow *and* too inflated a view of its own importance to act wisely. Our cleverness has given us enormous impact and power, but not much sense of responsibility in using it.

If we look at the cultures that did harmonize themselves with the world, they situated themselves within a more-than-human sense of community, a *sacred* sense of community that included not only physical human beings and other dwellers, but also their spiritual dimensions. We desperately need to expand our sense of the moral and sacred community. Pagan religion can help us relearn this vital lesson.

Second, the universal Pagan emphasis on harmony goes beyond harmony with the human and other-than-human community. It also focuses on internal harmony. Our society encourages excess and indulgence by the mundane self. From their earliest years in front of the television children are encouraged to see themselves as incomplete unless they possess things. Lots of things. Corporations hire psychologists to tell them how best to manipulate children into wanting their products. National child abuse is not too strong a term for this practice. Children grow up internalizing these attitudes as taken-for-granted. And today's Americans are unprecedented in their use of anti-depressants and other pills to get them through the day, as a strategy of filling inner emptiness with external possessions fails. Things often appear more promising before we acquire them than afterwards.

From a Pagan perspective there is nothing amiss with material well-being, but there is something profoundly sad about such well-being being considered the ultimate meaning of life, and possessions being sought to fill an inner need. In possessions the modern mind sees only surfaces – the glitter of the object and the reactions of those who see that you have it – but the needs they are intended to fill are usually internal. This is why consumerism cannot work.

Pagan spirituality honours and celebrates the material while placing it within a broader context which both underlines its importance and limits it. The material world *is good*. It is not a second best. But it exists within, is a manifestation of, and is supported by, a Good that is greater still because it encompasses the material world but is more than that. Once we appreciate this greater Good, our appreciation for and love of the material is different because we are not so dependent on it as a solution to our emptiness or a tool for meeting our wants. We are not so controlled by our desires and fears. I think it fair to say our appreciation for the material is *greater* because we respect the world of matter as having value beyond its ability to serve us.

What does Paganism offer us as individuals? Disharmony is a disruption of relationship, and while we are individuals, we are also who we are because of our relationships. When our relationships are amiss, so are we. And our relationships are frequently amiss.

I believe that within Gardnerian Wicca harmony is best understood from a NeoPlatonic philosophical perspective. Its rising levels of initiation, when understood wisely, take the practitioner ever closer to intimate union with the Gods. Within that union – and the more often it happens the better – the person is increasingly 'tuned in' to a harmonious relationship with qualities of the One as manifested through our Gods.[12]

This process is important because it is these qualities, which we all possess to some degree, that are most eternal. As we are awakened and gradually (oh so very gradually!) transform the rest of our lives, we become, in the words of our tradition, 'immortal'. This claim needs elaboration.

Mind, or consciousness, is energy, and each of us sends energy where our thoughts go. When we strengthen our connection with what is far removed from these ultimate qualities, we reinforce a self resting on an ultimate foundation of sand. I do not mean to deny the value of the temporary. Far from it. But the temporary is made lasting only through its integration into a larger context.

When we strengthen our connection with what is close to the One, that self and all its qualities are enriched with these characteristics. In a sense, it opens like a flower, its boundaries against the external world become more permeable. To a point these boundaries are necessary. But if not outgrown they can become prisons, and we become like a butterfly trapped in its chrysalis. The greater our capacity to love, to care, to show compassion and generosity, the greater the part of us that is eternal, because these qualities are most characteristic of the One. Our Gods help us grow there.

When I first encountered the Goddess, I also experienced perfect love for the first time. On a later occasion I told Her I hoped someday to be worthy of Her love. She replied, 'You have always been worthy of my love.' I immediately experienced a surge of pride, thinking 'I'm special after all!'

She responded: '*All* beings are always worthy of my love.'

It was one of the most profound experiences of my life.

This message is neither inferior nor superior to that of other religious traditions, assisting their members to become more loving, compassionate, caring people. Indeed, the very variety of spiritual practices that has developed within the human race seems to me one of the strongest arguments for the validity of Pagan spirituality. This is what we would expect in a world such as Pagans experience it. Here, my perspective is 180 degrees removed from that within many scriptural traditions, based on the revelations a small number of individuals supposedly made on behalf of the rest of us.

Energies far removed from love and compassion also have a kind of existence. Visit Washington, DC, and if you are sensitive, the sense of power as domination pervades the place, and has ensnared many. But power of this sort, like other low energies, exists only by acquiring energy from others. It is parasitic. Power seekers honour it, invest their lives in its pursuit, and feed it their own character, making sacrifice after sacrifice. Their sense of power is great, but they have become only its servants, residing within the rigid walls of a self-constructed cocoon. Few break free.

As I explained when discussing evil, these energies, as powerful and independent of us as they seem, appear largely to be our own creations. They are continually fed by our attention and striving. Here I think lies the source for problems with spiritual parasitism and the like, but exploring these matters distracts us from our present topic.

A Pagan View of Religious Pluralism

Religions are human creations, but they are not just human creations. They are the creative result of our encountering the More-Than-Human, and seeking to enter into better relationship with the Ultimate Context of existence. The Sacred responds and can even initiate, but the human component is essential, and is a source of enormous creativity.

As we seek to manifest our spiritual insights, we unavoidably colour and shape them with our individuality as well as the values and customs of our society and time. This enables the Sacred to enter into human life more fully and completely. Many of these encounters with the Sacred may be largely individual, and remain in the realm of the narrowly spiritual – important to the person having the experience, but not entering into society as a whole. But others enable us to come together as a religious community to celebrate, honour, and perhaps be transformed by that encounter. For this to happen spiritual insights must be put into terms to which the community as a whole can relate.

There is no error in saying that the meaning of the Good for me is harmony or love or salvation or enlightenment or any similar thing. As I emphasized above, the error only arrives when that becomes what I believe it should be for everyone else, and that all the others are in error. It is the error of saying that pepper is hot, and any fool who thinks it is sharp simply lives in darkness and delusion. Or vice versa.

Is a Hindu chant more or less 'spiritual' than a Gregorian chant? Is the Charge of the Goddess more or less spiritually true than the Sermon on the Mount? The question is mistaken at its core. As the More-Than-Human Sacred encounters the human, the result is a flowering of human potential elevated to its greatest capacity. A wonderful variety of religions has arisen within our world, each an expression of the people and time of their origination, of the Sacred that is most fully reflected through that particular tradition, and of all that has happened since. Religious pluralism is good because the Sacred far exceeds the capacity of any single tradition to fully honour all its aspects. The merely human cannot fully honour the super-human, but we can learn from and be inspired by one another.

Religion, then, is a kind of collective Sacred Performance Art.[13] I mean this term literally, but in no way disrespectfully. Religion is art because it focuses on what is beautiful as manifestations of and symbols for the Divine. This may be beauty in Nature, or it may be beauty created by human beings or, often, both. It can manifest both outer and inner beauty. But from the Acropolis to Chartres, from ritual robes to the costumes of those dancing the Orixas, from Tibetan and Navajo sand paintings to Greek sacred statues, from a Sundance to a Wiccan Circle Dance, beauty is central to religion. Even those religious traditions that emphasize the severe and spare, as did the Shakers, do so because from their perspective lesser beauty distracts us from the greater Beauty they identify with God. There is something beautiful in their simplicity, as there is in the lush energy of the statues carved in a Hindu temple's walls. It should hardly be surprising that religion inspires much that is finest in human art. It would be strange were it otherwise.

Performance is also central to religion because religions are more than systems of thought. Even more, they are forms of action. They all possess sacred rituals, sacred times and sacred relationships. They honour the Sacred through artistic action as well as in thought and deed. Ritual is the essence of religious performance, and even the simplest and sparest religious observances set aside special times and places where people meet in fellowship and communion to honour and strengthen their relationship with the Sacred. And in good ritual the Sacred responds – indeed, who comprises the audience may be the chief difference between ritual and theatre. Successful ritual brings us into that wider and deeper context. Theatre does not try to go there.

And, most fundamentally, religion is sacred. Both performance and art are in service to the More-Than-Human. In religion, performances must be connected with spiritual truths. Viewed from the outside, Greek tragedies or a Wiccan Priestess reciting the Charge of the Goddess are performances. But experienced from within, these events can be spiritually transforming, pointing to truths that must be experienced bodily as well as intellectually if they are really to be experienced at all. Art must manifest or point to beauty that is permeated by the Sacred or else it becomes merely decoration or personal expression. I am very fond of theatre, decoration and personal expression. They are often wonderful. But all are rooted in the cares and concerns of our day-to-day, largely taken for granted existence. They can even help us become better people. But in a non-pejorative sense, they are focused on the mundane.

Another complementary perspective offers us insight into the wonderful variety of religious forms and experiences. At its best each religion represents the connection of a way of life with the Divine. Each therefore exemplifies the highest kind of human creation. Perhaps our most appropriate role as human beings is to manifest the Sacred in human creations, thereby integrating the true, the good and the beautiful. At one time we did this in relative isolation, each band or society largely in ignorance of the practices of others. Today we are aware of the full variety of religious expression that is possible. Our challenge is to honour the deepest truths within them all while being true to how the Sacred speaks to us.

The secular alternative that ultimately we exist to propagate the species cannot explain one of our most interesting and almost universal traits: our capacity to care for what is of no practical use to us. Writing of the extinction of passenger pigeons, the greatest of American environmental thinkers, Aldo Leopold, noted: 'For one species to mourn the death of another is a new thing under the sun… we who have lost our pigeons, mourn the loss. Had the funeral been ours, the pigeons would hardly have mourned us. In this fact, rather than in Mr DuPont's nylons or Mr Vannevar Bush's bombs, lies objective evidence of our superiority over the beasts.'[14] We have the capacity to care, and care deeply, for beings who are of no utility to us. The capacity to love and care rests at the core of what it is to be human.

Whatever else it may be, the Sacred is true for us at levels far deeper than the worries and joys and concerns and plans of our day-to-day lives. It is the truth revealed by concern for and contact with Ultimate Contexts. In accomplishing this task religion addresses many levels and dimensions of our existence, helping put them into right relationship with one another and with All That Is, healing what secular modernity and our own narrow egos have torn asunder, and situating the fragments of our lives in a meaning that goes beyond our day-to-day concerns.

I am Wiccan. But I have respectfully explored, learned from and in some cases practised other Pagan traditions, especially those growing out of Native American practice or the African diaspora, and I have also learned much from a Buddhist teacher. In this regard I have gone as Spirit has led me. These experiences have often been as powerful for me as those of Wicca, although I have never experienced the Wiccan Goddess within any of them. And much as I honour these other traditions, my personal commitment is first to Her. Even so, I honour each as an expression of Spirit.

My personal experiences of Christianity have generally been weaker, despite my having tried for many years to follow and understand that path. I have felt what I would imagine a Christian would call the presence of God within a Christian church. And interestingly, once I became Wiccan, I found I had to take Christianity more seriously *because* we ourselves made no claims to exclusivity. After becoming Wiccan I had a powerful spiritual experience that probably would have led me to Christianity were I not already Pagan.[15] Instead, it helped me see a profound truth in the Christian way, a truth much less emphasized by Pagans: the power of forgiveness.

Christianity was not and is not my path. But for some it is a wonderful path. I believe Wiccans do not fully understand the implications of their own traditions when they see only Christianity's shortcomings. On the day when I finished the first draft of this chapter, I also read an account of the life of John 'Buck' O'Neill.[16] In 2006 O'Neill posthumously received the Presidential Medal of Freedom. He had been one of the great black baseball players back when black Americans were not allowed to play with white players. O'Neill had also been a major advocate for black athletes during those dark times. He was later inducted into the baseball Hall of Fame, and subsequently helped to get other players of the Negro Leagues inducted as well. At the age of 94, he spoke at an induction of seventeen black players from the Negro League into the Hall of Fame. Among other things, O'Neill said:

And I tell you what, they always said to me Buck, I know you hate people for what they did to you or what they did to your folks. I said no, man, I never learned to hate. I hate cancer. Cancer killed my mother. My wife died ten years ago of cancer – I'm single, ladies. I hate AIDS. A good friend of mine died of AIDS three months ago. I hate AIDS. But I can't hate a human being because my God never made anything ugly. Now, you can be ugly if you want to, boy, but God didn't make you that way.

So I want you to light this valley up this afternoon. Martin [Luther King] said 'agape' is understanding, creative – a redemptive good will toward all men. Agape is an overflowing love which seeks nothing in return. And when you reach love on this level, you love all men, not because you like them, not because their ways appeal to you, but you love them because God loved them, and I love Jehovah my God with all my heart, with all my soul and I love every one of you as I love myself.[17]

I chose these words by O'Neill in part because they came to me the day I first wrote this section. But, more to the point, to emphasize that it is in *this* dimension of spirit, and not theology, that the great spiritual traditions come together.

Philip Johnson

Gus has drawn attention to the importance of finding and expressing spiritual values that facilitate personal growth and well-being. In celebrating the Divine, the Earth and human diversity, Pagans treasure the freedom to explore and experiment in their spiritual journey. Pagans clearly intuit the heaviness of social and personal fragmentation that characterizes much of contemporary urban living and they find the shamanic way one of many helpful means for pursuing renewal. Gus presents a very generous outlook concerning the multitude of religious experiences that exist alongside Pagan ways.

Spiritual Phenomena

When Gus mentioned the value of trance experiences he correctly noted that some tensions exist between the shamanic and Abrahamic ways. It appears that particular personality types may have a predisposition for trance-mystical experiences, and some recent studies of modern-day Western church-goers suggest that, of those surveyed, very few are temperamentally inclined.[18] It is also true that most Christians have strong reservations about trances and feel that it is important to evaluate unusual spiritual claims and experiences. In those evaluative processes Christians feel constrained to ask probing questions about truth. Perhaps what also needs consideration is how we can rediscover ways that properly integrate intuition, reason and emotions.

As I have noted elsewhere in this book, the Gospels call for a way of living that involves loving God with our heart, mind, soul and strength, and loving our neighbours as ourselves. That thought is embedded in the early Hebraic tradition and is approved of by Jesus when conversing about putting life's priorities into perspective.[19] For Jesus this is wrapped up in the transformational power of God's kingdom breaking into our daily experiences. This holistic image of loving God and neighbours is foundational to an integral way of living and is at odds with the modern Western preoccupation with dualist models of humanity, the world and ultimate reality. The hyper-specialization of knowledge has sometimes encouraged reductionist explanations as well as diverting attention away from integrating new insights into a seamless understanding of the world. Some feel that our cultural alienation and dysfunction has much to do with the marginalizing of the intuitional, emotional and numinous. Today's trends in cultural change clearly signpost that many people are now looking for holistic ways.

The eighteenth century brought Western civilization into a period of accelerated cultural change known as the Age of Reason, which placed a strong emphasis on human rational capacities. It was also characterized by a good deal of scepticism towards Christianity. Christian intellectuals sought to critically engage with this perspective, with some mixed results, including an unwitting embracing of some cultural values that, in the long run, ended up distorting the holistic emphasis of Jesus' teaching. The Romantic Movement arose in reaction to the Age of Reason and emphasized intuition, feelings and the need to explore ways of recovering a seemingly lost world of strange, non-rational and hidden things. Writers such as Goethe drew on esoteric imagery to express this way of looking at reality through the depths of emotion, the wisdom of the body, and the paranormal. For those exploring the labyrinthine ways of the esoteric, the expectation has been that hidden truth can be accessed via avenues and techniques in which human reason is not the primary tool.

I believe that Gus is pleading for a unified understanding of personhood that can integrate feelings, intuition, imagination and cognition. It seems to me that an appropriate Christian response is to return once more to Jesus' emphasis on integrating the mind, heart and soul. The mind, intellect, reason, imagination and intuition are all the handiwork of God, and it is futile to divide and fragment these things, as has happened in dualist thought.[20] God has created us with a 'feeling intellect', so our capacity for intuition, emotion and reason should be exercised with gratitude. They are among the markers that point to us being created in God's image and likeness. By keeping feelings and reason in harmony it is possible to explore much more deeply how God unveils truth to us.

The spiritual life that Jesus insisted on is theocentric. Although there are many different elements that form part of the broad spiritual picture, the centre-point is always God. The human journey of life is sustained by the Holy Spirit, who guides Christians to follow Jesus' way. The Triunity of God is the start, centre and end-point in a direct and unmediated relationship with us. So the spiritual life is not centred in us or in our efforts at controlling life but in letting God be God in our lives. The priority is communion with God expressed in relationships.

In some respects this theocentric focus decentres the importance of extraordinary spiritual phenomena. That is, one does not have to expect to experience high-energy spiritual occurrences. Most people never experience visions, dreams, prophetic utterances or mystical journeys from Earth to heaven and back. However, this does not mean that unusual spiritual occurrences are impossible or irrelevant, but that the grounding of spiritual living relies solely on God's sustaining power being expressed in us in the routines of life. Our sufficiency for living is anchored in a grace-filled loving relationship with God through Jesus and the Holy Spirit. By way of response we offer ourselves as a sacrificial liturgy in all that we are and say and do.[21] In biblical imagery all women and men are viewed as priests before God. That thought is conveyed in the creation story in which humans work the Earth as a liturgical act. It recurs in the story of the people of Israel forming a new nation of priests, and Peter the apostle also imparts it as vital teaching.[22]

There is a wide spectrum of approaches and spiritual disciplines emphasized by different Christian movements that enables us to sense God's presence both within us and in the things of the world: prayer, meditation, praise, reflecting on scripture, Lectio Divina (a method of prayer and scriptural reading), devotions, monastic disciplines, art, music, spiritual retreats and making a pilgrimage to a place of sacred significance.[23] Sometimes through these things we may cross the threshold of an invisible realm and at other times that unseen world impinges on ours. But the importance of having theocentric motivations remains at the heart of this. It would be selfish and anthropocentric to use spiritual disciplines and seek other-worldly experiences in order to manipulate the unseen realm to gain control over our future and our well-being.

In Chapter 1 I indicated that there are extraordinary spiritual experiences referred to in the Bible in which people have revelatory visions and dreams, encounter angels, perform healings and prophesy. When these extraordinary incidents are reported in the Bible the reader is obliquely guided by the stories to ask a reflective question: Is this message and experience truly from God or is it something that springs from fallible, unreliable and even deceptive sources?[24] There are also specific passages that call for the testing of the claims of prophets, seers and diviners and prompt reflective questions about the context of the experiences, the reported content of what took place and the spiritual fruit that ensues in its wake.[25]

The need for holistic discernment is illustrated in the story of Saul, the first king of Israel. Saul emerged as a leader at a time when the nation had reached a low ebb. The leading spiritual figure of the day was a prophet, priest and judge named Samuel, who pleaded with the nation to have the right kind of spiritual priorities, but his advice went unheeded.[26] The institution of the monarchy was established as an attempt to redress social and political problems. Prior to his coronation, Saul appeared in the company of a band of itinerant prophets and he began prophesying. Those who were acquainted with him pondered: Is Saul among the prophets?[27]

Saul appeared to be a skilful leader when neighbouring states engaged in destabilizing actions. Yet as the burdens of office took their toll his relationships became strained due to suspicions of intrigue. As his fears about a rival claimant to the throne intensified, so his behaviour became more erratic. At one point Saul lapsed into an altered state of consciousness and lay naked on the ground for a day, prophesying.[28] This prompted people to ask once again: Is Saul among the prophets? At that time Saul was on the verge of a complete collapse, so his prophesying did not indicate a healthy spiritual experience.

The climax comes when Saul seeks the aid of a diviner to contact the deceased spirit of Samuel.[29] Although the practice is prohibited under Moses' law, God allows Samuel to appear.[30] Samuel points out the futility of the exercise: if the all-wise God no longer listens to you then there is no advantage in contacting a dead person.[31] The spirit of Samuel pronounces a word of doom and the next day Saul perishes in battle. What the story manages to do is to juxtapose Saul's initial spiritual qualities and experiences as a promising leader with those of his later madness and spiritual collapse. He could prophesy and yet was spiritually bewildered, and so his gift did not correlate with signs of an integrated spiritual life. The story also juxtaposes Saul's erratic lifestyle with the emergence of David as his eventual successor.[32]

In the Bible, then, extraordinary experiences are not taken at face value as being self-authenticating, but require reflection by all concerned on who God is and what has been revealed. Even Christian mystics, who operate inside a specific tradition and pass through to visionary encounters of union with God, make themselves accountable. St John of the Cross had beatific visions, but he still prayed, partook of the Eucharist and did not circumvent the traditions within which his spiritual life had been shaped.

Discernment

Biblical discernment prompts Christians to be cautious of spiritual deception and destructive beliefs and practices. Those who specialize in these matters use various reflective and evaluative questions such as: Does this glorify God or humans? Does it recognize Jesus Christ? Is this evidence of the power of the Holy Spirit or a human-devised way of creating special yet shallow effects? Is it about me gaining control and power over life and the world and others, or does it lead to Jesus' humble way of service? What do we find in the Bible that guides and teaches us about such matters? What is the attitude of the person claiming a divine experience? Is this person open and accountable or closed off from scrutiny? Are the fruits of God's Spirit of love, joy, peace, patience and gentleness being manifested? In what way does the experience promote spiritual growth and maturity?

However, there is a great temptation to simplistically divide the world up into two camps and locate serious errors in someone else's pathway while failing to recognize flaws in one's own household. Much careful probing is warranted because Jesus made it clear that not everything that God's people say and do is necessarily true, and the revelatory oracles of the non-Israelite seer Balaam indicate that not every unusual thing necessarily emanates from dark spirits.[33] This sort of evaluative discourse requires a good deal of reflection on the part of Christians. It must be applied prophetically in our own backyard before it is posed as a valid theological question for dialogue with practitioners of other pathways.[34]

Lastly, while Christians affirm the numinous in biblical times there seem to be those who struggle with unusual spiritual phenomena happening today. Here I am reminded of an intriguing story. About nine years ago I was invited to talk to a small group of Christians who were work colleagues in a secular publishing firm. As part of my formal presentation I briefly related one of my personal experiences in encountering angels. Afterwards, I was approached by 'Gerry', who wanted to tell me about his experiences. Gerry had been pursuing an approach to personal growth and spirituality that involved the shamanic discipline of vision quests. At one point Gerry encountered a spirit who called himself 'Michael'. Michael said he was an angel with an urgent message for Gerry: 'Follow Jesus.' Gerry began a period of critical reflection on this encounter and eventually decided that he would no longer use vision quests but instead become a follower of Jesus.

More than a year later, Gerry had an unresolved question that had been posed by his brother 'John'. Gerry's brother was convinced that 'Michael' was a dark and deceiving spirit. However, Gerry was puzzled since on the one hand he had followed the advice of 'Michael' while on the other he respected the opinions of his brother John. I indicated to Gerry that on biblical grounds it seemed highly implausible that a deceiving spirit would commend the way of Jesus. Gerry's experiences led to positive spiritual fruit. Gerry then introduced me to his brother John and we continued the conversation. John remained adamant that Gerry had encountered a deceiving spirit. It seemed to me that perhaps John's perspective suffered from a form of cognitive dissonance: he could not reconcile his beliefs with Gerry's experiences. God's actions in Gerry's life were clearly greater than John's theology could encompass.

Holistic Self

I believe that the kind of spiritual framework that we all yearn for, where we can find healing, meaning, values, integrity, renewal and growth, becomes available to us in the life of Jesus. That spiritual framework is not centred in the structures and organizational systems that come to mind when one thinks of the institutions of contemporary churches. This does not mean that community formation and the development of institutions are wrong or that Jesus advocated a privatized spirituality divorced from wider networks of relationships. Instead, the spiritual framework is centred in the person of Jesus and there are some key images and guidelines to be discovered from what he did and said.

Among the many empowering images that can be discovered in what Jesus said is the invitation to personal renewal or rebirth.[35] Those of us who have experienced tragedy, been wounded through broken relationships, or felt the frustrating burden of unresolved conflicts and doubts, would love to have access to an integrated and empowered spiritual life. In the life of Jesus we meet a person who was genuine in offering spiritual rebirth and an integrated lifestyle that engages the whole person – the feelings, the five senses and the mind. Jesus imparted wisdom for the mind, spoke about spiritual rebirth and growth, demonstrated a practical spirituality by healing those in pain and feeding those who were hungry, and gathered all of this together in his insistence that we love God with our heart, soul, mind and strength and that we love our neighbours.

Jesus started from wherever individuals happened to be in their lives and, in what seemed like moments of spontaneity, he invited them to 'follow'.[36] These invitations to follow were not couched in terms of being burdened or struggling to find perfection.[37] Instead Jesus formed friendships that were based on him being vulnerable towards others and being willing to accept them as persons who know what it is like to be a failure. His invitation to follow meant allowing his friends to be in a position to be accepted for who they were and explore who they might become through the transforming power of God's Spirit. Implicit in this process of inviting individuals to follow Jesus was the formation of a new community built around the love of God and love for others. This was an open community in which people could learn to deal with their failures and struggles in a context of continual acceptance and forgiveness.

What Jesus disclosed is that God creates spaces in which harmonious relationships can flourish. God is concerned not just with our souls but with the entire human being, body, mind and spirit; and also with liberating the entire creation as it languishes under the weight of a broken and lost harmony. God, who is the ultimate being, blesses us with significance and offers us the only worthwhile yardstick for establishing human dignity. So no matter what our social status, embittered circumstances or experiences of alienation and misfortune, we are loved by the most significant being of all.

The invitation that Jesus gave was about making people whole and renewing them, and it included the offer of healing the divisive things that fracture our lives and harm the Earth. Our need for renewal and rebirth indicates that there is a prior problem that we must come to grips with concerning our alienation from God and one another. If there were nothing fundamentally problematic about the universal human condition then presumably Jesus would not have illustrated for us in his actions and words the offer of forgiveness and rebirth. Here I find myself acknowledging that Jesus understands me and that I can indeed trust him as a gracious, loving and wise person. What Jesus then discloses about God and about my brokenness leads me to a place where I make an about-face in life and begin a fresh journey in complete dependence and trust.

If I am not convinced that I have a serious spiritual problem in the first place then implicit in my way of thinking is the belief that I know better than Jesus. Yet if Jesus is the clearest revelation of God to us, then if I am realistic and honest with myself I must face up to who I am in my brokenness. I must be open to receiving renewal from God to enable me to become the person I ought to be.

The experience of renewal that Jesus offers involves living by divine priorities that lead us to value ourselves holistically and to become agents of blessing towards others (including non-human sentient life). One facet of this integrated lifestyle concerns our outward integrity. When Jesus spoke about being recognized for our spiritual fruit he was indicating that, irrespective of the words we utter, our deeds show who we really are.[38] The public observance of religious ceremonies can easily be cloaked by a facade of piety, but time and again the Bible deconstructs that behaviour. The prophets who arose in the times of the kings of Israel repeatedly rebuked the political and religious leaders and the nation at large for pseudo-piety. It was easy to congregate at the right meeting place for worship and perform the ceremonies while hypocritically ignoring the injustices, abuse and suffering that were occurring around them in the lives of their neighbours.[39] In like manner, Jesus did not hesitate to challenge a feigned piety on the part of religious people and went as far as to warn of spiritual fraudsters who were deceived and led others astray.

Another facet of this lifestyle concerns our inner spiritual integrity. Jesus pointed beyond our being seen to behave piously in public and emphasized the need to examine our hearts. What we store in our hearts shapes our character and attitudes. Jesus reframed the Ten Commandments by saying that carrying hatred and anger inside us is just as bad spiritually as actually committing murder.[40] While Jesus pointed out that our spiritual problems arise from within us, he did not dwell on engendering more guilt over broken relationships, but emphasized that we can find forgiveness and restoration and be blessed through making a fresh start in life.

Jesus was sensitive to the damage caused by hurt, pain and alienation, and he placed the central emphasis on God's love and forgiveness rather than on reinforcing a sense of human worthlessness. This point is underscored in Jesus' story about the Prodigal Son, in which the estranged parent retained the hope of a restored relationship. When the son came back home he was not ostracized or derided for having led a wasteful, immoral life. The pain of separation gave way to the happiness of a renewed relationship.[41] In effect, Jesus demonstrated the love of God to others in what he did as well as what he said.

It is a sad truism that well-meaning Christians can sometimes inadvertently convey to others such an oppressive sense of all-pervading guilt that the good news of God's love is distorted. Those who harbour anger and guilt create turbulence in the world around them. So those who take the spiritual journey must realistically confront their inward pain and memories of bad experiences and find healing that rebalances their self-worth. The way Jesus approached people involved lifting them up, not lowering their self-worth. He encouraged and inspired people to become creative and reflective in considering how worthwhile life could be in a dynamic relationship with God. Jesus calls for a compassionate and challenging love that is extended even to those who hurt us.[42]

Jesus also held forth the prospect of us reconnecting with others and with the Earth as agents of blessing. The first humans we encounter at the start of the Bible were invited to join in the blessing of creation by imparting blessings on other people and animals and the biosphere at large. This notion of blessing was the foundation for what was a holistic spirituality, and the same model was set up as the way of life for the ideal king of Israel. Jesus points to these examples of blessing as being the expression of God's heart and love for the world. In his own life Jesus modelled this lifestyle of blessing both in the way he related to people and in the content of his teaching. The one who follows Jesus is to become an agent of blessing who spreads peace and harmony, and to do this one must be at peace within. It is through the action of Christ's Spirit that God's peace comes upon us. Then we are enabled, as Martin Luther put it, to become 'a little Christ' towards our neighbours. These deep and abiding concerns that shape our character should predispose us to understand people and circumstances through a spiritual lens and to express hope, compassion and gratitude and turn away from greed, anger and despair.

As we embrace spiritual rebirth so too we are called upon to treat others holistically. Jesus indicated the kinds of things we should be doing to express blessing to others in what is known as his Sermon on the Mount.[43] We are to express love for others and not merely for those who seem winsome and attractive. John the apostle captured the heart of this when he posed the question of how we can say we love an unseen God when we show no love for those around us whom we can see and who experience horrible deprivation.[44] We are to care for the marginalized and the powerless whose human dignity has been debased and denuded at the hands of others. In the midst of this we are to promote God's ways concerning equity, justice and peace. Similarly, in Jesus' story about the Good Samaritan, we are shown the importance of neighbourliness.[45] The story illustrates Jesus' point about loving God and loving our neighbour. Jesus links together personal renewal and social concern in a seamless way of life – another instance of 'both/and' not 'either/or'. If Christians do not manifest the 'both/and' in a holistic way, then we should not be surprised that many people look elsewhere to explore their spiritual questions.

UNICEF indicates that each year some ten million children under the age of five die from preventable diseases; that's equivalent to almost half the population of Australia dying in one year.[46] This statistic does not take into account the dreadful poverty that cripples the lives of many more people worldwide. The exploitation of others is a horrible reality that we must continually confront, but the danger is that we become complacent or indifferent to the plight of those who are disempowered and oppressed. Such exploitation reflects the perennial problem of humans devaluing one another with blithe disregard for what the original Genesis story affirms about us being made in God's image and likeness. When we exhibit contempt for other people we are also showing disregard for our Creator, in whose image and likeness all humans are made. A spirituality that has deep integrity is one that takes serious and practical steps to uplift people from their suffering and misery, and helps to reconnect them in positive relationships with God.

Pluralism

The reality of multiple religions on Earth stretches back to the ancient past. Yet it is only in recent times that most people living in Western nations have come into direct contact with devotees of the major religions. This sort of contact between people of different faiths will become increasingly common during the twenty-first century due to the development of our communications and transport systems. We all must face the challenge of learning to live peacefully and ethically alongside one another. Christians should without reservation uphold religious liberty for their non-Christian neighbours, and this need not involve compromising our conviction that Christ is the world's saviour. We all need to appreciate, honour and respect one another because we are all made in God's image and likeness. Our solidarity is grounded in the creation.

As neighbours we can learn from one another's cultures and appreciate our respective social, political, cultural and ethical achievements. We can be challenged by one another's dedication and passion, and come to understand how we can all contribute to social harmony. We need to cultivate an attitude of humility and respect for each other especially when misconceptions hinder relationships. Our different beliefs should also prompt us to reflect on how we live and on what we know and feel concerning divine truth. As we learn to befriend and respect one another, we will also come to realize that traditional believers from Buddhist, Hindu, Islamic, Jewish and Shinto religions maintain the exclusivity of their respective positions with just as much conviction and passion as Christians do.[47] If we do not take that to heart then are we truly honouring those who participate in different pathways from our own?

There are many people in the Western world who occupy a position that is warm towards religion and spirituality in general but is less well disposed when Christianity comes into view. It is not uncommon to hear it said that ultimately the truth content of all paths is essentially similar and that their social configurations and intellectual traditions are just products of culture. We are informed that no single tradition contains the truth but each one points in the general direction of it, or that there is a higher undiluted truth that rises above the religious divide. So any quarrels that have arisen among followers of different paths are largely due to believers on either side failing to realize that all religions are both culturally relative to each other and relative to deity. The relativist position points to the phenomenological fact that religions are indeed birthed in and shaped by human culture. The social sciences do enable us to recognize and reflect on how culture shapes religious communities.

However, it is a tricky path to tread if one insists that all religions are metaphysically relative. Some who insist that this is the case do not seem to fully appreciate that a total way of life carries with it explicit values and duties which affect everything for the believer. It is unhelpful to circumvent or ignore the unique claims made in each religious tradition. The idea that each particular religion claims to have exclusive and universal truth may disturb us. Yet could it be that another kind of intellectually and spiritually superior posture exists for those who claim a relative equality to the truth of every religion? Can we say we genuinely honour and respect Buddha, Shankara, Muhammad and Jesus if we do not let them be who they are, permit them to speak for themselves, and accept that each one made an exclusivist claim about ultimate reality?

CHAPTER 5
Jesus and Spiritual Authority

Gus diZerega

What is spiritual truth and how do we know it when we encounter it?

Many of the world's most important religions trace their history back to particular historical founders. Judaism sees its roots in the life and deeds of Moses, Christianity looks to Jesus, Islam to Muhammad, and Buddhism to Siddhartha Gautama. Adherents to these traditions believe their principal founders were divinely inspired or descended or had attained ultimate spiritual insight. Claims to spiritual authority within these traditions rest on their founders.

While they often acknowledge the importance of inspired teachers, Pagan religions are markedly different in this regard. They are not built around a set of teachings originating with an individual. Occasionally a branch of Paganism, such as Hermeticism, is identified with revelatory pronouncements by a person or deity, but even in these cases the level of doctrinal specificity is far more general than with, for example, the Bible.

While individuals have certainly played important roles in establishing particular Pagan traditions, as Gerald Gardner did with my own, their insights are not considered infallible. I suspect no Gardnerian believes Gardner was divinely descended (as Christians believe about Jesus), was inspired by direct contact with a divinity who used him as a conduit for teachings (as Jews, Muslims and Mormons do their founders), or was enlightened (as Buddhists do Siddhartha Gautama). It certainly is no tenet of our religion. I do believe Gardner was divinely guided, but that is quite a different matter. His being divinely guided does not mean his words are uniquely authoritative, only that his actions served spiritual purposes beyond his ken.

Nor did Gardner ever intimate even this much. He said, I believe truly, that he was initiated into a New Forest Coven in England, that it was in decline and that he was afraid a very old religion was on the verge of dying out. With the repeal of England's anti-Witchcraft laws, he decided to make Wica's (one 'c') existence public, and began to initiate others into its path. In this way Wicca (two 'c's) was born, a religion with its roots in Gardner's practice, but in some ways elaborated by him to make it more accessible. Gardner's claims were remarkably matter-of-fact for a man who can be credited with playing a seminal role in creating modern NeoPaganism.

Nor did Gardner claim he was making public any new religious insights or dispensations. Quite the contrary. He was hoping to assist in preserving the 'Old Religion', a religion with roots in the earliest periods of human history. He evidently believed Margaret Murray's theory that Witchcraft was a survival of pre-Christian religion, a theory that hardly anyone today accepts, even those of us who believe there is considerable evidence for the antiquity of key elements in our tradition.[1] But the fact that most of us believe Gardner was wrong here in no way weakens our belief in our religion.

How can that be?

Potentially more devastating to the value of our tradition in the eyes of some is the theory that Gardner made it all up. I believe this conjecture is wrong, and cited sources in the controversy in Chapter 1. But let us assume for the moment that Gardner did make it up. *What then?*

While I would be disappointed to learn our founder was such a trickster, it would have no impact whatsoever on my regarding myself as a Gardnerian Witch. To those who see the historical veracity of their beliefs to be crucial to their truth, this attitude probably seems inexplicable. I hope to show why it is not.

First and foremost, for me and a great many other Gardnerians, and other Pagans, the truth of our practice is attested by the fact that our deities come. We personally experience their presence, and we normally do so in ritual space established according to the teachings of our tradition. That the Gods come is all the proof we need that our practice carries with it some spiritual authority.

But there is a great deal more to say here to assist the understanding of those who have not themselves experienced our Gods, or perhaps any Gods at all.

Authority in Pagan Spirituality

Another important issue is whether NeoPaganism is in fact Paganism in the sense of belonging to the long spiritual traditions embracing polytheism and no firm divisions between the material and spiritual realms. Is it genuine? Significantly, once practitioners of traditional Pagan customs are aware of what we do, many recognize us as fellow practitioners of spiritually harmonious paths. So I have been told by a Voudon Priestess in New Orleans, and by Native Americans. Other Gardnerian Wiccans have been told the same by traditional tribal peoples in Africa and Latin America. They recognize a common foundation despite different mythologies, and in some ways different practices. We are all Pagans.

So a question about spiritual authority among Wiccans is in many ways a question about spiritual authority in Pagan spirituality. To explore this issue I want to take a brief excursion into history.

Institutions, Religion and Authority

As I described earlier, organized religions arose as societies became more complex, and particular practices became codified and organized under the authority and guidance of individuals who were specialists in these practices. Whereas shamans had intensely personal connections with Spirit, as religions developed they became increasingly institutionalized and their practices standardized. Personal inspiration has always had a potentially tension-filled relationship with established spiritual leaders. Institutionalization exacerbated this. Jesus' problem with the Pharisees was only one example among many such.

I do not mean to demean religious organizations. They are necessary to facilitate spiritual connections for those who have neither the time nor perhaps the inclination or aptitude to enter into more personal spiritual involvement. By offering a common framework they also enable a larger community to come together, and that community assists one another in focusing on spiritual contexts when the stresses and strains of daily existence threaten to narrow their focus. In addition, they can facilitate working out more explicitly the spiritual insights that underlie their practices. But religious institutionalization necessarily involves distancing many ordinary practitioners from direct contact with Spirit, with the institution's leadership and interpretations intervening.

This tension between individual experience and group institutionalization is unavoidable. It arises from our being individuals who are also social beings. In coping with this tension, Pagan religions tend to favour the individual, and monotheistic religions the institutional. But these are only tendencies. Charges of impiety were levied against Socrates. Some monotheists follow very individualized paths.

Institutionalization divides laity from priesthood and ministers from congregation. Inevitably the leaders are considered authorities by many lay people. Because the presumption of wisdom is attached to the position, not the person, people holding these positions are often perceived as possessing more wisdom than they do.

As religions developed into organized bodies of practice governed by special authorities, privileges inevitably became attached to those exercising leadership responsibilities. With these privileges came the temptations of power and status. Some spiritual people probably became corrupted and some non-spiritual people were attracted to positions of spiritual leadership in order to profit from the privileges and respect accompanying their position.

Human history is filled with examples where religions ceased being spiritually oriented, becoming instead tools for other interests – usually political – or vehicles by which leaders enriched themselves at the expense of their community as a whole. Often both. So while religions began as forms of community spiritual practice, and may remain as such for individual practitioners, institutionally religions can pursue very mundane ends.

When shamans lost their connection with Spirit, they could no longer heal, and their divination was worthless. Their failure was readily apparent. But when an organization went astray, and people believed their personal access to Spirit was through it, and they themselves had had little direct experience with which to challenge organizational authority, serious trouble brewed. People tend to trust big organizations to which they have an attachment until evidence to the contrary is utterly overwhelming. Even then some are wilfully blind. When an organization claiming spiritual authority goes sour, the stage is set for serious abuses of spiritual authority.

The history of these abuses has led secularists to emphasize the horrors committed in religion's name. While the exclusivist claims of monotheistic traditions to spiritual superiority and even domination have led to more horrors than within Pagan or Buddhist traditions, they are not absent even here. In practice, Buddhism has not always been peaceful or tolerant.[2] We Pagans should never forget that the Aztecs with their massive blood sacrifices and ritual warfare and Carthaginians with their sacrifice of infants were also Pagans. A corrupt shaman can injure a relatively small number; but a corrupt religious institution can injure thousands. Sometimes millions. Corrupt secular institutions have injured even more.

In addition, people within traditions that have become corrupted can still have powerful experiences with spirits. I previously discussed how spirit forces far removed from their ultimate source in the One may need to acquire energy in parasitic or other harmful ways. Therefore experience of spiritual presences need not mean one is on a good spiritual path. There is too much evidence to the contrary. So the presence of spirits need not be a sign of a good path. But there is a criterion.

The most fundamental teachings of the world's spiritual traditions emphasize qualities such as peace, harmony, compassion, love, forgiveness and generosity. Here is a valid criterion for spiritual truth accessible to any person with even a little ethical clarity. Does your religion increase your capacity to practise qualities such as these? Does it broaden the number of people and other beings to whom you relate in this way? In examining a spiritual tradition, do its spiritual authorities exhibit these same qualities? If so, it is probably not, or at least not too, corrupted. Otherwise beware. The source of the tradition may be valid, but its current expression corrupt.

While I try most of the time to rely on Pagan sources, I think a statement from Jesus' Sermon on the Mount is appropriate: 'By their fruits ye shall know them.' These sentiments are echoed within many Pagan traditions. For instance, part of our 'Charge of the Goddess' goes as follows:

> *I am the gracious Goddess who gives the gift of joy unto the heart of man; upon Earth I give knowledge of the Spirit eternal; and beyond death I give peace and freedom and reunion with those who have gone before; nor do I demand sacrifice, for behold I am the Mother of all living, and my love is poured out upon the Earth.*

She then describes how She can be most appropriately honoured:

> *Let my worship be within the heart that rejoiceth; for behold, all acts of love and pleasure are my rituals and therefore let there be beauty and strength, power and compassion, honour and humility, mirth and reverence, within you.*
>
> *And thou who thinkest to seek for me, know thy seeking and yearning shall avail ye not, unless thou knowest the mystery; that if that which thou seekest thou findest not within thee, thou wilt never find it without thee, for behold I have been with thee from the beginning and I am that which is attained at the end of desire.*

Pluralistic Authorities

I am inclined to think there is an even deeper dimension to understanding spiritual authority. People vary in their character, talents, and in many other qualities. It would be surprising if one spiritual tradition were to fit everyone equally well. I know for myself that becoming Pagan challenged my personal tendency towards being judgmental and self-righteous precisely because it acknowledged the truth of other spiritual traditions and made no exclusive claims for itself. Once I was a Wiccan I had to confront my emotional antagonism to Christianity, rooted in the painful aftermath of a youthful flirtation with Fundamentalism. If Wicca was valid, it followed there was spiritual truth in Christianity. Not as much as most Christians claimed, but much more than I had once thought.

I also began a still continuing process of confronting and gradually overcoming my judgmental tendencies. Had I become Christian I may well have had these same qualities reinforced. It seems few Christians 'judge not that ye be not judged', and I doubt I would have been among them.

If a religious practice increases a person's capacity to demonstrate loving-kindness, peace, compassion, harmony and the like, this is evidence that it is a good path *for that person.* The same religion may influence another person differently, bringing out pride, scorn, aggressiveness and dishonesty. I live up to some Christian standards better as a Pagan than I ever did as a Christian. People are different, and while the greatest religions have developed enormous differentiations over the course of their existence in order to respond to human diversity, it may well be that not every religion equally fits every person.

I suspect this is so. We are mere humans, and Spirit is superhuman. It seems hubristic to claim that *any* human practice, even a particular religion and perhaps even all of them together, encompasses all that is spiritually important. The truth may be instead that, since no single religion can give adequate coverage to every dimension of the spiritual in human life, *all of them together* are needed to do so. It may well be that it takes an entire planet and all that flourishes on it to truly do justice to how Spirit manifests in a material world.

To think it is all about us is Narcissism. We Pagans have a myth about that.

Mythos and *Logos*

At the time of their founding Christianity and Judaism emphasized the importance of history to the truth of their traditions, in contrast to the Pagan religions. I agree this marks a significant difference between the Abrahamic and Pagan traditions. But with Christians at least, this difference has grown over the past several hundred years because early Christians also made use of mythic reasoning. As time has passed, Western Christianity has become less mythic. As it has done so, Pagan traditions have become more opaque to it.

If we were to go back to the Middle Ages or into Classical Antiquity, both Pagan and Abrahamic, we would encounter a view of spirituality very much at variance with that held by many modern monotheists. In *The Battle for God,* Karen Armstrong describes two ways of conceiving knowledge: *mythos* and *logos*.[3] Before modernity's rise, 'myth was primary' because it provided a way to understand the spiritual meaning embedded within life itself. Myth concerned itself with the meaning *in* life, not the meaning *of* life. *Logos* in this usage refers to reason, understanding the rationally verifiable relations between things.

Myth is not primitive science because it focuses on inner meaning rather than exterior event. Science explores externals: what can be seen, measured, repeated and predicted. Myth is a culturally and psychologically framed way of illuminating patterns and depths of inner meaning. The hagiographies of Saints would be a pretty noncontroversial example of Catholic Christian myths, but the early church even considered basic elements of Christian theology to be myths. For example, St Gregory of Nyssa (335–395) honoured both *mythos* and *logos*. While not challenging the historicity of the crucifixion and resurrection, according to Armstrong, Gregory 'had explained the three hypostases of Father, Son, and Spirit were not objective facts but simply "terms that we use" to express the way in which the "unnameable and unspeakable" divine nature (ousia) adapts itself to the limits of our human minds'.[4]

This kind of thinking is in accord with Pagan philosophers of the time, such as Sallustius. It is also in accord with English Wica. Of Sallustius's essay, *About the Gods and the World*, Gerald Gardner wrote, 'it might have been spoken at a witch meeting, at any time, as a general statement of their creed.'[5]

Using NeoPlatonic terminology, Sallustius wrote that there were five basic kinds of myths: theological, physical, psychic, material and mixed. I will not go into these categories, except to note that for the ancients, myth was anything but simple and straightforward. In his text Sallustius applied all these various categories in analysing myths about Kronos.

Sallustius makes two important points relevant to this chapter. First, to the question 'Why are the myths so strange?' because they depict the Gods engaged in adultery, robbery and the like, Sallustius answers: 'Surely it is intended that the obvious absurdity and contradiction will alert the individual's soul that the words are veils, mere cloaks wrapped around an inner mystery.' The koans used in Zen meditation could be similarly described. The famous question 'What is the sound of one hand clapping?' cannot be answered by reasoning it out. On the surface it is a contradiction. In Zen practice the solution arises not from rational deliberation but rather in a flash of insight.

The way to spiritual insight is *not* through the discursive intellect. In my view this is because the intellect breaks apart and separates things into categories, and so cannot penetrate deeply into spiritual awareness of interconnectedness. Valuable as the discursive intellect is in dealing with the mundane, it can be misleading when relied upon to comprehend the Sacred. I suspect this is why the great Catholic theologian St Thomas Aquinas never finished his *Summa Theologica.* During Mass on December 6, 1273, St Thomas had an experience after which he stopped writing, explaining, 'All that I have written seems to me like straw compared to what has now been revealed to me.'[6] Secularists and *logos*-dominated theologians suspect Thomas may have had a stroke or a breakdown.[7] I've never met or heard of a stroke victim who spoke that way, but I have had mystical experiences that make Thomas's words sound very reasonable.

I think Sallustius offers an interesting insight into these kinds of events. He writes, 'Myths also represent the activities of the Gods. For one may call the world a myth, in which bodies and things are visible, but souls and minds hidden; the outer shell veils the inner realities.' It seems St Thomas may have been privileged to experience some inner realities.

As to the variety of myths, Sallustius teaches: 'Every kind of myth has its special appropriateness: theological myths suit philosophers, physical and psychic myths suit poets, myths of a mixed nature suit mysteries and their initiatory rites, since the intent of every mystical ceremony is to unite us with both the universe and the Gods.'

In answering the question of why rely on myths instead of straightforward narrative, Sallustius argued, 'The first benefit from myths is that we have to search out their meaning and so do not leave our minds idle; the very inquiry is a useful exercise.'[8] This reasoning should be familiar to anyone acquainted with Jesus' parables. Sallustius writes also that they have been used by 'inspired poets, the best of philosophers, and by those who established the mysteries and initiatory rites. The Gods themselves employ myths in giving oracles.'

In a mythic context, faith was a confidence in the deeper truths made accessible by myths that were not literally true. *Myth was never intended to be taken literally*, though some people probably always have done so, even in Classical times.[9]

Myth was distinguished from reason, or *logos,* by Pagans and most early Christians, and both were considered valid forms of knowledge. Because it focused on the meaning embedded within that world, not on its surfaces, myth was not in conflict with accounts of the material world. It did other jobs.

Consider how time appears from the perspectives of *mythos* and *logos*. To use a Christian example, the Bible says, 'One day is... as a thousand years and a thousand years as one day' (2 Peter 3:8). From this perspective, time is more than an empty filing system in which events can be organized sequentially. This is subordinate to, a part of, and embedded within divine experience. Charles Taylor, a Christian philosopher, argues that from this perspective, events in the Old and New Testaments 'were linked through their immediate contiguous places in the divine plan'. Thus, the sacrifice of Isaac and Christ's crucifixion 'are drawn close to identity in eternity even though they are centuries (that is, eons or *saecula*) apart. In God's time there is a sort of simultaneity of sacrifice and crucifixion.'[10] This is mythic reasoning, not *logos*. Sallustius's discussion of Kronos gives us a Pagan perspective on time that is in no sense contradictory to this one if God is taken as the One.

Logos understands time as secular and homogeneous, an empty, passive stage onto which all things appear and disappear, never to be repeated. As Taylor describes it, 'events now exist only in this one dimension, in which they stand at greater and lesser temporal distance and in relations of causality with other events of the same kind... this is a typically modern mode of social imagination, which our Medieval forebears would have found difficult to understand, for where events in profane time are very differently related to higher time, it seems unnatural just to group them side by side in the modern relation of simultaneity.' Thus, 'Premodern understandings of time seem to have been multidimensional.'[11]

By focusing only on sequence, secular time shatters our connection to this kind of mythic awareness, removing things and events from any meaningful context except the sequential cause and effect most easily analysed by *logos*. Myth is abandoned in favour of history. Attention to the meaning *in* events is replaced by attention to the meaning *of* events, something external to them. Referring again to Taylor's discussion, modern time has become empty as well as homogeneous. Time's emptiness points to how 'both space and time come to be seen as "containers" which things and events contingently fill, rather than as constituted by what fills them. This... is part of the metaphysical imagination of modern physics, as we can see with Newton.' This 'step to emptiness is part of the objectification of time that has been so important a part of the modern subject of instrumental reason'.[12] Objects and time have surfaces without depth, and can best be studied and understood from the outside.

From the standpoint of a purely transcendental view of divinity, a *logos*-centred approach is no problem. God is entirely outside the world, which is simply a divine artefact, devoid of meaning beyond that which its Creator gives it. In terms of logic, *logos* suffices for this kind of radical and utterly transcendental monotheism. But there is a deep irony here.

With the rise of *logos* to full interpretive authority over scripture, the door is opened wide to pure secularism because inner meaning is now gone from within the world. It is easy for God to become the God of ever narrowing gaps and also, ironically, a God whose goodness is defined in terms of will alone, because nothing is supposed to limit God, not even reason. Reason can explain the world, but it cannot account for the Sacred. This superficially seems akin to *mythos*-centred arguments, but whereas *mythos* argues that meaning is embedded in life, this alternative argument finds it only in a divine will that is itself unlimited and therefore ultimately arbitrary. These are hardly the only ways to interpret these matters, but they are common ones, and to the extent that a Christian thinks in these terms, he or she cannot easily understand a Pagan perspective.

When so many Christians accepted the basic logic of the sciences for interpreting scripture because it apparently described a history of the physical world, the potential for future conflict between science and religion was unintentionally created. In a world of surfaces, of objects and 'its', statements must be of objective fact, *or they are wrong*. When the revealed source is taken as an authority for detailed statements about the physical world, the stage is set for trouble.

By 1860, well over a hundred different *logos*-centred attempts had been made to calculate Earth's age in linear time based on biblical evidence. The findings ranged from 5,400 to nearly 9,000 years.[13] All were attempts to combine reason as *logos* with biblical accounts to derive the Earth's age. The resulting errors point to the spiritual inadequacy of logo-centric reasoning for questions of biblical interpretation.

If *logos* becomes the sole source of truth open to human understanding, and the apparent facts within a divinely inspired text do not match up with what empirical investigation has revealed, either the text must be rejected or the evidence of the senses and understanding must be rejected in favour of the authoritative claims of the text. Jonah *had to* be swallowed by a whale. The sun *had to* stand still for Joshua. The earth *had to* be created only about 6,000 years ago. Otherwise the Bible was simply false. Seeking to subject all knowledge to *logos* resulted in abandoning *both logos and mythos* in favour of the ego's will to believe.

Implicit in the movement away from embracing both *mythos* and *logos* to *logos* alone was a paradoxical tendency to embrace the irrational if spirituality was to survive. From the standpoint of *mythos*, faith can mean a confidence in the deeper meaning of events despite surface appearances because we have personally encountered or intuited that meaning. On the other hand, faith can be maintained by a will to believe despite the evidence because a previously accepted authority commands as much. The two kinds of faith are different, and in the modern world the second has radically displaced the first. Pagans, however, prefer the first.

I am not trying to tell Christians how to interpret scripture. That is their concern. I *am* telling them that over the centuries they have interpreted scripture in different ways, and that when they emphasized a mythic dimension as well as a historical one, they were in harmony with thousands of years of Pagan tradition and *also* not so likely to run into basic difficulties with modern science. Sallustius's physical science has long since been superseded, but his flawed science in no way invalidates the basic mythic points he was trying to make so long ago.

From a Pagan perspective, the price paid for a *logos*-centred spirituality is unacceptably high. Divinity is within the world as well as transcendental to it. The world *is* alive. It has interiority. It is not simply surfaces. A mind focused on its sense of separateness from the world, and which sees the world as consisting of objects in physical relation to one another, cannot get us very far in understanding the meaning of existence.

I am also not trying to say there is no role for *logos* in spirituality. Far from it. This chapter is itself a *logos*-centred defence of the necessity for both *logos* and *mythos*. But by itself *logos* cannot situate us in an internally meaningful world, and Pagan panentheism implies that the world is meaningful immanently as well as transcendentally. From a Pagan perspective *logos by itself* is not a valid way to spiritual authority because it focuses on the surfaces of objects, not their internal relations of meaning.

Pagan spirituality is rooted in *mythos* without rejecting *logos*. Armstrong writes, 'In the pre-modern world, both *mythos* and *logos* were regarded as indispensable. Each would be impoverished without the other. Yet the two were essentially distinct... They had separate jobs to do.'[14] This is why so many of the ancients treated myths as allegory, for much of what was most meaningful resisted being written down without risk of distortion. It is why Plato emphasized that he never wrote down his most important teachings and often resorted to myth, as with the myth of the cave in his *Republic,* to get a point across in ways that straight description could not.[15]

Myth has Pagan origins. It developed in oral cultures where stories could be more easily remembered than an analytic argument, and where inspired poetry could lead to insights that could not be made by logical argument alone. It is well known today that adequately translating some poetry is essentially impossible. It is too deeply rooted in its language, culture and time. Myth is like this, only more so, because it represents how members of a culture seek to understand that which is beyond words and description.

Myths enable Spirit to communicate with us in ways that are inaccessible to a *logos*-centred way of understanding. They are superficially concrete and practical, but they take us deeper than can the abstractions of *logos*. *Logos* can bring us a better understanding of the abstract, the theoretical, and also of surfaces. But Spirit is ultimately concrete, manifesting through encounter, love, mystery, tragedy and joy.

Mythos's relation with *logos* was always a source of tension in written traditions, which encourage a different kind of thinking. That knowledge of the Sacred could seemingly be reduced to a text encouraged people to think that all truth was there in the words on the page, and not in the interaction of text, reader and experience. Wiser readers knew differently, but not all readers were wise. With the translation and printing of scripture, the Reformation greatly increased the power of *logos* to guide our understanding of the Sacred. At the same time, the Protestant emphasis that everyone should read the Bible for themselves vastly expanded the number of people struggling to determine scripture's meaning. For many, spiritual experience through ritual, celebration and encounter in the world was replaced by reading about *others'* spiritual experiences. People were told to discount their own whenever they could not be squared with a 'proper' interpretation of the text. Philip describes just such an instance in Chapter 4. I think I can safely write that we Pagans generally think this was a tremendous loss, not because there is no value in studying sacred texts, but because they were often studied so narrowly.

Paganism and Modernity

I have discussed the relationship between *mythos* and *logos* at such length because, along with being a religion primarily of experience and practice, NeoPaganism is a return to mythic spirituality in the context of the modern world. The Goddess is Mother, Maid and Crone. The Oak King and the Holly King battle one another on the equinoxes; first one triumphs, then, six months later, the other prevails. Always and forever. The Goddess of life descends to the underworld to encounter the Lord of Death. The Goddess is eternal, and the God eternally dies and is reborn. These are mythic images. They are not stories by moderns seeking to return to the past, let alone attempts to compete with scriptural stories. They are ways by which, through symbol and ritual, we can gain a deeper understanding of the inner truths of physical existence. And for us they work.

I know Pagans who are chemists, computer scientists and medical researchers, often PhDs, people deeply schooled in mathematics and the physical sciences. They have no problem with these myths because they do not see them as competitive explanations for the physical world compared to science, but rather as aids to focusing on different levels of meaning and significance.

A *logos*-centred understanding of the Sacred either becomes completely cerebral, and so abandons the heart, or it ultimately turns its back even on *logos* itself to embrace the will to believe as a substitute for any understanding at all. A *logos*-centred world has blinded many to the meaning inherent in the world within which we live. With its attention only on externals and boundaries, a *logos*-centred view of the world rejects feminine values of intuition and receptivity that open us up to the meaning in the world. We can only understand a person when we open ourselves up to them. The same is true for the world.

Spiritual authority is important in Pagan religion, but its character is very different from that commonly associated with scriptural monotheism. And it does not bring us into conflict with other kinds of knowledge.

Philip Johnson

There once was a non-white swarthy male who lived on the social fringes of a relatively obscure province. He wandered around villages and towns as a penniless and homeless story-teller, sleeping out in the open, or sheltering in the homes of those who would invite him to stay over for a while. He befriended some strange, rough and listless peasants who set off a chain reaction of new relationships. He flouted all kinds of social conventions by the company he kept and the way he behaved around women, migrants, the sick and the poor. He gained some notoriety for his antics in open public spaces, and at parties, weddings and funerals. Some people found his stories and exemplary behaviour endearing while others suspected that he was mentally unstable. He was chased out of some villages accompanied by insults and murderous threats. Gossip about him spread and eventually the ruling elite took notice. They were alarmed by the social disturbances he seemed to cause, so they conspired to have him arrested on trumped-up charges. He was dragged before a kangaroo court, falsely accused and found guilty, and then executed as a seditious criminal – he was Jesus of Nazareth. This image of

Jesus as a homeless itinerant may be surprising but it is there in the Gospels: 'Foxes have holes and birds of the air have nests, but the Son of Man has no place to lay his head.'[16] Let us explore the possibility of more surprises here.

Secular Grip

Through a long chain of events that began in the sixteenth century, the authority of the church in modern European society was gradually displaced. The processes that unfolded in this chain of events swept aside the earlier Medieval and hierarchical understanding of both the supernatural and the natural world. Protestants encouraged people to read the Bible in ways that challenged Medieval customs. The centrality of the individual's standing before God spurred on church reforms, but soon non-theistic theories emerged as new areas of knowledge appeared to contest what had been previously understood about God, the Bible and the Earth. Scientific discoveries, market economic models, secular systems of governance and an emphasis on the freedom of the individual to choose became central components in new all-encompassing non-theistic narratives.

Today we are in the midst of entirely new processes of cultural change while at the same time remaining heirs to what has gone before us. The non-theistic temper of recent centuries still influences the way many people understand Christianity. Various popular discourses indicate that people are reacting against their negative personal and cultural experiences of Christianity. The quest to re-enchant the world that searches for an immanent deity is in reaction against negative images of monotheistic transcendence. Some incline towards a monist understanding of reality, while others are exploring new dualist forms of Gnosticism. What they hold in common is the rejection of the concept of a personal, omniscient and omnipotent God who seems disconnected from life on Earth. The rhetorical styles used in some (but not all) discourses of rejection seem heavily reliant on secular postures. Let the spiritual seeker beware: the same axe that Richard Dawkins wields against monotheism he also uses to discredit polytheism and PaleoPagan beliefs.[17]

What is registered as a lack of belief relates to images of the God-of-the-gaps or monarchic images of hierarchical oppression. When new discoveries eluded scientific explanation it was easy for well-meaning monotheists to try to bridge the gap by pointing to God's mysterious handiwork. That line of thinking was doomed to end up in a cul-de-sac once those gaps were closed by scientific models and developments. So it is no wonder that God seems to have vanished. This is due to a stunted theological view that devolves from a secularized understanding of how the world works.

In Chapter 2 I indicated the problems that were associated with monarchical and hierarchical images of God. It is easy to forget that both in Classical Antiquity and in Christendom the human social order centred on kingship and a hierarchical society. In Antiquity the supernatural order was understood in similar terms: a 'high god', subordinate deities and lesser beings. In Christendom ecclesial structures were developed using hierarchical models that were paralleled on imagery of God, the heavenly court of angels and so on. That social order functioned in agrarian-based societies with feudal systems of governance. Once that social order was overturned, the connection between the older social order and the presumed heavenly hierarchy was broken. These archaic images of gods and goddesses or of God and angels make no sense in a technologically driven and democratically influenced model of society.

The current reactions against the transcendent order seem to be centred on non-theistic understandings of the cosmos and of a rejected hierarchical transcendence, and on truncated theistic responses. However, both the God-of-the-gaps and the hierarchical imagery have no connection with the primary image of God that is represented to us in Jesus. Jesus is represented as God present with us in powerlessness, humility and vulnerability.

The need for personal renewal is widely sought and there is a diversity of opinion about how it is accessed. Some feel that the locus for such renewal comes through an esoteric unity with personified cosmic energy or in a state of depersonalized consciousness. Those approaches are based on a metaphysical reunion that stands in deep tension with the Christian understanding of God. I wonder if some seekers have unwittingly committed themselves to concepts that undervalue their own humanity by de-emphasizing a personal God. To rise above the cacophony of conflicting human opinion we really need to connect relationally with a personal God as the prime point of reference for finding universal meaning. A personal God who understands our frailties can show us how to relationally experience spiritual renewal.

Mythopoeic Thought

Gus draws attention to mythopoeic thought as a neglected approach to understanding the cosmos. Mythopoeic thought understands the world in an intuitive way that is open to transcendental realities being experienced through our senses and also in other states of consciousness. Specific myths become the narrative form through which mythopoeic understanding of reality is usually presented. Myths employ both imaginative and symbolic language to refer to the interrelatedness of the natural and the supernatural.

There is a Christian way of understanding myth that points us to God and complements other ways of thinking through matters of the heart and mind. Mythopoeic thought was part and parcel of the Classical Mediterranean and Ancient Near Eastern cultures. The Hebraic thought contained in the Old Testament illustrates the cultural experiences of the Hebrews in different parts of the Fertile Crescent, while later New Testament writers operated throughout the regions of Asia Minor and the Eastern Mediterranean. As mythopoeic thought created a shared cultural 'dialect', those who composed the biblical books understood and interacted with it. The biblical writers passed on revelatory messages about theopoetic or ultimate truth using both figurative and discursive discourses. They were keen for their contemporaries to experience God's transformative ways and they communicated ultimate truths in poems, symbols and images, stories, factually oriented narratives and reflective logical discourse.[18]

In the Bible mythopoeic thought is transformed into a new theocentric perspective. The ancient Hebrews did not hesitate to interact with the matrix of ideas held by neighbouring cultures. For example, the creation stories of Genesis do not merely show us Hebraic monotheism, but unite symbol and reality together concerning the Earth and the cosmos and carry them forward to offer an entirely new and transformed perspective from the polytheist creation myths of Mesopotamia and Egypt.[19] Hebraic mythopoeic thought also placed a very strong emphasis on ethical accountability before both God and the community, which differentiated it from some of the emphases found in the myths of neighbouring cultures.

Mythopoeic thought has a niche in the history of Christian theology. One of the prime movers in this direction was the Lutheran pastor Johann Valentin Andreae, whose extensive corpus of theological writings used myth as 'the vehicle for showing how the various realms of human existence and knowledge both reflect the Gospel and are reflected in it'.[20] In the twentieth century the informal literary club known as the Inklings included C. S. Lewis, J. R. R. Tolkien and Charles Williams, and each in their respective books employed mythopoeic thought interrelating symbols, archetypes and the gospel.[21] In another vein, John Drane, Ross Clifford and I have examined Christian symbolism and archetypal imagery in tarot cards.[22]

Gus refers to remarks from Karen Armstrong concerning Gregory of Nyssa's stance on non-literal Trinitarian language as another instance of mythopoeic thought. Here a brief clarification is needed. Gregory of Nyssa was among those who approached theology with an emphasis on the ineffable (known as 'apophatic theology'). For the Greek fathers the doctrine of the Trinity was 'a matter of religious experience – liturgical, mystical, and, often, poetical'.[23] John Meyendorff indicates that, for Gregory of Nyssa, in 'God's being... the ultimate meaning of hypostatic relations [was] understood to be totally above comprehension, definition, or argument'.[24] Meyendorff goes on to say that knowledge of God transcendent is only possible as far as revelation occurs 'inasmuch as the immanent Trinity manifests itself in the "economy" of salvation' and 'inasmuch as the transcendent *acts* on the immanent level'.[25] Meyendorff adds that this theological tradition 'affirms the full and distinct reality of the Triune hypostatic life of God'.[26]

Gus also points to the linear view of time and history that is a strong feature of Christian historiography.[27] He indicates that mythic thinking about time surfaces in the biblical verse that says 'one day is as a thousand years' with the Lord. He also refers to Charles Taylor's remarks about the simultaneity of the sacrifices of Isaac and Christ. I would like to gild the lily a little more.

The pre-Christian Greco-Roman writers of history – Thucydides, Polybius, Livy – looked for cyclical patterns in the past. The biblical view offered a centred, linear understanding of history in which the world has a beginning, its focal point is the incarnation of Christ, and its events are consummated in the return of Christ at the end of time. However, recurring patterns of history appear as a secondary motif in both the Bible and early Christian thought. In the Old Testament, corporate cyclical patterns are evident in the many stories told about the formation of Israel and its subsequent fortunes under the kings. The book of Judges is replete with dramatic cyclic stories about the emergence and recession of Israel's various tribes as they repeatedly oscillated between serving God and lapsing into idolatry.

In early Christian practice, liturgy developed as a means of re-presenting the life of Jesus through the seasons and from this a church calendar emerged. The rotation of the events of Christ's life follows a cyclic pattern but with the crucifixion and resurrection as the focal point and with the consummation of history still held in view. Irenaeus was a second-century Christian theologian who conceived of a theory of recapitulation in which all the stages of human life are sanctified and shaped by the patterns in Jesus' life. Jesus' story is then repeated throughout the personal stories of each believer and each stage occurs within the linear movement of time. Irenaeus's theory reflects mythopoeic thinking about the Christ event and its incorporation within the lives of individual believers. However, he did not regard Jesus Christ as a mythological person but held to his historical existence. Here is another instance of what we have encountered on other topics: *both* mythopoeic thought *and* historical data held together.[28]

Another example of the way mythopoeic thought about time has appeared in Christianity is found in the novels of Charles Williams. In *Many Dimensions* an ancient stone is discovered that allows an individual to move in time, place and thought. After using the stone one of the characters meditates:

> *The past might, even materially, exist; only man was not aware of it, time being, whatever else it was, a necessity of his consciousness. 'But because I can only be sequentially conscious,' he argued, 'must I hold that what is not communicated to consciousness does not exist? I think in a line – but there is the potentiality of the plane.' This perhaps was what great art was – a momentary apprehension of the plane at a point in the line. The Demeter of Cnidos, the Praying Hands of Dürer, the Ode to a Nightingale, the Ninth Symphony – the sense of vastness in those small things was the vastness of all that had been felt in the present.*[29]

In *Descent into Hell* Williams explored normal time and the 'eternal now'. The lead female character encounters a *doppelgänger*, which is a classic image of a rejected self. An intuitive poet helps her in this encounter by taking up in his imagination all her fear so that she is set free to meet her other self. She is then empowered to act in a substitutionary way in the present by helping a past ancestor face death without fear.[30] Chad Walsh makes the following observation about Williams' novels:

> *He is unwilling to grant that it [time] is final. He grounds his conviction in the faith that all times are encompassed in God, and the ever-present now of eternity makes travel between past, present and future a simple possibility and fact.*[31]

Williams' imaginative exploration of time and eternity evidences very integral thinking on his part. Walsh notes:

> *His imagination and his religious faith are so mingled and merged that it is fruitless to attempt any analytic separation. One has the impression, uncanny at times, that he simply pictured what he himself saw… The feeling produced by his novels is that he has not replaced one reality with another, but simply forced our eyes wider open.*[32]

Mythic Archetypes

People worldwide use stories and symbols to help make sense of their inner being, their communities and the Earth. Unlike the negative perception that a 'myth' is something false, myths are technically stories that shape a culture and carry forth ideas that affect the way people relate to the world and each other. They point beyond the surface using the imagination to uncover what is happening in the cosmos, why these things are happening, where these things are headed, and who is affected and how to respond. Myths point to the underlying realities of our relationship with the cosmos and the supernatural, with the Earth and its creatures, and they provide meaning for human activities. Much of the current interest in myth has been stimulated through the popular diffusion – and sometimes the misreading – of ideas handed on from scholars such as James Frazer, Joseph Campbell, Carl Jung and Mircea Eliade.[33]

Although I have disagreements with the theories and conclusions about myths found in the writings of Frazer, Campbell, Jung and Eliade, I do feel they have made some points that connect with a Christian understanding of matters. What has emerged from various lines of inquiry that these and other scholars have undertaken is that myths and symbols highlight the human condition, the yearning for healing and for reconnection with a transcendental realm. Some of these writers suggest there are recurrent patterns or motifs in myths that include nostalgia for a lost world, hopes for a utopia and heroic figures rescuing others or defeating monsters. These motifs are technically referred to as 'archetypes'.

For religious studies theorists like Eliade, archetypes refer to a paradigm about the divine origins of archaic societies, institutions and rituals.[34] Myths provided the framework through which the gods discoursed with humans, and the archetypes uncovered in the stories point to the spiritual needs of those communities. In Jung's work archetypes refer to universal symbolic patterns in the subconscious life of humans which shape our psychic experiences. Jung felt there is a common psychic life which draws on universal symbols that express needs for transformation. He saw archetypes emerging from the subconscious in dreams, myths and rituals.[35] Other studies suggest that in the world's folklore and fairytales one can discern patterns to the stories' motifs which express yearnings for a reality that is beyond the grasp of rational discourse.[36] Many of these ideas resonate with people and the Australian film producer George Miller (*Mad Max*, *Babe*) has come to understand his own story-telling along the lines of Jung's archetypal theory.[37]

Although I believe there is a danger in over-simplifying and decontextualizing myths from their cultural contexts and making dubious inferences from them, it is interesting to note that similar yearnings are expressed symbolically in many different stories. As a Christian I find it fascinating to read myths that refer to a lost Paradise from archaic times replete with a symbol of a cosmic tree standing at the centre where humans meet the Divine. Similarly, the recurrent figure of the hero defeating monsters, pursuing an epic quest, and delivering others from harm resonates with things that I read in the Bible.

It is in light of these ideas about mythic archetypes that J. R. R. Tolkien considered the significance of motifs in fairytales and their fulfilment in the Gospels:

> *The Gospels contain a fairy-story, or a story of a larger kind which embraces all the essences of fairy-stories. They contain many marvels – peculiarly artistic, beautiful and moving: 'mythical' in their perfect, self-contained significance; and at the same time powerfully symbolic and allegorical… The birth of Christ is the Eucatastrophe*

of man's history. The resurrection is the Eucatastrophe of the story of the Incarnation. This story begins and ends in joy. It has pre-eminently the 'inner consistency of reality'. There is no tale ever told that men would rather find was true, and none which so many sceptical men have accepted as true on its own merits... This story is supreme; and it is true. Art has been verified. God is the Lord of angels and of men – and of elves. Legend and History have met and fused.[38]

In a similar vein C. S. Lewis wrote about the fusion of myth into history:

The heart of Christianity is a myth which is also a fact. The old myth of the Dying God, without ceasing to be myth, comes down from the heaven of legend and imagination to the earth of history. It happens – at a particular date, in a particular place, followed by definable historical consequences. We pass from a Balder or an Osiris, dying nobody knows when or where, to a historical Person crucified (it is all in order) under Pontius Pilate. By becoming fact it does not cease to be a myth: that is the miracle... We must not be ashamed of the mythical radiance resting on our theology. We must not be nervous about 'parallels' and 'Pagan Christs': they ought to be there... If God chooses to be mythopoeic – and is not the sky itself a myth? – shall we refuse to be mythopathic? For this is the marriage of heaven and earth: Perfect Myth and Perfect Fact: claiming not only our love and our obedience, but also our wonder and delight.[39]

The observations of Tolkien and Lewis redirect our attention to considering God's revelation of himself in history in the life of Jesus.

Divine Revelation

Earlier in this book I noted that God as Triunity has three centres of personhood which are in a unified relationship. As God has chosen to create the cosmos, some kind of dynamic relationship must develop between Creator and creation, and that is precisely what is imaged in the Bible. Creation has occurred through the free initiative of God. God is interested in developing relationships with every aspect and dimension of the creation. It is in light of this dynamic backdrop that the concept of revelation emerges. As a concept, revelation is concerned with making a disclosure or unveiling what was previously hidden, obscure or unknown. God is the initiator of revelation and is the centre-point of what is unveiled or disclosed to those who are in relationship with him.

God's self-disclosure is facilitated in various ways in the context of the creation. Without the creation there would be no relationships and hence no revelation. In Chapter 3 it was briefly noted that one of the images used to depict the entire creation is that of a unified web of relationships which is pictured as a harmonious, inclusive and integrated household. As all sentient life belongs in the household and God is open to relating with all things, then the whole creation becomes the arena in which revelation can occur. Since God is both transcendent and immanently related to the creation, various modes of revelation are possible.

One mode is in the overall sphere of creation, where glimpses of the breathtaking beauty and grandeur of God can be discerned. This is illustrated in some poetic passages in the Bible, which refer to the glory of God filling heaven and Earth.[40] The natural world signifies God's grandeur and goodness and the Psalmist gladly declares that the heavens display God's glory and righteousness.[41] In what is sometimes called zoo-semiotics – symbols and signs in sentient life – we are pointed to the wisdom and presence of God.[42] That God cares for all sentient life is revealed through provisions made in the Earth's natural cycles.[43]

Humans have an innate sense for the Divine by virtue of having been created in God's image and likeness. As we saw earlier in this book, we are hard-wired for God, who has put 'eternity' in our hearts. Our yearning to be united in relationship with God is innate, from our stirrings inside our mother's womb through to our awareness of God's presence everywhere.[44] How we respond to this innate sense of God's presence and revelation in the natural realm is another matter. As we suffer the blighted effects of broken relationships with God, the Earth and each other, the human tendency is to withdraw in favour of autonomy.

We have also noted elsewhere in this book that it is possible for humans to encounter God anywhere, anytime, and sometimes divinely initiated disclosures have occurred in the form of unusual sensory experiences such as visions and dreams. Some of these divinely initiated encounters have happened to individuals endowed with the gift of prophecy, dream interpretation, and so on. Those who experienced these things have often been important actors in families and communities in which sensitivity to divine revelation and guidance has been most apparent in their listening to these messengers and acting on what God has disclosed. These messages and experiences form part of the anthology of diverse books that have been collected together to form the Bible. Christians hold that the Bible is God's word, based on its own declarations and the attitude of Jesus concerning scripture. At a subjective level Christians also affirm that God's Spirit bears witness within us to trust and heed scripture. So the sacral locus is found in reading this broad collection of stories, poems, songs, aphorisms, visions, prophecies, letters and historical narratives written by those who encountered God and imparted teaching and guidance.

The primary mode of God's revelation, however, occurs in the life of Jesus. God is a personal being who builds relationships with others and, as we have noted, humans are hard-wired for relationships with the Divine. It makes sense that God would initiate contact with humans and that he would do so through the life of a particular person. Through Jesus God helps us to see how spiritual renewal is needed and how we can find spiritual transformation in an unmediated relationship with God. It is in the mode of personal revelation through Jesus that the other modes of revelation – the sphere of creation and our innate sense of God – come together in a seamless garment.

We lack unity and harmony between the sexes, between communities and nations, between humans and animals and the biosphere; and when left to our own devices our plight worsens. It is not difficult to point to the suffering caused by individual and social irresponsibility, moral indifference to the plight of the oppressed and marginalized, and the power-grabs that many pursue in order to control others. The vested interests of groups we belong to as well as those we privately entertain tend to be self-serving and yield discrimination, exclusion and exploitation. Humans are very efficient at creating misery and hell. If those of us living in the 'free' nations of the Earth stick to the maxim that personal growth is all about my freedom to choose what to do, wherever, whenever and with whomsoever I wish, then we are perpetuating the problem of disunity and an absence of harmony and authentic spirituality. This sort of behaviour is disastrous, yet it is all too common today for people to be reluctant to take responsibility for their own actions.

We need to encounter someone who can show us a holistic way of living and relating to each other, to the Earth and, most importantly, to God. God's concern and care for the Earth and for humans has been disclosed and unveiled in the life, teaching, crucifixion and resurrection of Jesus. Jesus presents us with an array of images of who God is: vulnerable, humble, powerless, open to us, understanding, and willing to live alongside us. Jesus shows us through the concrete example of his life and teaching how relationships with God, humans and the Earth are meant to function. Jesus modelled for us how God's Spirit brings about human transformation, and how we can have access to spiritual power for daily living. Jesus' invitation is clear: 'Follow me.'

Truth is a Person

At the heart of the Gospels are the dramatic events of Jesus' arrest, execution, burial and resurrection. Those narratives do provoke a lot of questions, and for those of us living in the shadow of the Age of Reason there are some critical matters connected to historical inquiries. It is appropriate that we wrestle with what is written in the Gospel documents, consider if their contents are believable, and explore how these books were composed, copied and circulated. When the evidence is sifted some useful answers to those questions emerge.

The Gospels are the primary sources for Jesus' life and these books were composed and in circulation within a generation of the events. As ancient books were copied and recopied by hand, it is possible to work out a good pedigree for the texts from the earliest surviving manuscripts, many of which predate Emperor Constantine. It is also possible to illuminate the social and political background to the Gospels by looking at Roman and Jewish sources from the first century, as well as evidence from archaeological findings.[45]

The resurrection of Jesus from the dead is an extraordinary event for which there is both circumstantial and direct evidence. His grave was discovered to be vacant and the immediate band of disciples had no fathomable motive for creating a hoax.[46] It is remarkable that the beliefs they attested to in these texts and forfeited their lives over actually survived the ravages of periodic persecution from the reign of Nero until the fourth century.

When the combined weight of evidence is reflected on, it is difficult to sustain the popular allegations that the texts were 'doctored' under Constantine's reign or were simply borrowed mystery-religion myths that Paul used to invent a historical character.[47] These books were not written by the victors of history but by people from the first century participating in a marginalized group who were subjected to both Imperial persecution and religious discrimination. In light of Gus's comments I find it is also quite striking that one Gospel writer declared that the *logos* is more than reason or words but is actually the person of Christ.[48]

CHAPTER 6

Paganism, Christianity and the Culture Wars

Gus diZerega

The United States and many other Western nations are confronting major cultural challenges unimagined when the dominant guiding philosophies and religions of our time first developed. For most of the last 2,000 years of Western history, issues concerning gender, sexuality and the environment have not been culturally divisive. They are now. In addition, questions of cultural diversity have taken on new meaning as many immigrants come not only from other Christian cultures, but from non-Christian ones as well. It seems to me these issues fall into two broad categories: the rise of the feminine to challenge a pathologically patriarchal society and the rise of spiritual diversity. That is how I will address them.

The 'Culture War'

In agricultural and post-agricultural societies women have consistently been relegated to second-class status. In countless ways sexual double standards have prevailed. Even where such double standards did not exist, values associated with males were all but universally given greater social preference, often by women as well as men. Not coincidentally I think, Nature was also often perceived as feminine, and also suffered from the general triumph of patriarchal values. These attitudes extend back far more than 2,000 years, and infected Pagan, monotheistic and Buddhist societies across the board.

While there had been earlier hints of changes to come, beginning in the 1960s issues of gender, sexuality and nature entered the arena of cultural and political discussion in a big way. They remain there. Because they challenged religious and cultural assumptions that were traditionally taken for granted, they provoked a fierce response from those claiming the mantle of cultural and religious conservatism. Much of this attack claims to defend religion against 'secular humanism'. To give but two examples, Pat Buchanan, a leading American conservative, wrote:

> *In politics conservatives have won more than they have lost, but in the culture, the left and its Woodstock values have triumphed. Divorce, dirty language, adultery, blasphemy, euthanasia, abortion, pornography, cohabitation and so on were not unknown in 1960. But today they permeate our lives…*
>
> *We can no more walk away from the culture war than we can walk away from the Cold War. For the culture war is at its heart a religious war about whether God or man shall be exalted, whose moral beliefs shall be enshrined into law, and what children shall be taught to value and abhor. With those stakes, to walk away is to abandon your post in time of war.*[1]

And two days after 9/11, while the nation was still in shock, the two most prominent religious leaders of the Christian Right, Pat Robertson and Jerry Falwell, discussed the atrocity. Falwell said the US deserved it, adding 'I really believe that the pagans and the abortionists and the feminists and the gays and the lesbians who are actively trying to make that an alternative lifestyle, the ACLU, People for the American Way, all of them who try to secularize America… I point the thing in their face and say you helped this happen.' Robertson replied: 'I totally concur…'

Notice the centrality of sexuality, gender and the Divine Feminine in these arguments. I shall return to this issue shortly. Buchanan, Falwell and Robertson's conflation of secularism with new religious movements is fascinating. It is also a complete confusion. Their error has two dimensions.

First, the secularization of politics and the secularization of society have different causes. The first arises from people's abundant experience of politics' corrupting influence on religion, and the violence that flares when advocates of competing faiths seek political power to enforce their views. During the American Founding era, Baptists were among the strongest advocates of a separation of church and state, and no one would call them secularists.[2] But Americans' historical memories are short, and many have forgotten their wisdom. Not only is the secularization of politics not connected to the secularization of society, the actual relationship may be *inversely* connected: removal of religion from normal politics helps preserve its vitality. Certainly it is the case that in European nations with long histories of religious involvement in politics, the proportion of their populations who are religious believers is smaller than in the US.

The secularization of society has different roots. It is embedded in the growing belief that the transcendent 'God-of-the-gaps', thought to intervene at those points where science could not understand the world, was no longer plausible. For many people there no longer appeared to be any gaps that were unlikely to be bridged someday by growing scientific knowledge. For them, religion in its entirety was ultimately based on factual errors and preserved by wishful thinking. This secular outlook emerged from within a *logos*-centred culture that had no comprehension of other kinds of truth beyond science and blind faith. It is little connected to politics: many western European nations have state-supported churches, but are even more culturally secular than the US.

Even so, contemporary culture warriors prefer to conflate these two different streams, thereby offering people a false choice of integrating religion into politics or seeing it gradually disappear within society. In my judgment this is because they must now rely on the power of the police to offset what they have lost in freely given allegiance. A Pagan response to these issues is interwoven throughout my discussions in this book. Here I want to focus on a still deeper error.

The Entrance of the Divine Feminine into Western Culture

What we have today in the United States and elsewhere is a *three-sided* struggle. One side, that of Buchanan, Falwell and Robertson, defends a pathological patriarchal mindset that now sees itself challenged not only by secular institutions, but also by the rise of feminine spirituality within all levels of Western religious life. While they claim to speak for Christianity, a great many Christians oppose them, including my co-author.

Traditional secular society, typified by modern science, is the second side. Its weakness lies in its inability to comprehend the internal dimension of life. Focusing only on exteriors that can be measured and predicted, it offers us power and material prosperity, but at the cost of denying life any ultimate meaning. Many scientists are not secular in this sense, just as many Christians are not members of the 'Christian' Right.

By presenting us with a false dichotomy, the patriarchs of the 'Christian' Right argue that it is they and they alone who defend the existence of any spiritual reality against forces of atheism. But the third player in this struggle, manifesting through the rise of feminine spirituality, confronts them in the centre of their citadel, offering a powerful challenge to those whose religion has lost touch with genuine spirituality, subsisting instead on the emotional addictions of the will-to-believe, anger and self-righteousness. This reality underlies the culture warriors' consistent and confused conflation of secular modernity with the 1960s counterculture, for the counterculture was *also* a rejection of the dominant cultural ideals in the US and other countries. It was at its core a resurgence of feminine values and consciousness as a desperately needed corrective to a culture that was powerfully out of balance.

Many cultural streams arose during the 1960s – but these streams generally flowed into a common river, which was able to change a person's, or even a culture's, mental landscape. I think this list covers the most important cultural strands of the 1960s:

• the rise of the civil rights movement

• the rise of the peace movement

• the rise of the environmental movement

• the rebirth of feminism, particularly a feminism that did not argue just that women could be like men, but also that where differences between the sexes existed, those associated with women were just as valuable as those associated with men

• interest in altered states of consciousness

• interest in alternative spiritual perspectives such as Buddhism, Hinduism, Native American, NeoPagan and later the New Age

• the rise of rock and roll, as popular music became increasingly sensuous and visceral[3]

• growing interest in nontraditional and holistic approaches to health, including acupuncture, energy work, body work and other forms of healing increasingly common today

• long hair became acceptable to men – before then it was regarded as feminine (except on Jesus)

• increased concern with 'right livelihood' as an alternative to pursuing a career, a stance pioneered by the hippies

• introduction of the pill, which gave women control over their bodies to an unimagined degree

None of these trends were without precursors, but during this time they entered the cultural mainstream and reinforced one another, forming a coherent style of relating with the world and with others that was receptive, intuitive, connective, sensuous and non-lineal, and which emphasized personal experience over abstract information. Whether symbolically (as with long hair), viscerally (as with rock and roll), or explicitly (as with environmentalism and sexuality), there was a shift to honouring the concretely and sensuously physical, and coming into harmony with it, rather than exalting the abstract and impersonal over the world of matter. If we were to seek a single term to encapsulate these values, it would be 'feminine'.

During the 1960s, *feminine* values first effectively challenged on a mass scale the dominant patriarchal technocratic ideals of the left, centre and right, which exalted power and control. In doing so they injected new life into the core of American and other mostly Western countries' culture, politics and religion. They also raised a deep and unsettling challenge to structures of power and authority justified by habits of thought that were thousands of years old.

The sole and tragic exception was the cult of revolution. But revolution and violence were rejected by most countercultural young people. For example, when in 1969 this self-proclaimed vanguard proclaimed Chicago's 'Days of Rage', hoping to lure 20,000 radicals to 'begin the revolution', 300 showed. Two months earlier, at Woodstock, New York, some 400,000 young people had participated in a mammoth peaceful gathering. Compared to Chicago, this was a ratio of about 1,333 to one. A week after the fizzled 'Days of Rage', *millions* of Americans participated in the anti-war moratorium.[4]

In my opinion, contemporary cultural and political battles over sexuality, gender, ethnicity and nature cannot be understood without first recognizing them as evidence of the deep changes in human awareness initiated in many Western nations during the 1960s. They continue to challenge a one-sided masculinity so inhuman that even its major advocates often live lives in stark contradiction to the values they preach. For example, in the US the highest divorce and murder rates occur in states associated with the Religious Right.

The rise of NeoPagan religion constituted one important dimension of what I like to term the rise of the Divine Feminine. This feminine spiritual current also began making itself felt in more established religions. Increasingly women became ministers in Christian denominations, where their presence had long been marginal, and the issue simmers even within Catholicism. Feminine as well as masculine aspects of God began to be emphasized in some Christian traditions. In the 1960s women began attending rabbinical schools, leading to the ordination of the first female American Reform rabbi in 1972. Similar trends began changing new religions that were entering from abroad, such as Buddhism. Western Buddhism differs from traditional Asian Buddhism particularly in the much more prominent role women play in the Sangha.[5] But NeoPaganism is the most unambiguous expression of this spiritual development.

NeoPaganism and the Divine Feminine

Along with our polytheism, nothing makes contemporary Wiccans and many other NeoPagans seem more unusual than our focus on the Goddess as our primary deity. For us She is the most important expression of the Sacred. She is central to who we are.

From its very inception women have played a uniquely powerful role in NeoPaganism. In traditional Wicca the High Priestess has always been the coven's major authority. Who serves as High Priest is her choice. Other traditions established after the Gardnerian generally preserved women's dominant role. The most well known American Pagan is Starhawk.[6] In some cases 'Dianic' covens were established in which only the Goddess is worshipped in Her various aspects and all members are women, and feminist Wicca has grown in popularity among feminists with a spiritual commitment.[7] In short, concerning the role of women and the feminine in religion, NeoPaganism is at the cutting edge.

Thousands of Years in Three Paragraphs

The feminine has also long been associated with the Earth. Mother Earth is a concept found in many cultures. It probably seemed to many that the rain, falling from the sky, impregnated the Earth, thereby bringing forth plants from the darkness of the earthly womb. As the Earth was experienced as alive, it was easy to conceive Her in gendered terms.

With the rise of agriculture there was almost certainly a rise in the ambiguity with which people, men in particular, approached the feminine – human and earthly alike. It is easier to live with natural cycles than to try to control and override them, as indicated by the evident decline in human stature and health that coincided with the rise of agriculture. Power increasingly became rooted in controlling land, and the greater importance of certainty of descent from the father encouraged the placing of women under greater control. Politics became increasingly rooted in domination and military force because it was hard for farmers to move. This gave men an additional edge. Because societies were more stationary, they were vulnerable to natural cycles in ways that more mobile kinds of life had not been. Increasingly the Earth, the basis of life, was seen as withholding, inconstant, and increasingly in need of control.

The natural and social miseries accompanying agricultural life in early city states and empires contrasted powerfully with the unchanging procession of the eternal stars, which were seemingly free from corruption and decay. And of course the Earth was feminine, the sky with its fertilizing rain, masculine. As a result, I suspect the widespread belief that the heavens were unchanging and perfect compared to the mutable and miserable character of life on Earth also contributed to this apparent dissociation of transcendental conceptions of Spirit from the world which, even if it remained inspirited, was of a distinctly lesser, and feminine, character.[8] The abstract and universal became exalted far above the concrete and local. As institutionalized religions became more closely associated with political and economic power, we can hardly be surprised that interpretations of the Sacred veered in this direction.

Spirituality and Modernity

We are no longer such a society. Most of us today seek nature out for personal healing, peace and beauty. The declining importance of physical strength as a means of assisting success or justifying domination, combined with women's growing educational and economic opportunities, has compelled a re-examination of age-old gender relations and their justifications by women and men alike. Old bastions of patriarchal superiority have been undermined. War, the 'sport of Kings and Republicans', has become suicidal and its emphasis on technology rather than strength has weakened its monopolization by men. Modern science, once thought of as objective evidence for the superiority of men and 'masculine' styles of thought, has been shown to rely on the 'feminine' as strongly as on the masculine.[9] Finally, the liberal values of human rights and equality, although originally conceived in abstract terms basically compatible with patriarchal styles of thought, gradually became centred on the concrete as well, where they further challenged old notions of domination and hierarchy.

Small wonder those believing in extreme patriarchal values feel threatened. As the fall of Communism demonstrated, even the most powerful institutions survive only when people believe they are legitimate or, through inertia, when no alternative arises. Today patriarchal domination is increasingly perpetuated by instilling fear in as many people as possible: fear of a vengeful deity, of other cultures and of those who are different within our own culture. If this extreme patriarchy is secular it seeks empire; if 'spiritual', apocalypse. What unites them is a love of domination and what preserves their alliance is their desire to dominate *different* aspects of human life. They offer no positive vision.

In the US, the Bush administration with its mishandling of every challenge that has come its way exemplifies the deep moral and intellectual rot at the core of those who rail against feminine values. Nor, it seems, can they walk their own talk. From businessmen who depend on government contacts rather than competitive excellence for their wealth, to military 'experts' who avoid ever serving their country, to moral exemplars with worse divorce and similar records than most of those they criticize, the pattern is clear and unequivocal.

Today's cultural tensions arise from the rapid degeneration of a pathologically patriarchal society that has lost its way morally and spiritually. Having nothing to offer besides claims to dominate others, its representatives rail against corrective currents which, taken together, are manifestations of the Divine Feminine. The best evidence for this concerns abortion and contraception. The *only* thing that seems to lower abortions in a society is the availability of contraception.[10] Yet many 'culture warriors' seek to ban or limit contraception despite it guaranteeing that many women will therefore seek to terminate their pregnancies. Opposition to female sexuality trumps their supposed commitment to life.

They emphasize 'traditional' religion. But it is not traditional, marking instead the advanced degeneration of efforts to ground religion only in *logos*: the abandonment of both *logos* and *mythos* in favour of blind and irrational faith. James Dobson, Paul Weyrich, Don Wildmon, D. James Kennedy and similar sorts argue that evangelical Christianity requires 'conservative views on politics, economics and biblical morality'.[11] For them, religion becomes a political party dedicated in part to attacking the feminine in whatever form it manifests. I emphasize again that these people do not speak for all Christians, or even all evangelicals. Philip Johnson makes this clear. But they speak insistently and loudly and mislead millions.

Beginning in the 1960s, I think Spirit offered the modern world an opportunity to regain its cultural, psychological and spiritual balance. To do so, feminine values must become equal to the masculine in the sacred and spiritual as well as in other dimensions of human life. The issues of transcendence and immanence, of the masculine and feminine, symbolize this tension. I am on secure ground when observing that purely transcendent images of deity tend to be associated with masculine, even patriarchal, theologies. And transcendence marks the ultimate boundary – an unbridgeable one – hence its appeal to a one-sided metastasizing of the masculine, with God being far more easily conceived as hierarch than as loving.

At the centre is a struggle over whether boundaries must be tightly closed or whether greater openness is needed. A purely transcendental outlook favours inviolable boundaries. To the degree that immanence exists, boundaries become porous. Immanence means that a dimension of the Divine is in everything and no boundary is ultimately total.

Sexuality concerns boundaries at every level: psychological, physical, social and, I would argue, energetic and spiritual. *This* is why the culture warriors are so obsessed with anything that empowers women. Of course, like men, women combine feminine and masculine elements within any given individual. But symbolically they epitomize the feminine.

Part of today's religious and cultural turmoil is caused by the fact that most existing religions are split between older more patriarchal forms and newer ones that have developed better understandings of the Sacred. Paganism seems different only because older forms of EuroPagan practice had been suppressed. This plus its polytheism made NeoPaganism far more initially accepting of the Divine Feminine than most other traditions. But this potential exists in all genuine spiritual traditions.

Gays and Religion

Nothing threatens an embattled and insecure patriarchal mindset more than homosexuality, particularly male homosexuality. The blurring of sexual and gender boundaries can be very threatening to those who are insecure in their own identity. (The rest of us can only wonder why, with so many problems in the world, some people focus on who other people want to sleep with.) We see the clash between pathological patriarchal and more balanced and feminine oriented kinds of spirituality manifested in current controversies about the role of gays in religious communities.

Many mainstream churches have been deeply divided by issues such as gay marriage and gay clergy. These issues have been largely absent in the NeoPagan community. In 1984, when I first became involved, gays were very visible within the NeoPagan community. Some have been among our most respected leaders and teachers. For virtually all of us sexual orientation is not an issue.

To be sure, among British Traditional NeoPagans there were initially some tensions when the gay community began demanding to be more visibly accepted by their straight friends and neighbours. The reason is interesting theologically. I want briefly to describe it.

Much NeoPagan symbolism and ritual is rooted in the differences between and attaining harmony with the masculine and the feminine. Gardnerian and most other NeoPagan traditions emphasize the relationship between the Goddess, the Divine Feminine, and the God, the Divine Masculine, as their way of honouring the Sacred as immanent in the world. Every British Traditional Esbat includes a symbolic sexual union of the sacred male and female and 'conjoined they bring blessedness'. The changing of the seasons and rhythms of life are also structured around relations between the sacred feminine and sacred masculine. Gender duality permeates our rituals. In addition, as Gardner handed down our tradition, initiations are cross gender: woman to man, man to woman.

The role of gay Wiccans has therefore been a matter of controversy in Gardnerian circles. Some gays who were attracted to our practice said they felt out of place, particularly with respect to initiation symbolism, and wondered whether we would accommodate them. In California, where I practised at the time, the issue was resolved by leaving it to the prospective initiate to determine whether he or she felt primarily connected to the masculine or feminine. The sexual duality of the feminine and the masculine *as qualities* is fundamental to our practice, but many believed how it is connected to physical gender is not. As a California Gardnerian of my acquaintance explained, 'it is absolutely essential that both the God and the Goddess be represented – but doing so is more complex than external gender'.

Some other Gardnerians took a more conservative approach, insisting gender polarity be maintained even if it meant otherwise well-qualified people would not join. But unlike within the monotheistic traditions, being gay was not considered to be a spiritual or any other kind of shortcoming; rather, this particular kind of Pagan practice was just not for them. I have spoken with gay Pagans who said that because they respected traditional Gardnerian Wicca they did not want to join, as they believed it would dilute the tradition's focus. There are other traditions that do not have this requirement, and even very gay-friendly traditions, such as Minoan for men and Dianic for women. Nor are such traditions considered theologically inferior to those that are heterosexual.

Outside Gardnerian and other British Traditionalist groups there was even less controversy. The only one I remember was a May Pole celebration. Traditionally women carried their ribbons in one direction and men carried theirs in another. At a public festival some gay Pagans insisted on carrying their ribbon in the direction they felt most suitable. The celebration went just fine, but it was a simple celebration rather than a magickal working attempting to accomplish some outcome separate from the dance itself.

On the other hand, a magickal working organized in advance would have found everyone on the same page with respect to this question. If any disagreed, etiquette would have led them to not be involved, *whatever* the decision. I think few would argue when I say that NeoPagans in general have little or no problem with gay issues, and for the most part never have had.

This leads me to a final point at which our experience differs from that of many more mainstream religions.

From a NeoPagan perspective, no tradition claims to have the ultimate spiritual truth for humanity. The Sacred exceeds our understanding, and when we seek to integrate our lives more fully into the Sacred, we should do so humbly, respectfully regarding how Spirit speaks to others. The breathtaking variety of practices and traditions within Pagan spirituality is a sign of immense richness, not of disorder. If you do not want to work with me in a way we both find fulfilling, neither you nor I are necessarily spiritually injured. It is up to each of us to find the path most fitting for who we are.

The existence of all gay or all straight or mixed covens is what we might expect to find. And we do. People work with those with whom they feel most comfortable, and while for most of us gender orientation is not an issue, if for some it is, this is not a problem. There are also individuals who may work in a mixed coven for some purposes, and a homogeneously gendered one for others, depending on the dimension of the Sacred on which they want to focus.

After all, as the Lady says in the Charge of the Goddess: 'all acts of love and pleasure are my rituals'. Perhaps, as a consequence, there is more sexual variety within the NeoPagan community than any other of which I have heard, and less judgment on others' behaviour. We probably have a higher percentage of gay, bisexual and lesbian people within our community than is found in society at large. They are welcome and they know it.

Boundaries

We return now to the issue of boundaries. I have argued that NeoPagans emphasize the Sacred in its immanent aspect. When clearly understood and apprehended, the world and everything in it is a manifestation of the Divine. So ultimately distinctions are not primary characteristics of reality. There is no transcendent/immanent distinction except at the 'denser' levels of physical manifestation.

Further, when we ask why there is a physical reality, given this underlying monism and the obvious suffering and pain it appears to entail, only one answer seems to me to make sense: to manifest good things that could not otherwise be manifested. And when I try to figure out what those good things are that might outweigh such enormous suffering, the only one clearly to shine forth for me is that in the context of diversity, love can manifest in more ways. Love treasures and takes delight in the singular, the individual, the unique, as intrinsically valuable and good.[12] As She once told me, 'All beings are worthy of my love.'

Love opens us up to experiencing the intrinsic value of the loved. This, I suspect, is the primary spiritual task facing each of us.

Even our beloved's shortcomings – and we all have them – enable us to develop compassion, a quality that would remain unrealized within a world characterized by simple unity. Individuality and diversity can only be fully honoured spiritually when we open ourselves to including ever wider and deeper dimensions of the world. But open hearts cross boundaries while still respecting them. In a paradoxical way, the qualities of monism are most fittingly manifested within a world of diverse individuality.

The hippies' insight to 'make love not war' was right, though they usually lacked the maturity, experience and wisdom to follow their vision during the dark years that followed – years that are still very much with us. But the seeds were planted, and their shoots are still growing, spreading and flowering. The men of privilege and pride, now as well as then, see only weeds where we see flowers.

Interfaith

Spiritual boundaries have long plagued humanity. It is difficult for many to acknowledge that a spiritual path they find enormously fulfilling may not be equally fulfilling for others, or that paths trod by others may be as valuable as their own. It usually takes respectful dialogue to bring home to people within different religious communities the depth of spiritual commitment often held by people within other faiths.

This is scarcely confined to religion. One characteristic that fundamentally distinguishes the modern mentality from those that preceded it is a recognition that our similarities as people are fundamentally more important than our differences. As Europeans are learning (and some Americans are forgetting), those similarities even trump claims of national loyalty and identity – legitimate claims to be sure, but not all-embracing ones. Respecting human equality and ethical worth makes possible the richness of creativity and cooperation that characterizes the modern world. For the Sacred to manifest even more fully in our world, we have now as a people to embrace this same insight with regard to Spirit.

Many Pagans, Wiccans in particular, have been active in interfaith work, assisting people within other traditions to know something of our beliefs and practices. Two worldwide organizations have particularly benefited from our presence, the United Religions Initiative (http://www.uri.org/) and the Council for a Parliament of the World's Religions (http://www.cpwr.org/). In part, our involvement has been for self-protection. Given Jerry Falwell and Pat Robertson's vicious claim and the supercharged emotions of the time, our efforts may have proven vital. Their absurd and, I would say, sacrilegious charges went nowhere.

But I believe there is more in our involvement than simple self-interest.

Interfaith work may be an area in which Wiccans can be of great service to the larger spiritual community. Most Wiccans have no problem acknowledging that other faiths also possess spiritual truths, perhaps truths as important as our own. *It is what we would expect.* While some are led to our path following unpleasant experiences of another religion, if they are attentive I believe they are ultimately healed of these antagonisms, and are able to recognize the Sacred in that other religion as well as with us.

Religious traditions are different ways in which human beings have sought to come into greater relationship with the Sacred. All are potentially sources of spiritual insight that may be slighted or even unknown within other traditions. It is fitting that NeoPagans have taken a leading role in seeking to help preserve minority spiritual traditions throughout the world. The Lost and Endangered Religions Project associated with the CPWR is a case in point.

The richness of humanity's religious experience means that when people enter into genuine fellowship with one another, all parties are changed. Wiccans involved with interfaith work have developed a deeper appreciation for people within other faith traditions even as they have demonstrated to others the value and beauty of our own. That has been my own experience in interfaith dialogue, an experience I have heard described by others.

We make no efforts to convert another, and others do not seek to convert us. Nor do we ever try to find a common all-embracing 'religion' that somehow combines May Poles with Masses, Drawing Down the Moon with gospel hymns, ritual drumming with sermons. If we do something together, and sometimes we do, it is in a way that honours the individuality of all our traditions.

Seen from this viewpoint, perhaps Spirit is like a photon. Perform some experiments and a photon appears to be a wave, extended in space. Perform others and it appears to be a particle, with well-defined tiny boundaries. The human mind cannot conceive how it can be that both photons do not appear overly troubled by our inability to understand them.

If this is true for a photon, among the simplest of physical entities, how much more true may it be of the human encounter with the More-Than-Human? From one perspective our religions are unique ways in which we address our relation to the Sacred. From another, all are interconnected threads in the divine web through which humankind, and all kind, take their place in the all-encompassing Sacred. Both are true.

Philip Johnson

Gus and I agree that Christians and Pagans face the challenge of learning how to peaceably coexist, and this is highlighted by debates on religion in the public square, gender and sexuality, interfaith relations and cultural change. In the midst of rapid cultural change these topics generate tensions between the two communities. Gus suggests that modern cultural imbalances are being rectified via the immanent Divine Feminine.

The problem of religion in the public square is illustrated by Gus quoting various politically conservative Americans such as Pat Buchanan, the late Jerry Falwell, Pat Robertson and James Dobson, most of whom are evangelical Christians.[13] They lament the erosion of respect for Christian beliefs and are alarmed by America's social, moral and religious plurality. Gus quotes Falwell, who interpreted the events of 9/11 as divine retribution on America. Falwell claimed that God's protective hand had been withdrawn because Christian values were being undermined by Pagans, feminists, lesbians and others. Gus also alludes to remarks made by other spokesmen who have asserted that evangelical theology requires that one holds to conservative views on politics, economics and morality. I speak as an 'outsider' with respect to America, and although there are comparable debates in Australia, England and New Zealand, the political contexts are quite different.

Every religious community – including Pagans – has its fair share of 'uncles' who make inappropriate statements. I repudiate Falwell's remarks about the American tragedy of September 11, 2001 as gratuitous and repugnant, and many other Christians feel the same way. To be fair, we must acknowledge that on September 14, 2001 Falwell publicly apologized, saying: 'I would never blame any human being except the terrorists, and if I left that impression with gays or lesbians or anyone else, I apologize.'[14] Yet he did maintain until his death a story about the destiny of 'Christian America' that I will examine later.

Political Stereotypes

Part of the tension between the Christian and Pagan communities focuses on the Religious Right, which is becoming globalized.[15] The prime movers are identified as born again or evangelical Christians but the movement also includes conservative-thinking Roman Catholics and Mormons. Some critics assume that evangelicalism and the Religious Right are synonymous and portray them as a monolithic movement. Tabloid media footage of ham-fisted preachers rousing an audience with moralist rhetoric perpetuates a hostile image.[16]

Many evangelicals (including myself) are critical of the Religious Right. Contrary to media stereotypes there is no evangelical consensus on politics. Falwell and Robertson do not speak on behalf of all evangelicals because political views are actually quite diverse, spanning theocracy-dominion, conservative, moderate, reformist and left-radical convictions.[17] This internal diversity has not curbed the Religious Right's influence, but over the last 40 years academics and pastors have challenged their fellow evangelicals about the blind-spots created by marrying the church to social and political conservatism.[18] Media images firmly linking Reagan, Bush and the Religious Right obscure from the public's memory the fact that two Democrat Presidents were evangelicals: Woodrow Wilson and Jimmy Carter.

Any Christian stance on politics must be open to scrutiny, and whatever is ethically corrupt, theologically dubious and politically naïve must be challenged. Evangelicals have had a mixed legacy of good and bad activity since the movement emerged in the eighteenth century. In response to the liberating message of Jesus, evangelicals have tackled major social injustices with positive enduring outcomes for human welfare and for civil rights. Other activities have been failures or have produced mixed results when problems were not comprehensively addressed.

Here are some of the serious blind-spots: evangelicals joined in anti-Masonic, anti-Mormon and anti-Catholic campaigns in the nineteenth century. White evangelicals supported segregation and apartheid, and some even joined the Ku Klux Klan. There are evangelicals who promote anti-Semitic conspiracy theories about history and modern international affairs. Some have been oppressive towards women. Others exploit the environment's natural resources, convinced that the Earth has a 'use-by date' in the not-too-distant future. There are disturbing cases of Pagans and Wiccans being vilified in towns and cities spurred on by rumours, innuendo and unbecoming behaviour. The list goes on to include many other woes, some of which Christians have repented while others remain to be renounced. Some reflect the abuse of power, xenophobia, intolerance and selfishness.

Yet there are also many positive actions which express compassion and produce spiritual nurture and growth: the abolition of slavery, support for animal rights, the creation of relief agencies and benevolent societies, the push for prison reforms, the promotion of literacy, the founding of trade labour unions and the introduction of factory reforms. Evangelicals have participated in the peace movement, opposed bride-burning in India, resisted the opium trade and halted female infanticide and child foot-binding in China. Anna Howard Shaw was an American evangelical suffragette leader, while Catherine Booth and Phoebe Palmer were nineteenth-century preachers, social reformers and supporters of Christian feminism.[19] When Georgia experienced the gold rush of 1828, efforts were made to evict the Cherokee Indians from their tribal lands. Evangelical missionaries allied themselves with the Cherokee Chief John Ross in petitioning Congress to oppose President Jackson's policy and that of the state of Georgia. Sadly they were unsuccessful, but this is a striking case in which evangelicals were defenders of indigenous people.[20]

Political Naïveté

Christians who participate in grassroots politics today often lack a theologically mature social ethic. James Skillen has pointed out that the problem is aggravated by church leaders who are unclear about the role of government in society.[21] Activists often fail to evaluate their own discourses about why government should be concerned about a narrow list of moral issues to the exclusion of other problems. Mark Noll argues that the fundamental problem that needs addressing is why American evangelical political causes are based on questions of personal morality rather than on any deep theological evaluation.[22]

Political naïveté can also lead well-meaning evangelicals into having idealized dreams. David Kuo was an enthusiastic evangelical filled with great hope when he joined the staff at the White House in the Office of Faith-Based and Community Initiatives during the administration of George W. Bush. His disillusionment with the political intrigue and exploitation of voter sympathies ought to serve as a strong reality check to the utopian dream that a compassionate, godly nation will emerge if evangelicals take influential posts in Congress, the White House and the Supreme Court.[23] Evangelicals seem to have forgotten the sagely quip that televangelist Rex Humbard made in 1980: 'If I got into politics I'd be like a blacksmith pullin' teeth.'[24]

I am not suggesting that Christians should withdraw from political participation. My point is the need for theological maturity, and for more reflection on values and the realities of political life. Our social backgrounds, hand-me-down family attitudes, peer thinking and personal experiences play a major part in forming our political and social values. In most Western countries evangelicals are strongly represented among the middle classes. When a particular social class or personality type dominates a local church then social stratification sets in. So Christians cannot automatically assume that their inherited values are in the first place biblical – some may be and others may not. Put another way: are today's urban/rural middle-class values compatible with those taught by Jesus, the apostles and prophets?

Secondly, assuming biblical values have been identified, why should any non-Christian have to observe them unless they follow Jesus? Are they essential to reforming an intractable problem that only legislation can remedy? If Christian values are imposed by law, how will non-Christians recognize the gospel? Can Christians be more effective by serving the community than by relying on any government? God expects Christians to live by Jesus' message, and it is dangerous for Christians to expect the government to do the tasks Jesus gave to the church to fulfil. Thirdly, the claim that evangelicals must espouse conservative political values is a dangerous assertion that masquerades as a biblical ideology. Noll points out that all too often the rallying cry for 'Christian politics' is merely a cloak for justifying self-interested politics with God-talk.[25]

'God's Country'

The leaders of the Religious Right promote a parochial vision of 'Christian America' established in colonial times. American history does include explicit Christian elements in it such as the Pilgrim Fathers and the Puritans. Yet the Religious Right's story is deeply flawed because the early colony was also home to unorthodox religious teachings such as astrology, Freemasonry and Pow-Wow healing.[26] The Founding Fathers – Benjamin Franklin, Thomas Jefferson, Thomas Paine and George Washington – espoused Deism. Since unorthodox, Deistic and non-Christian religious beliefs were present in pre-Revolutionary America, it seems that the constitutional guarantee of religious liberty was not designed for the sole benefit of Christians.[27] Some of the best insights into this matter have come from evangelical historians.[28]

American national life has also developed a civil religion. Elements of it appear in the vague references to 'Nature's God' or 'the Creator' in the Declaration of Independence of 1776, in the Pledge of Allegiance, and in the national motto 'In God We Trust'. It also emerges in presidential rhetoric when the White House adopts pastoral and priest-like roles. When the tales of 'Christian America' and civil religion converge, the Religious Right assumes that biblical and national values are one and the same. Civil religious sentiments however are devoid of orthodox belief and marrying the two things together produces a distorted gospel.[29]

In the early twentieth century the Afrikaners thought that God had appointed them to rule South Africa, but their story was morally bankrupt. Neither has God chosen the USA or Australia to receive any special favours. I believe that those who tell the 'Christian America' story are unaware that they are actually putting forward a romanticized story of how they feel things ought to be. For conservative Christians bewildered by widespread cultural change, this story seems inspiring, but as other evangelicals have already shown it is a misleading myth. In the face of cultural change the preceding myth lends itself to a siege mentality.

Jesus and Politics

Jesus saw that there were legitimate tasks for governments to perform and accepted that one's civic duty included paying taxes.[30] He recognized that those who govern have spheres of authority and that God's people are meant to be good citizens who promote peace and harmony. Although Jesus upheld the belief that there is a genuine need for government, he did not bestow legitimacy on any particular political party or system. Jesus' teaching does not require uncritical or passive acceptance of the actions of those in government. He did not refrain from being critical of social injustices, the abuse of authority, or the efforts of imperial leaders to deify themselves and their regimes. For a political power to see itself as being on a par with or greater than God was repugnant to Jesus. So the antics of Herod Antipas, the ruler over Galilee, drew biting criticism from Jesus.[31]

Many of Jesus' earliest followers became socially marginalized as he called into question all kinds of barriers erected by hierarchy, patriarchy, ethnicity and privilege. He subverted the status quo by welcoming the rejected and the disempowered, including women, non-Jews, political and criminal outcasts, the sick and the poor. His prophetic message about God's new community focused on a just and peaceful society that is spiritually centred in relationship with our Creator.

Jesus illustrated aspects of this new community through the

parables he told about transformed attitudes that translate into social conduct, such as love for one's neighbour (meaning whoever is in need of help), love for enemies and pursuing justice for the vulnerable.[32] For example, to act counterculturally in oppressive situations means that, like Jesus, one does not seek power over others, but instead stands in partnership with the vulnerable, weak and powerless. Jesus refused to be drawn into the nationalist plots of his Jewish contemporaries, who wanted him to lead an anti-imperial uprising as their king.[33] While his actions put him on a collision course with the political and religious establishment of the day, Jesus repudiated the need for the seizure of political power because such activity cannot establish God's new community. Jesus told Pontius Pilate that 'my kingdom is not from this world'.[34]

It would take another book to properly examine the ethical and political implications of Jesus' teaching, and what applications they have in our context.[35] Likewise, it would take a book to evaluate church–state relations since Jesus' day. The Roman emperor Constantine favoured a united empire with a united church as the sole religion. Under this model, the civil rights of those outside the state-church's membership were repressed, including dissenting church groups and non-Christian religious practitioners. The Anabaptist and Mennonite Reformers critically challenged the idea centuries later.[36] These 'radical' Reformers and later dissenters made a substantial contribution to contemporary ideas about religious freedom. Gus reminds us of the 'forgotten' ways of the Baptists and, if space permitted, we could learn from Roger Williams' Baptist colony of Rhode Island.[37]

Let us also remember the positive Christian input that shaped rights, duties and liberty in the common-law. Modern civil rights owe something to Christians such as Cardinal Stephen Langton, the father of the Magna Carta; the Dutch lawyer–theologian Hugo Grotius, the father of international law; John Locke, who powerfully influenced American constitutional thought; and Lebanese diplomat Charles Malik, who assisted in drafting the UN Universal Declaration of Human Rights.

Other Christians have not had any experience of the social privileges accorded a state-church. Since the seventh century the Copts and Churches of the Ancient East have operated as minorities inside the Islamic world. Many Christians learned to cope under the repressive anti-religious policies of the Marxist states of Eastern

Europe and Chairman Mao's Cultural Revolution. Jesus' way works for people who have no ballot box and who live in contexts of vulnerability and powerlessness.

Divine Feminine and Immanence

I accept that patriarchal attitudes have had to be challenged and that some important moves for cultural change have emerged in recent decades in the area of women's status and social roles. The stories of women who have acted as agents of change in modern society are many and varied. Among the throng of early nineteenth-century voices were women from the English, Australian and American evangelical sub-cultures.[38] If we burrow into church history there are several pioneering examples of Christians upholding the rights of women.[39] Women today find themselves participating in structural contexts created and led by males. Church debates about ordaining women tend to be polarized and often fail to grasp that women are meant to be in equal partnership with men in God's new community.[40] What was revealed about holistic equality both by Jesus and in the creation story is far from being realized in today's church and world. As with other topics in this chapter, it would take another book to examine properly the negative and positive legacies of the churches concerning women.

Gus refers to the innovations of the counterculture and invites us to see how the marginalized ways of the Divine Feminine are re-emerging in human consciousness. Gus contrasts cultural change, immanence and the feminine with the debilitating impact of patriarchy and its oppressive images of transcendence. The perspective that Gus offers is an interesting one and it prompts me to refer back to remarks I made earlier in this book about discernment. Within the Christian tradition, the capacity for discernment and the ability to challenge are anchored in various biblical themes such as promoting justice, pleading for equity, mutual service, repentance and embodying truthfulness. Yet they are not defined by merely locating accountability inside the Christian community. They also rest ultimately on knowing the 'inconvenient truth' that we are accountable to God for what we do and say.

I believe that what we may sense as immanence in our culture has to be related back to the transcendent. Otherwise we may be projecting out from our inner being all kinds of things that can be dark and untrue, or we may be divining signs and symbols and justifying this with God-talk that later on proves to have feet of clay. If we cast our minds back to the 1920s in Weimar, Germany, some new religions emerged offering the promise of spiritual renewal based on racial theories, Nordic myths, yogic powers and ideas about purging reality through ritual esoteric practices. These groups wanted to dismantle and obliterate both Judaism and Christianity. From our vantage point today, we can look back in horror at what finally coalesced into the Aryan mysticism of the SS in the Nazi regime.[41] However, it is vital that we are not blind to untruth in the present as there are many dark, destructive and harmful things subsumed under the canopy of 'spirituality'. The question that confronts us is: How do we discern what is good or bad in immanent forms of spirituality, particularly if there is little place for rational cognition to evaluate things, and if there is no accountability to a transcendental source?

I am reminded of Georg Hegel and Thomas Altizer, both of whom bore witness to what they believed was the immanent spirit's work. Hegel was persuaded that the immanent world spirit operated through four historical epochs that would take us to the final goal of freedom. At the start of the nineteenth century, Hegel looked forward and felt that the immanent spirit was positively at work in the fourth epoch in the Germanic nation. After two World Wars we look back and see the precise opposite to Hegel. In the mid-1960s Thomas Altizer came to notoriety as a 'death-of-God' theologian. In his *Gospel of Christian Atheism* he said that the immanent spirit was awakening us to the death of God's transcendence. Altizer's curious death-of-God theology did not survive the 1960s yet, paradoxically, while he predicted the end of transcendence, many young people were moved by the Beatles' search for transcendental experiences among India's gurus! These two examples are salutary reminders that we can be premature in linking the spirit to a cultural trend. What we intuit as being the work of the immanent spirit may in the march of time turn out to be the exact opposite. Again, this draws us back to the question of how we discern truth and if we are over-confident when interpreting the signs.

Gender, Sexuality and Tolerance

I appreciate Gus's points about Pagan attitudes to gender, sexuality, gays and toleration. It is clear that in matters of sexuality there are considerable differences between Christian and Pagan views.

The Christian mosaic is variegated. There is a sad legacy within Christian history of negative attitudes towards sexual pleasure, and the treatment of women has many dark, inexcusable and tragic corridors to it. Attitudes among Christians towards gay, lesbian and transgendered people are also polarized. On the opposite side of the coin, there is a significant biblical line on a holistic understanding of what it is to be fully human, and an entire biblical book celebrating erotic love (Song of Songs). The creation discloses that both genders are made equally in the image and likeness of God. The masculine and the feminine equally reflect the Divine; one is not subordinate to the other. Heterosexuality points us back to our image-bearing likeness to God, so both genders together – not apart – fully encompass it. Fully expressing who we are does not require us to conform to whatever other people suppose we should be because the source of our dignity is rooted in the very being of God. So sexuality is a blessing of creation, not a curse.

What does become a curse to us is our decision to turn away from the partnership in life that God invites us to share. Our relationships with one another, with the natural realm and with God are broken. This is negatively expressed in physical, emotional, mental, spiritual and sexual ways, which leave us in a space that God never intended for us. The decisions we make about expressing our sexuality are impacted by the damage done to our whole being as image-bearers of the Divine. Our relationships have moral consequences. Our desire to dominate or misuse other people points to a distorted sexuality. We can misuse the blessing and the mystery of sexual intercourse, and even the most libertine Pagans seem to accept there are some boundaries and some forms of unacceptable sexual activity (such as paedophilia). We need the transcendent to show us the difference between the blessed and cursed expressions of sex and sexuality.

I suspect that a lot of evangelicals do not understand why religious liberty is important for all people in civil society. Aside from ensuring that religious groups are not violating the basic civil and criminal laws of the land, religious liberty in society should be open and non-repressive. Christians can and should affirm religious liberty for all. To take that stance does not involve diluting the gospel message or denying the uniqueness of Jesus Christ. The gospel cannot be forcibly imposed and attempts to do so effectively wreck the open invitation from Jesus for people to start life afresh in a journey of discovery and growth.

In light of Gus's discourse on the Religious Right I feel constrained to ask about some things that appear to me to be critical difficulties. I appreciate the criticisms he raised about patriarchy and the abuse of power. I noted that some evangelicals had supported the Ku Klux Klan, which most Christians deplore. I appreciate that many Pagans share the same concerns about extremist groups and hold to green-left political stances.

However, I feel that there are unresolved questions about darker elements in the worldwide Pagan community concerning patriarchy, power and prejudice. Jeffrey Kaplan points to periodicals such as *The Odinist* in which 'a pronounced warrior ethic' is espoused 'which emphasized the desire to one day strike back in some form at the dominant culture for its perceived injustices'.[42] Margot Adler notes from the same publication that what distinguished Odinism 'is that for the first time a religion has declared itself founded upon the concept of race, with its correlation to culture and civilization'.[43] In this particular case the group held to the Aryan race myth and Adler also noted that the publication included articles attacking liberal values and defending the goals of apartheid. Graham Harvey notes that 'many Heathens hold views on race and sexuality which are considerably to the right of the political centre', and that 'some certainly hold neo-Nazi views'.[44] I acknowledge that many Pagans in Heathenism and Ásatru have commendably distanced themselves from racial supremacist views. While Gus describes a fairly widespread acceptance of gay and lesbian people, Harvey points out that they are not welcome in The Odinic Rite and the Hammarens Ordens Sällskap.[45] How far does the manifestation of the Divine Feminine reach when there are minor sections of the Pagan community who assert patriarchal power, favour racial pride and purity, and repudiate multiculturalism and pluralism?

I wonder to what extent the Pagan community fully experiences internal peace and harmony, particularly as Internet forums such as Witchvox disclose divisiveness in the 'Witch Wars' and use the criteria of anti-cult literature to warn against cult-like leaders abusing coven members. It seems that the machismo factor is unresolved. Pagans uphold the Wiccan Rede – namely 'that you harm none' – and hold to the karmic principle that your actions will rebound on you in a threefold manner (the law of the threefold return). How do Pagans then reconcile upholding the Wiccan Rede with the retaliatory practice of casting spells – or, as it is technically known, the practice of hexing or bitchcraft?[46] To what extent is hexing open to abuse and disrespect? If the karmic impact of the threefold return is ethically and experientially true then why would anyone even countenance hexing in the first place? These matters seem to me to point to deep tensions among Pagans about power and the limits of tolerance shown towards each other.

Boundaries and Bogeyman Stories

I believe that at times our communities are aggravated by deep-rooted suspicion and ridicule. I am not accusing Gus of generating a bogeyman and I do not hold all Pagans or all Christians responsible for circulating hostile tales. However, 'big bad wolf' stories are found within both communities and they inflame the tensions. I will summarize elements of extreme bogeyman portraits from both Christian and Pagan material.[47]

According to some Christians, Pagans worship the devil, use demonic rituals, lead an immoral life, and recruit or corrupt children through Halloween festivities, TV shows like *Charmed*, and the Harry Potter novels. Pagans threaten the wider community as Witch-chaplains are now appointed to hospitals and the armed services. They reject America's godly heritage that began with the Pilgrim Fathers. Former Pagans (now happy Christians) confirm in their autobiographies that Paganism is dangerous and spiritually bankrupt. In the worst hyperbole, Pagans are cardboard cut-out models of Gothic monsters.

According to some Pagans, Christians are hostile bigots. The church is guilty of colossal atrocities in history, hates other religions, oppresses women and destroys the Earth. Bible-bashers stir up community opposition to individual Pagans and group events. They are undermining the separation of church and state, and will create a Religious Reich to impose their puritanical religion on everyone. Former Christians (now happy Pagans) confirm in their autobiographies that the church is intolerant and spiritually bankrupt. In the worst hyperbole, Christians are cardboard cut-out models of Fascists.

Here each side curiously mirrors the other's story by pointing to the presence of the 'other' in the public square: 'they' represent a threat that must be negated. The constructed story reconfirms the group's identity in contrast to what is rejected about the opposition. It allows the storytellers to feel they can regain some social control and power and mobilizes them to resist alterations to civil rights in the public square. I wonder why partisans on both sides exhibit fundamentalist tendencies and seek power over each other; and why such 'masculine' aggressive energy is expended in mutually wedging opponents in the public square. Are we willing to relinquish these spiritually unedifying bogeymen? Are both communities prepared to listen to Jesus?

Responsive Thoughts

Lainie Petersen

As I began to read this dialogue between Mr Johnson and Dr diZerega, I found myself considering the interfaith dialogue that has been part of my life for the past fourteen years. At the age of twenty-four, after many years of being an evangelical Christian, I began to explore NeoPaganism and Western Esotericism. While never really identifying as a Pagan, my drift from evangelical Christianity was profound: I joined several esoteric orders, organized an annual convention of occultists, read tarot cards professionally, and was eventually ordained a priestess in a NeoGnostic church. During this time, I would have considered any suggestion that I might return to orthodox Christianity to be laughable.

Yet, a few years ago, I inexplicably found myself being drawn back to Christianity. (This was not the same Christianity that I had practised as an adolescent, which had been an odd mélange of modernist Bibliolatry, cowering fear, irrational confidence in a misanthropic God and more than a touch of obnoxiousness.) Instead I was drawn to the person of Jesus Christ who, in his perfect love, became one with humanity in order to reconcile us and the whole creation to the God who is Creator. Unlike my sudden conversion to Christianity as a teenager, this return to my Christian faith was a slow and gradual process, almost like a lover's wooing of his beloved, and quite unlike the hasty 'decision for Christ' that I made as a fourteen-year-old girl.

Because my reversion to orthodox Christianity was accomplished slowly, there was no sudden transformation in my personality or behaviour. While most of my esoteric practices have given way to Christian disciplines, my friendships with Pagans and esotericists are still quite intact. I keep tabs on the esoteric community while also involving myself in regular fellowship with Christians. Curiously, my friends within the Pagan and esoteric communities have been supportive of my return to orthodox Christianity, demonstrating that the love of true friends is not something that is easily lost. Similarly, many of my newfound friends within the Christian community have been respectful and curious about my previous path, and have strongly supported my continuing relationships within the Pagan and esoteric communities.

Reading this dialogue has, then, been poignant, refreshing and affirming. Poignant because while I now identify with Mr Johnson's religion, there was a time when Dr diZerega's would have been closer to my own. I find this dialogue refreshing because, at its core, it is not about the authors convincing each other (or their readers, for that matter) of the truth. Instead, they each seek to make themselves understood by their readers and each other. Finally, I find this dialogue affirming in that it speaks to my own spiritual quest. Both reason and direct experience of the Divine have had considerable impact on my journey, and I see both expressed in what has been written by these two men. For these gifts alone, I am grateful for this dialogue.

Jesus and the Nature of Spirituality

I appreciate the distinction that Dr diZerega makes between 'spirituality' and 'religion', noting that one is personal, the other communal. I was particularly touched by both Dr diZerega's and Mr Johnson's descriptions of their own spiritual practices because, despite each man's adherence to a different religion, there were similarities in their practices. Both expressed gratitude towards their deity/deities and both expressed a desire to interact with their deity/deities through their day-to-day activities. To be sure, there are differences in how each of them understands the significance and purpose of their spiritual practices, and these cannot be ignored. But their mutual desire to honour and relate to the Sacred is evident, and it is something that I think most, if not all, religious people can understand.

I am particularly intrigued by Dr diZerega's remarks about how, for Pagans, spiritual practice is given higher priority than any sort of orthodox belief. As I noted at the beginning of this response, my teenage spirituality was formed by a peculiar brand of Protestant evangelicalism that is practised in the United States. Within this particular religious context (particularly in the 1980s when I was a teenager), a significant amount of emphasis was devoted to right believing: the emphasis on the Bible as the 'Word of God' meant that much of our time and energy was to be spent in making sure that we had the 'right' understanding of biblical texts. In addition, a cottage industry in 'discerning' heresy had cropped up in the evangelical community, with various factions accusing each other of errant doctrine and practice. All of this concern about 'being right' in my beliefs meant that I was unable really to develop spiritually. It also contributed significantly to my decision to leave evangelicalism for the greener pastures of Western Esotericism and NeoGnosticism, in which practices of sacrament, ritual, prayer and meditation were seen as the way to obtain knowledge, as opposed to simply reading and studying sacred texts.

But as Mr Johnson notes in this chapter, as well as in Chapter 5, there is a more holistic approach to Christian spirituality than the one I had learned as a teenager. This approach acknowledges that, although we are a 'religion of the book', the concept of *logos* has a much deeper meaning than words on a printed page. Jesus describes himself as one who 'fulfils' the law: the written *logos* is fulfilled (not supplanted) by the willingness of God to incarnate and dwell with his people. It is in the person and activity of Jesus that Christians are to find their spirituality, and it is through his incarnation, death and resurrection that we are enabled to become his disciples. As a discipled community, our religion informs our spirituality and, in turn, our spiritual practice deepens our relationship with and knowledge of our God. I know I have found that observing regular times of prayer, devotional (rather than intellectual) reading of scripture, and a commitment to acts of mercy and charity has deepened my commitment to, and understanding of, doctrinal orthodoxy.

The Divine and Humanity

As Dr diZerega notes, '... on these matters human language is probably not up to the job of doing the subject justice'. I would agree with his assessment wholeheartedly. As Mr Johnson notes, even the apostle Paul recognized that there are certain aspects of God and God's nature that are hidden from humanity. Still, humanity wishes to understand, apprehend and know God, and for Christians (and other religions of the book) language is an important part of forming that understanding. Language can be used in the writing of sacred scriptures, in developing theologies, in offering prophecy and in providing instruction and edification to others. Language is, however, specific to its time and culture. As such, what we communicate about God via language is necessarily limited.

One particular difference between the way Christians and NeoPagans (and other types of Pagans as well) conceive of deity/

deities is that Pagans are eager to speak of and to regard deity/deities as female. While I feel that the trend towards gender-inclusive language in the Christian church has often been poorly considered and executed, I am acutely aware of the problems associated with speaking of God using only male-gendered language, including its negative effect on anthropology as well as a skewed image of who and what God really is. While I intend to address the issue of the Divine Feminine later in this chapter, I am pleased to note that both men recognize the problem of a deity who is supposed to be without gender, and yet is popularly regarded as male by most of 'his' followers.

The human tendency to gender God is, however, not entirely a matter of sexism; it also reflects humanity's sincere desire to know and relate to God. As humanity is male and female, and this distinction is hard-wired into our very being, we are uncomfortable when asked to relate to a personal being if we cannot identify its gender.[1] Yet, as Mr Johnson notes, while the writers of the Jewish and Christian scriptures wrote of God using language that was usually masculine, this was not always the case. Furthermore, there are limits to the ways in which the Christian God is willing to allow his creation to regard him as having a gender: idols, images and other objects that might have encouraged intimacy by giving God a 'face' are not permitted. God seeks intimacy with humanity, but on his own terms. He resists the sort of intimacy that would tie him to a gendered body, and instead directs us to worship and relate to him in ways that differ from how we conduct our human relationships.

The reasons why I, as a Christian, depend heavily on God's revelation of his nature to me (rather than on my own attempts to understand and conceive of God) are addressed, in part, by Dr diZerega and Mr Johnson's dialogue on the problem of evil. Though I would note that theodicy is an incredibly complex issue which is not easily addressed, I was pleased to see that both men chose to address the topic by looking at spiritual causes of evil. As one might expect, I do accept that humanity (along with all of creation) is 'fallen', which is to say that it no longer exists in the same state in which God had created it. Nor does it function as God had originally intended it to. This, then, brought about a very real limitation of natural (and human) resources and an obsession with self-preservation which, as both authors note, distinguishes humanity in some very destructive ways (which I will address in the next section on Nature). While I am open to mystical experience (and have indeed had such experiences), my openness is tempered with an awareness of my own fallen nature, and as such, I rely on other forms of God's revelation, including scripture as well as the larger community of the present and historical church. Again, this does not preclude other forms of revelation, but it does explain why I (and I believe most Christians) prioritize God's revelation through scripture and community over that of personal experience and natural creation.

Nature

When people have asked me about where I feel closest to God, my reply is always the same: by water. Being by the ocean is best, a visit to a large natural lake is a close second, but even a river or a large water fountain will do. I see God's majesty in the crash of the waves and I marvel at the way the mist from rapidly moving water will sprinkle my skin. Nothing else feels like it. Curiously, I don't usually have any profound theological thoughts when I am near water (i.e., I don't muse on baptism or suchlike), I just find myself in awe at the magnificence of this precious element and the many forms in which it can exist and move. For me, spending time near and in water reminds me of God's care and delight in the creation of water, the many geographical forms in which water is contained, and the wonder of my own body that both needs and delights in it.

Both Dr diZerega and Mr Johnson rightly note the unfortunate human tendency to exploit and abuse nature in order to satisfy human desires and (at least as we humans perceive them) needs. While Dr diZerega's understanding of nature and its relationship to the Divine differs from Mr Johnson's (and my own), there is nonetheless a commonality between both worldviews: nature ought to be respected, cherished, preserved and cared for. The reasons, however, for why Christians and NeoPagans ought to possess such a high view of nature are very different. For Christians, nature was created by God for his own glory, and for humankind (created in the image of God, unlike the rest of nature). Humankind is given stewardship over nature, though after humanity's fall we see that stewardship shattered and, ultimately, abused.

One of the more interesting aspects of the authors' dialogue is its discussion of death and the role that death plays in their understanding of nature. Dr diZerega cites the common NeoPagan Wheel of the Year as a celebration of the cycles of nature while Mr

Johnson, in the section entitled 'Relationships: God, Humans, Nature', describes creation's fall as a steady decline. In particular, Christians view the entrance of death into the human condition as a consequence of sin. It is a spectre haunting the human race and is a reminder of the broken relationship between humanity and God: it is *not* good. We are comforted by Christ's resurrection (which is not the same as rebirth), but we also suffer when we lose someone to death. This is perhaps one of the most significant differences between NeoPaganism and Christianity, and if true interfaith dialogue (and possible cooperation) is to take place, I believe this difference should be taken seriously.

I raise these concerns not because I wish to be contentious, but because I actually see concern for the natural world as one area in which Christians and Pagans need to be talking, and acting, together. Despite our theological differences, we can all acknowledge that we must share this planet, and that we must assume responsibility for its care and use. I would also note that there is nothing in either Pagan or Christian ethics and thealogy/theology that should preclude this sort of cooperation. However, I do believe that in order to avoid misunderstandings, Pagans and Christians must fully understand each other's motives for protecting nature, as well as our assumptions about nature. When these things are understood, I believe our cooperation in the area of environmental stewardship will be much more effective.

The Culture Wars

It was within the chapters on culture wars that I found myself beginning to have difficulties. As I read, I found myself succumbing to 'debate' mode, in which I was more interested in disproving some of the statements being made than in trying to understand the position of the author. I suppose it is fitting, then, that the title of these chapters included the term 'wars', because I believe my initial reaction is indicative of why Pagans and Christians so often end up talking past each other. In any case, after a strong cup of tea, and a few clarifying emails from our editor, I was able to reassess the material in these chapters, and offer the following response.

Dr diZerega and Mr Johnson are from two different countries: the United States (diZerega) and Australia (Johnson). As such, they are both operating within different cultural and political contexts. While this can make for a refreshing exchange of ideas, it carries with it a strong risk of misunderstanding as well. I think that both authors did a good job of acknowledging that they are approaching this topic from different cultures. In addition, I think that both men realize that there is an unfortunate tendency for both Pagans and Christians to make sweeping generalizations about the political and cultural views held by both groups. I do, however, want to respond to a couple of aspects of this dialogue.

When I was asked to write this chapter, my gender was noted as a possible asset to the project. While I firmly do not believe that there is any one 'woman's perspective' (any more than there is any one 'man's perspective'), I do appreciate having the opportunity to respond to the significant gender issues that are inevitably raised in Pagan and Christian dialogues. As a Christian, I am very sensitive to the charges that Christianity is inherently misogynistic, yet as a feminist trained in church history, I am fully aware that these charges are not entirely without merit. My Christianity, however, tells me that there are profound spiritual reasons for disharmony between the sexes, and my Christianity also offers me hope for their reconciliation.

I am aware that NeoPaganism prides itself on its openness to the Divine Feminine, as well as to female leadership within its many communities, and Dr diZerega rightly notes that this openness is something that is not disputed within NeoPagan communities. By contrast, the status of women within the Christian church has been uneven throughout the centuries, and in recent years has become a matter of much contention within the evangelical community. I am unhappy with this ongoing tension within Christianity, and do confess to sometimes looking back with great fondness to the NeoPagan and Occult communities in which women's leadership is the norm. However, I also found myself questioning some of Dr diZerega's assertions regarding gender differences and 'feminine values' (such as intuitiveness, receptivity, sensuality, etc). I found his statements troubling because this emphasis on gender distinction/essentialism is being used against women who might seek leadership roles within the church, or mutuality (instead of subordination) in their marriage relationships. I personally fail to understand what makes receptivity and intuition explicitly 'feminine' values, just as I fail to understand why, say, assertiveness and rational thought are 'male' values. Within Christianity, *both* sexes are supposed to demonstrate the fruit of the Spirit (which includes love, joy, peace, kindness and self-control). Despite the efforts of some neopatriarchalists, there is no prescribed way to be male or female outlined in the scriptures: men and women are both to be conformed to the image of Christ.

My second concern with these chapters was what I regard as the over-identification of individuals such as Jerry Falwell and Pat Robertson with the 'Christian' side of the culture wars. To his credit, Dr diZerega notes that many Christians, including Mr Johnson, do not subscribe to the views of these men or their particular brand of political Christianity. At the same time, I have to wonder why the spectres of Falwell and Robertson were even raised. The 'culture wars' are indeed real, but they go much deeper than the relatively small segment of Protestant fundamentalism represented by these men. (Conversely, I also think that an appropriate Christian response to Robertson and Falwell needs to go beyond a shrug of the shoulders and the comment, 'Well, they don't represent me'. Christians should have acted more strongly against the 'Religious Right' and its excesses, and there is no excuse for this not happening.) I think that a more thoughtful dialogue could have ensued on this topic had less bombastic culture war leaders been selected for discussion.

Conclusion

In closing, I would like to say that reading these chapters has accomplished what I believe the goal of all dialogues should be: my understanding of Paganism, and Christianity, has increased. Despite being made aware of some of the significant differences between these pathways, I was also moved when something that the authors (particularly Dr diZerega) said about their spirituality resonated with my own experiences. As I noted at the beginning of this chapter, many of my most beloved friends are NeoPagans, and my love for them is unchanging, despite my own shift in spiritual practice and religious belief. I do believe that it is this sort of love and appreciation for the other that can sustain this conversation between Pagans and Christians. I certainly hope that it will.

Don Frew

The Nature of Spirituality

Upon reading Philip Johnson's first chapter on the nature of spirituality, I was struck by the similarity of approach to the ultimate Divine between him and Gus, indeed between him and me. Only a few things stood out for me as a Pagan. Philip wrote:

> *God is understood to be both transcendent and immanent, which is a paradox that we cannot fathom. What we come to understand, however, is that God is not identical with the cosmos (hence transcendent), but also that God is not a remote being uninvolved in the Earth (hence immanent).*

The Pagan in me immediately spoke up and said, 'What "paradox"?' I, too, understand the Divine to be both transcendent and immanent. What else could be meant by 'all-encompassing'? Gus mentioned our prayer to the Dryghton. It begins:

> *In the name of Dryghton,*
> *the ancient providence,*
> *which was from the beginning,*
> *and is for eternity,*
> *male and female,*
> *the original source of all things;*
> *all-knowing, all-pervading, all-powerful, changeless, eternal…*

We take very seriously the 'all-' in this conception of the Divine. 'All' necessarily includes everything, both material and immaterial, both conceived and inconceivable, both transcendent and immanent. It strikes me that the idea of this somehow being a 'paradox' betrays a deep-seated, fundamental belief in the separation of spirit and matter – the 'Fall' at the heart of most Christians' relationship to the world.

While many attempts to bridge this separation are made in many Christian scriptures about God being present in all things, as Philip mentioned, I don't believe it is ever overcome. There is always a sense of God being omnipresent, but as a visitor or observer, not as an essential part – indeed, the essential part – of all material things.

This distinction between differing views of the world – between a world that is a fundamentally good manifestation of the Divine and a world that is a fundamentally flawed (and ultimately damned) creation of a separate Divine Being – is at the heart of the differences between Pagans and Christians.

The other thing that really struck me about Philip's comments was his encounters with 'spirits' and other spiritual beings. I encounter a manifestation of the Divine and it's a Goddess or a spirit. He encounters such a being and it's an angel. Just how much are we letting the terminology of our faith traditions create differences that aren't really there? How many of the perceived differences between our faith traditions are just the result of using the 'wrong' words to describe the right thing?

If I described my first experience of the Goddess to a Christian, but identified the being with flowing dark hair in white robes and sandals as Jesus instead of Morgaine, I would be welcomed with open arms as having been touched by the Lord, but it's just a matter of labels. How do we *know* I didn't experience Jesus, just in the terms he knew I would understand and accept? And if that's the case, couldn't the converse be true as well? We may be creating and focusing on differences that aren't really there.

The Divine

Philip's second chapter, on the Divine, opens with a lengthy defence of the idea of the Christian God not having gender, or being beyond gender. Philip says:

> *Unlike many of their ancient near-eastern neighbours the Israelites refused to make carved or physical representations of God.*

True, but God 'himself' made a physical representation of God in the form of Jesus. When he chose to manifest on Earth as a living being, he chose to do so as a human male. How can this *not* be interpreted as the male being closer to the identity of God or being preferred in some way? He could have come as a woman, or he could have come twice, as both man and woman, but he didn't. For Pagans, all the discussion that Philip so eloquently presents doesn't eliminate this fact, which is overwhelmingly off-putting to us.

In this chapter, Philip also says:

> *Another major aspect concerns the understanding of God as Trinity. This is an unfathomable mystery about God's oneness and unity that has exercised the best efforts of great thinkers, but which defies our capacity to comprehend or fully analyse it.*

Again, like his statement above about the 'paradox' of transcendence and immanence, this 'unfathomable mystery' is a commonplace in most Pagan mythologies. As Gus explains, many deities are aspects of each other, or emanations of each other, or even offspring of each other. That a being can be both one and many seems to us to be obviously true, and reflects the fact that reality is not hierarchical or separated into layers; rather it is a continuum, something like a spectrum. While we may talk about individual levels of being, from the Divine to the material, it is akin to talking about colours, such as yellow and orange. Yes, for the sake of conversation, they are distinct colours, but the reality is that there is no precise demarcation between them; one slides into another. Light, the most common analogy for the Divine, is both white and all the colours of the rainbow; one and many simultaneously.

What is puzzling to me as a Pagan is why a concept that is so widely accepted in the many Pagan religions as a common aspect of the existence of the Divine in its many forms should be so mysterious in Christianity. What is different in our views of the world that leads to this?

I couldn't agree more with Philip's emphasis in this chapter on the importance of returning to an awareness of the immanence of the Divine:

> *The Pagan emphasis on the immanence of deity easily triggers important critical theological responses. However, I wonder if we could also see this as a cultural signifier to a church that has over-emphasized transcendence and de-emphasized immanence? The solution is not to concentrate on immanence and downplay transcendence but rather to recalibrate theology and the spiritual life so that we once again have a balanced 'both/and' portrait.*

I have spoken at many interfaith events on this as the central message that Wicca brings to the community of faiths. The concept of immanence is found, I believe, in all faiths – some just focus on it more than others. A focus on the immanence of the Divine necessarily leads to concern for the environment, for social and economic justice, for equal rights, etc.

Philip writes that:

> *[Panentheism] defines God and the Earth as mutually necessary: God depends on the organic processes of the universe to grow and change just as much as the processes require God.*

I am confused by this. For me as a Pagan, to say that the world is a fundamentally good manifestation of the Divine, but that the Divine is also more than the physical world (just as we are both our physical bodies *and* something more than that) is just a statement of what 'is', not what is 'necessary'.

In discussing the question of evil, Philip says that:

> *Christians feel the acute tension in reconciling suffering and evil with the image of an all-loving and all-powerful God. If God is benevolent and powerful then why are evil and suffering permitted?*

Many people throughout Christian history have asked this same question. Some have responded by lapsing into a dualist heresy and explaining that the material world was made by a lesser, evil god. Pagans respond by looking at the ultimate Divine in a different way. My all-loving, all-powerful, benevolent force is the source of existence. I don't conceive of it in any way, shape or form, as a sort of person who is looking over my shoulder and deciding whether or not to intervene to make my life better or worse. I understand that Philip doesn't profess such a simplistic view, but it seems to be bound up with his approach to the question of evil. To ask 'Why are evil and suffering permitted?' is to a priori assume that God is making a decision to allow or forbid the evil.

This has always been an area of Christianity that has confused me, and it is tied up with the question of what I call 'operative prayer'. Many times I have been at interfaith events where I have participated in a Christian service in which we have been asked to pray to God for, say, peace in the Middle East. What does this mean? Was God not going to get around to peace in the Middle East, but because he heard us pray for it, he'll do something about it? Or is he weighing the prayers for and against peace, and the side with the most prayers wins? What conception of God as ultimate Divinity allows our prayers to him to make any difference *at all* in the outcome of things?

When a person survives a bus crash and tells a news reporter that they just thank God for saving their life, aren't they saying that God deliberately chose *not* to save all the other folks who died in the same crash?

I'm sorry, but I just don't get it. A Pagan view of the Divine believes there is a divine order to all things, stemming from a divine source, and that order and that source are both fundamentally good, but individual free will and illness can act out of harmony with that divine order and produce chaos, if not evil.

We don't see the ultimate Divine as being moved by prayer. We address our prayers and our magicks to more immediate manifestations of the Divine, whom we relate to as the Gods and the spirits of nature. Through meditation and ritual I can build a closer relationship with a God or Goddess, but I don't usually think that they are watching over me all the time, orchestrating the good and bad events of my life. They interact with me through and in the areas of their expertise and manifestation. If I am cultivating a relationship with a healing deity, for example, I do expect them to keep me healthier than I might be otherwise and to help with my healing of others, but I don't expect them to keep my car in good running condition or get me a job.

Not to be vulgar about it, but as a Pagan I am quite comfortable with 'S___ happens' as an explanation for most things. As Gus has pointed out, physical embodiment invites certain problems and when we encounter such problems, most Pagans don't respond by asking 'Why?'; rather they ask, 'What can I do about it?'

Nature

While Philip's discussion of Nature expresses the side of Christianity that sanctifies and cares for the natural world, he acknowledges that there is another side that takes a purely utilitarian view and treats the Earth as a resource to be used until Christ's return. As a Pagan I applaud the presence of the former, while fearing that the latter will always keep the former in check and limit Christianity's effectiveness as a force for Green change in a world facing global warming.

I must say that I was a bit miffed when Philip appeared to 'pass the buck' for this environmentally darker side of Christianity:

There is undeniable evidence of anthropocentric and negative attitudes towards the Earth among Christians. In past eras some Christians were influenced by NeoPlatonic dualist views that devalued the natural world and regarded God as remote from the Earth.

As a Gardnerian, whose philosophical roots are solidly grounded in the NeoPlatonic teachers of late Antiquity, I am tempted to trot out the many, more current scholars who point out that Christians projected *back* such views *onto* NeoPlatonism in an effort to establish a Classical philosophical precedent for their beliefs. It was the NeoPlatonists, whose argument that the material world is a fundamentally good manifestation of the Divine, who most strongly influenced the creation of modern Wicca. However, I should not stray too far afield in this response and more on this topic could be its own book.

I feel that there is also a bit of 'passing the buck' in Philip's litany of ancient Pagan cultures whose practices were less than ecological. Modern Pagans freely acknowledge that many ancient and indigenous cultures did not practise ecologically sound lifestyles, but such cultures also operated with *considerably* less scientific knowledge about the world than we have now. They simply didn't understand how they were affecting their environment. Now we know better and we can change. This is one of the many reasons that Witches such as Gus and myself are *Neo*Pagans. A Pagan view of the world necessarily looks to knowledge about the world, first from experience and now from science, to tell us about the world. As we learn more, our approach to and actions in the world must change if we are to continue to be in a loving, respectful relationship with Her.

A Pagan approach *demands* such a response to new information. Sadly, until very recently, the Christian approach has been to suppress any new information that contradicts current beliefs. We need look no further than the current US administration's response to global warming to see a clear, frightening and dangerous example of particular Christian beliefs trumping scientific knowledge. (I am aware that the current administration represents only a very narrow view of only a particular brand of Christianity, but it illustrates how dangerous certain beliefs can be.)

Conclusion

I keep having a 'Yes, but…' response to Philip's words. He is clearly portraying the best of Christianity to us in his writing, and I have no doubt that he and many like him live up to the principles he espouses in these chapters. But I can't help feeling that he is downplaying a dark side to Christianity that has historically been open to great abuse. When he says:

> *The other critical phrase that is used refers to humans being made in God's image and likeness. Much learned discussion has ensued over what this means because the creation story does not present a specific definition. The consensus is that humans are God's representatives, so they are to care in the same way that God does by being equitable, merciful and loving. In other words humans must image the loving and gracious characteristics of God towards the rest of the creation. In light of these details it is possible to understand that human dominion involves a serious moral trust, which carries with it the further thought that we are accountable to God for our actions.*

… my immediate thought is, 'But isn't God also described in the Bible as vengeful, wrathful, jealous, etc.?' If we are made in the image and likeness of God, as Philip says, to act as God does and manifest his characteristics toward the rest of creation, then doesn't that include these qualities that we would nowadays call negative? If it doesn't, then who gets to choose? Tyrants throughout history could console themselves with the belief that they were following God's example in carrying out the worst of atrocities.

Conclusion

Gus diZerega

Philip and I have tried to make our practices and beliefs accessible to readers from the other's faith community while being true to our own experience and understanding. I hope I have succeeded in helping Pagan readers come to a deeper appreciation of our religious traditions or, if they are already well versed in these issues, that they feel they were well argued by me. I hope my Christian readers now more sympathetically understand a religion in many ways different from their own.

I do want briefly to return to the issue of panentheism. Philip suggested panentheism 'defines God and the Earth as mutually necessary', thereby slighting God. For me, this argument preserves a dualism between the Sacred and the world, the transcendental and the immanent, that I am trying to avoid. They are necessary aspects of the *same* unity. Here is an area where many Christian and Pagan perspectives differ, but not in the way most might think. I would warn us all that on these matters human language is probably not up to the job of doing the subject justice.

To close, I want to deepen my argument that Paganism is a worthy spiritual tradition, without arguing that Christianity is not.[1] For many Christians my most challenging claim is that there is nothing amiss with spiritual pluralism. How is it possible for many religions to harmonize with spiritual truth?

I begin with a frequent observation. Over time religions either differentiate, or use violence to impose conformity. Christianity had many branches before becoming unified through the might of the Roman state. A major schism occurred with the separation of Orthodox from Catholic Christianity. In the West Protestantism split from Catholicism, and then itself fractured. With the coming of religious liberty, still more differentiation followed.

This differentiation has been a problem no Christian has solved to general satisfaction. In Pagan traditions there is even greater differentiation, but Wiccans do not worry that if Ásatru is valid, Wicca is not. Nor so far as I know do practitioners of Ásatru worry that if Wicca is valid, Ásatru is not. When Wiccans, Ásatru, Druids and other traditions gather at festivals, I have never seen panels discussing who is spiritually most correct. Conflict occurs *within* a tradition when members disagree as to what constitutes proper practice, but I have never heard anyone argue that those with whom they disagree are spiritually lost.

A Pagan perspective *decentres* religions just as, on the individual level, spirituality decentres the self. There is no point at which all religions converge, except, I think, that virtually all acknowledge the Ultimate Source is all good, loving, beautiful and true. And further, to the degree to which we incorporate or harmonize with these characteristics, we and others are the better for It.

These remarks bring me to Petersen's very perceptive observations. Good as they are, I think two misunderstandings and one deeper issue emerge. We see one another's remarks through our own frames, so I may misunderstand her, in which case I apologize.

While Christians and Pagans differ over death's spiritual significance, we mourn as much as anyone when a loved one passes. But we mourn *our* loss primarily. They have moved on.

I also think Petersen misunderstands my reference to feminine values and how they apply to biological women. I argue for balance between and respect for masculine *and* feminine values in *both* men and women. Applying gender labels to these values is almost universal across cultures, but you can substitute 'yin' for 'feminine' and 'yang' for 'masculine'. Alas, I cannot delve more deeply now.

Finally, she says she is surprised I refer to Falwell and Robertson regarding the 'culture war'. I am American. They and their followers dominate one of two American political parties, blame Pagans and feminists for 9/11 (the 'apology' Philip mentioned was for upsetting people, not for being wrong), and seek to undermine our Constitution. The term 'culture war' comes from them and their conservative Catholic allies like James Buchanan, not from us. For millions these people *are* Christianity. But as Mrs Petersen grants, I *explicitly* deny they represent Christianity as such. If I thought they did I would not be writing here – nor would I have been invited to do so.

A Divine Network

Increasingly, the modern world understands much of the social and natural world in terms of interconnected networks. The most exquisite and intricate order can arise without deliberate planning as long as participants adhere to certain fundamental values that generate order when followed. I believe this concept of networks helps us understand spiritual reality.

The deeper our individual encounter with Spirit, the more we describe our experience as being beyond words. But religions are held together by practices and doctrines rooted in written or spoken teachings. Any given religion therefore can *never* do more than honour *some* aspects of divine reality, as seen from its own vantage point.

Human religions reflect distinctions we see in every other dimension of life, from our basic individuality to the wonderful variety of human societies and natural environments. Of course, all those societies are afflicted with people's being out of harmony with the Sacred. But just as coming into greater spiritual harmony does not abolish individuality, so a variety of religions honouring the Sacred need not imply they should all become the same.

Religious diversity comprises humanity's *spiritual* network. Like any network, each religion connects to some degree with others, and yet remains distinct. As in any living network, at any given time some nodes grow, some are stable and some decline.

Human institutions easily become perverted to serving goals that are different from their initial ideals, and religions are no different. Networks of different religions help to limit this weakness, even if they cannot eliminate it entirely. By showing other ways in which Spirit is honoured, each helps keep others in line when corrupt or spiritually dead leaders and members threaten to turn them towards serving the mundane. Taken together, humanity's religious traditions help keep any single religious tradition in better harmony with its own spiritual insights.

As long as its members seek to set a good example rather than attack us, Christianity is good for Pagans. Early Christian philanthropy impressed Classical Pagans, and many began developing greater philanthropic awareness as a result, an awareness that might have flowered wonderfully had they been permitted to continue practising Pagan religion. And Pagans can be good for Christianity in similar ways. Today many Christians are becoming aware that the world is more than an accumulation of resources for our use. As issues of ecology and extinction enter more distinctively into the church's purview, its concept of the divine community may widen to include the other-than-human.

If so, it will have adopted a position often considered characteristically Pagan although scarcely denied in scripture.[2] Such a development no more makes Christianity Pagan than a greater emphasis on philanthropy made Pagans Christian. Rather, these are examples of a focus in one tradition helping to invigorate a potentiality within the other which so far has remained weakly expressed.

In such a world of mutual respect between Pagans and Christians, Muslims and Buddhists, Hindus and Jews, the possibilities for human reflection of the Divine will have grown more than ever could have been the case with any one religion on its own.

Philip Johnson

As this dialogue draws to a close I must express my gratitude to Lainie Petersen and Don Frew for sharing their impressions. All that remains for me is to briefly reply to parts of Don's commentary.

I referred to God's transcendence and immanence as a paradox and Don questions why I use that term. He suggests this is linked to the separation of spirit and matter, which in turn relates to the Fall. Actually I had two things in mind when using the word 'paradox'. The first is that God is ineffable, and Christians are peering 'through a glass darkly'.[3] Our finitude often leaves us facing paradoxes about ultimate matters.

The second is that I freely admit that I do not know how God can be transcendent in being and ontologically distinguishable from the cosmos while simultaneously being omnipresent throughout the creation. I am content with the biblical witness to transcendence and immanence and admit that *how* this is so is quite beyond my comprehension. It is in like manner that I later remarked that God's Triunity is an unfathomable mystery. Along with many Christians down the centuries, I am happy to accept mystery and paradox. The best I can do here in regards to transcendence and immanence is to point to Richard Bauckham's analogy of art and the artist:

> *Certainly we find God in all things, as the artist who has put himself into his creation, but we find God in all things only by distinguishing all things from God, distinguishing the work of art from the artist, distinguishing the gifts from their giver, distinguishing the creatures themselves from the divine source of all their being and goodness and beauty.*[4]

From Bauckham's analogy we are helped to understand that the stuff of the cosmos does not consist of divinity or have latent or intrinsic divine qualities embedded in its atoms. The Christian understanding is that matter is not the substance of Spirit appearing in another form (as diamond and carbon are allotropic: the same substance taking different forms).

The distinction between God and the cosmos has nothing to do with the theology of the Fall but is inherent in the concept of the original creation, and this is borne witness to in biblical revelation. The Fall is about a fracturing of relationships that has led to a breakdown in what was originally good, harmonious and unified. The Fall has nothing to do with the separation of Spirit from matter or the withdrawal of God from the creation. The biblical witness is that, post-Fall, God continues to be active and present throughout the whole creation. The creation however is not God's body; it was not made with divine substances, nor because of the Fall has it lost any pre-existent divine qualities.

Don correctly sees a fundamental difference between our understandings of God and creation. However, I feel that it is unhelpful to characterize the Christian view of the creation's destiny as 'ultimately damned'. To take that understanding is to completely ignore the fundamental biblical theme that, since the Fall, all of the creation is included in the process of divine redemption, which the incarnation of Christ powerfully reaffirms. The biblical witness also points to the eschatological transformation of the entire creation. The Earth and animals are not destined for a cosmic refuse heap, and if some Christians hold that view then they do so in total contradiction to the biblical witness.

Don feels that the Christian view of omnipresence largely indicates that God's presence is like that of an observer. I did indicate that this kind of view has much more affinity with Deism or even a God-of-the-gaps outlook. Perhaps that is an understanding that has been conveyed to him by some Christians, but it is a truncated view that is out of kilter with the biblical witness. Although Don does not see sufficient evidence of it, all I can do is repeat what I wrote earlier: God is intimately at work throughout the whole Earth blessing, nurturing, sustaining and maintaining all life (for example, Psalm 139). This is the classical Christian view.

On the topic of panentheism Don finds my admittedly cursory discussion a bit confusing. It is a topic that requires a book-length discussion. However, I would make this important clarification: my remarks were not directed at Pagan understandings of panentheism. In Chapter 2 I began by mentioning three theologians: Cobb, Hartshorne and Fox. My critical remarks that immediately follow refer to the positions that these theologians have taken *inside* the Christian community. In my endnote, bibliographical direction is given to four publications for further details. I did not comment on what Pagans understand about panentheism. The internal Christian dialogue on panentheism is complex but it indicates a profound division between advocates of classical Christian thought and Christian advocates of panentheism.

Don feels that I am passing the buck on the environmental debate. I feel that the context of my remarks has not been fully appreciated. I began by referring to the criticisms raised by secular critics, environmentalists and animal rights advocates who claim that Christian beliefs are the root cause of the problem. Bibliographically I drew attention to Lynn White, Peter Singer and Stephen Wise as examples of this perspective and my reply came accordingly. My wife and I encountered these entrenched attitudes when studying the inaugural course in animal law at the University of NSW in 2005.

I urged a wider understanding of the matter, which acknowledges that ecological damage has been common across many civilizations. I then offered a theological understanding based on the book of Genesis to help illuminate why human activities in the natural world have often been harmful. The problem is a human one and not a religious one. My argument, then, had nothing to do with passing the buck by relocating the source of the problem in pre-Christian cultures.

My available space has almost run out, which means that I have reluctantly passed over some of Don's interesting comments in silence. I hope that this dialogue has clarified some matters and offered a fresh insight into some of the distinctive practices and beliefs of Pagan and Christian pathways. Although this book is now finished, the task of dialogue between both communities must go forward. I pray that you have been challenged by what you have read, and especially that you may follow what Jesus affirmed about loving God with our whole being and our neighbours as ourselves.

Endnotes

Introduction

1. Barry A. Kosmin, Egon Mayer, Ariela Keysar *American Religious Identification Survey*, The Graduate Center, City University of New York, http://www.gc.cuny.edu/faculty/research_briefs/aris/key_findings.htm

2. Estimates of the number of Wiccans in the US, Ontario Consultants on Religious Tolerance, http://www.religioustolerance.org/wic_nbr2.htm

3. See Philip Johnson, 'Wiccans and Christians: Some Mutual Challenges', available at http://www.jesus.com.au/html/page/wicca and later abridged in Fiona Horne (ed.), *Pop! Goes the Witch*, New York: Disinformation, 2004, pp. 196–202.

4. Gus diZerega, *Pagans and Christians: The Personal Spiritual Experience*, St. Paul: Llewellyn, 2001.

5. For general background see Gerald R. McDermott, *God's Rivals: Why Has God Allowed Different Religions? Insights from the Bible and the Early Church*, Downers Grove: InterVarsity Press, 2007; Avery Dulles, *A History of Apologetics*, 2nd ed., San Francisco: Ignatius Press, 2005.

6. See, for example, Richard Fletcher, *The Barbarian Conversion: From Paganism to Christianity*, Berkeley: University of California Press, 1999; Carole M. Cusack, *Conversion among the Germanic Peoples*, London and New York: Cassell, 1998.

7. See Karen Jolly, Catharina Raudvere and Edward Peters, *Witchcraft and Magic in Europe: The Middle Ages*, London: Athlone, 2002; Joseph Klaits, *Servants of Satan: The Age of Witch Hunts*, Bloomington: Indiana University Press, 1985; Walter Stephens, *Demon Lovers: Witchcraft, Sex, and the Crisis of Belief*, Chicago and London: University of Chicago Press, 2002.

8. See 2 Kings 22:8–13.

9. See Bill Ellis, *Raising the Devil: Satanism, New Religions, and the Media*, Lexington: University Press of Kentucky, 2000; Bill Ellis, *Lucifer Ascending: The Occult in Folklore and Popular Culture*, Lexington: University Press of Kentucky, 2004.

10. These include: J. P. Moreland and Kai Nielsen, *Does God Exist: The Great Debate*, Nashville: Thomas Nelson, 1990; Gary Habermas and Antony Flew, *Did Jesus Rise From The Dead? The Resurrection Debate*, San Francisco: Harper and Row, 1987; Gregory A. Boyd and Edward K. Boyd, *Letters from a Skeptic*, Wheaton: Victor, 1994.

11. For apologetic texts see, for example, Brooks Alexander, *Witchcraft Goes Mainstream*, Eugene: Harvest House, 2004; Craig S. Hawkins, *Witchcraft: Exploring the World of Wicca*, Grand Rapids: Baker, 1996.

12. On the divinatory nature of conspiracist interpretations of history see Brian P. Bennett, 'Hermetic Histories: Divine Providence and Conspiracy Theory', *Numen*, 54, 2007, pp. 174–209; Paul Coughlin, *Secrets, Plots and Hidden Agendas*, Downers Grove: InterVarsity Press, 1999.

13. Eric J. Sharpe, 'Faith at the Round Table', *Areopagus*, 7, 4, 1994, p. 34.

Chapter 1

1. *Hermetica: Introduction, Texts, and Translation*, Walter Scott, trans., Boston: Shambhala, 1993; *The Hymns of Orpheus*, Thomas Taylor, trans., Los Angeles: Philosophical Research Library, 1981.

2. The closest to a genuine European survival is Lithuanian and Latvian Romuva. See Jonas Trinkunas (ed.), *Of Gods and Holidays: The Baltic Heritage*, Lithuania, Tverme, 1999. See also Carlo Ginzburg, *The Night Battles: Witchcraft and Agrarian Cults in the Sixteenth and Seventeenth Century*, John and Anne Tedeschi, trans., Johns Hopkins University Press, 1992 and Ginzburg, *Ecstacies: Deciphering the Witches' Sabbath*, Raymond Rosenthal, trans., NY: Pantheon, 1991.

3. Stephen Toulmin, *Cosmopolis: The Hidden Agenda of Modernity*, Chicago: University of Chicago Press, 1990.

4. On Gardnerian Wicca see Margot Adler, *Drawing Down the Moon: Witches, Druids, Goddess-Worshippers, and Other Pagans in America Today*, Revised ed., Boston: Beacon 1986, pp. 62–66, 80–86, 118–19. Adler's book is the best introduction to the variety of Pagan practices in the US today. See also Sabina Magliocco, *Witching Culture: Folklore and Neo-Paganism in America,* University of Pennsylvania, 2004. Among its other substantial strengths, Magliocco's book is an excellent description of Wiccan practice within the Gardnerian tradition.

5. Some argue Gardner 'made it all up'. See, for example, Aiden Kelly, *Crafting the Art of Magic Book I – A History of Modern Witchcraft 1939–1964*, Llewellyn 1991. He did not. Adler briefly discusses the issue in *Drawing Down the Moon*, op. cit., pp. 80–86. Don Frew offers a careful rebuttal in 'Methodological Flaws in Recent Studies of Historical and Modern Witchcraft', in *Ethnologies*, Vol. 20, no. 1–2. (Summary available online at http://www.fl.ulaval.ca/celat/acef/201a.htm.) The best available indepth study of Gardnerian Wicca's origins is Philip Heselton, *Wiccan Roots,* UK: Capall Bann Pub. Co., 2000. Unfortunately some relevant material is considered oath bound, and so not able to be published. Serious students of craft history are invited to attend lectures on these topics held in Pagan conferences such as Pantheacon in February in San Jose, California.

6. Gerald Gardner, *The Meaning of Witchcraft,* New York: Magickal Childe, 1959, pp. 186–89.

7. Quoted in Adler, 2004, p. 86. Doreen Valiente wrote many excellent books on Witchcraft. I recommend them all.

8. For a more detailed examination of traits shared by Pagan religions in general, see my *Pagans and Christians*, op. cit., pp. 3–83.

9. Gus diZerega, 'Nature Religion and the Modern World', *Sacred Cosmos*, November, 2000.

10. David Abram, *The Spell of the Sensuous*, NY: Pantheon, 1996.

11. Jordan Paper, *The Deities Are Many*, Albany: State University of New York Press, 2005, pp. 103–120.

12. *Pagans and Christians*, op. cit., p. 24.

13. Martin Buber, *I and Thou*, 2nd ed., NY: Scribner, 1958.

14. Robert C. Fuller, *Spiritual but not Religious*, New York: Oxford University Press, 2002.

15. Matthew 23:13–26.

16. See, for example, Paul Heelas and Linda Woodhead, *The Spiritual Revolution*, Malden and Oxford: Blackwell, 2005; Rachael Kohn, *The New Believers*, Sydney: HarperCollins, 2003; Christopher H. Partridge, *The Re-Enchantment of the West*, 2 Vols, London: T & T Clark, 2005 and 2006; Adam Possamai, *In Search of New Age Spiritualities*, Aldershot: Ashgate, 2005; Wade Clark Roof, *Spiritual Marketplace*, Princeton: Princeton University Press, 1999.

17. See John Drane, *The McDonaldization of the Church*, London: Darton, Longman and Todd, 2000.

18. Cheslyn Jones, Geoffrey Wainwright and Edward Yarnold, *The Study of Spirituality*, New York: Oxford University Press, 1986.

19. Richard F. Lovelace, 'Evangelical Spirituality: A Church Historian's Perspective', *Journal of the Evangelical Theological Society*, 31/1, March 1988, pp. 25–36.

20. Luke 10:27–28.

21. Job, Song of Songs, Proverbs and Ecclesiastes.

22. 1 Timothy 3:16.

23. Genesis 16:7–14; Genesis 41; Isaiah 6; Ezekiel 1; Daniel 2 and 10.

24. Exodus 3:1–14; Ezekiel 8:1–4; Acts 8:39–40; 2 Corinthians 12:1–6; Revelation 1:10ff.

25. I have briefly sketched three such encounters in Ross Clifford and Philip Johnson, *Riding the Rollercoaster: How the Risen Christ Empowers Life*, Sydney: Strand, 1998, pp. 74–75.

Chapter 2

1. Virginia Ramey Mollenkott, *The Divine Feminine: The Biblical Imagery of God as Female*, New York: Crossroad, 1987.

2. A good discussion of theology from a panentheistic perspective is Charles Hartshorne, *Omnipotence and Other Theological Mistakes*, Albany, NY: SUNY Press, 1984.

3. Jordan Paper, *The Mystic Experience: A Descriptive and Comparative Analysis*, Albany: State University of New York Press, 2004.

4. Paper, *The Deities Are Many*, p. 129, and *The Mystic Experience*, pp. 75–135.

5. Contrast Paper, *The Mystic Experience*, pp. 54–57 with Steven Katz, 'Language, Epistemology and Mysticism', *Mysticism and Philosophical Analysis*, Steven Katz, ed., London: Sheldon Press, 1978 and John Hick, *An Interpretation of Religion*, New Haven: Yale, 1992, pp. 172–89.

6. For more about this experience, see *Pagans and Christians*, op. cit., pp. 91–92.

7. Polymnia Athanassiadi & Michael Frede, ed., *Pagan Monotheism in Late Antiquity*, Oxford University Press, 2001.

8. Don Frew, 'Gardnerian Wica as Theurgic Ascent', presented at the *Pagani Soteira* symposia, 6/29/2002 and 7/27/2002.

9. Lucius Apuleius, *The Golden Ass*, Robert Graves, trans., Middlesex, England, Penguin, 1950, p. 228.

10. Sarah Iles Johnston, *Hekate Soteira: A Study of Hekate's Roles in the Chaldean Oracles and Related Literature*, Atlanta, GA: Scholars Press, 1990; Robert Von Rudloff, *Hekate in Ancient Greek Religion*, Victoria, CA: Horned Owl Publishing, 1990.

11. See Socrates' *Apology*.

12. Adam Smith is justly famous for giving the first detailed description of such orders in his *Wealth of Nations*. His metaphor of the 'invisible hand' captures its sense. But the concept is useful far beyond economic theory, as Smith himself knew. For three otherwise quite different contemporary studies, see F. A. Hayek, *Law, Legislation and Liberty, Vol. I: Rules and Order*, Chicago: University of Chicago Press, 1973; Steven Johnson, *Emergence: The Connected Lives of Ants, Brains, Cities, and Software*, NY: Scribner, 2001; and Albert-Laszlo Barabasi, *Linked: How Everything Is Connected to Everything Else and What It Means for Business, Science, and Everyday Life*, NY: Penguin, 2003.

13. diZerega, *Pagans and Christians*, op. cit., pp. 117–31.

14. Aristotle writes, 'There are others, however, who regard the control of slaves by a master as contrary to nature... the relation of master to slave is based on force, and being so based has no warrant in justice.' *Politics*, Ernest Barker, trans., London: Oxford University Press, 1958, p. 9. Aristotle then attempts a rebuttal of this position.

15. Charles Darwin, *The Descent of Man*, NY: Penguin, 2004, pp. 144–57.

16. Ecclesiastes 3:11.

17. St Augustine, *Confessions*, Book I.1. from *Augustine Confessions Books I-XIII*, translated by F. J. Sheed, Introduction by Peter Brown, Indianapolis: Hackett Publishing, 1993, p. 3.

18. Andrew Newberg and Eugene D'Aquilli, *Why God won't go away: Brain Science and the Biology of Belief*, 2nd ed., New York: Ballantine, 2002. Dean Hamer, *The God Gene: how Faith is hardwired into our genes*, New York: Doubleday, 2004.

19. Exodus 3:3–6.

20. Sebastian P. Brock and George A. Kiraz, eds., *Ephrem the Syrian: Select Poems*, Provo: Brigham Young University Press, 2007. Glen Cavaliero, *Charles Williams: Poet of Theology*, Grand Rapids: Eerdmans, 1983.

21. Ian T. Ramsey, *Religious Language*, London: SCM Press, 1957.

22. Mary Daly, 'The Qualitative Leap Beyond Patriarchal Religion', *Quest*, 1 1974, p. 21.

23. Hosea 11:9.

24. Exodus 20:3–5.

25. Tikva Frymer-Kensky, *In The Wake of the Goddesses*, New York: Free Press, 1992; Aida Besançon Spencer, Donna F. G. Hailson, Catherine Clark Kroeger and William David Spencer, *The Goddess Revival*, Grand Rapids: Baker, 1995.

26. Isaiah 66:12–13.

27. Isaiah 42:14.

28. Isaiah 46:3–4.

29. Psalm 22:9–10.

30. Job 38:29–30.

31. Luke 12:27–28.

32. Proverbs 8 and 9.

33. Deuteronomy 32:11; Psalm 91:4.

34. Matthew 23:37.

35. Hosea 14:5, 8.

36. Genesis 16:13–14.

37. Martin Luther, *Luther's Works: Lectures on Genesis*, vol. 7, St. Louis: Concordia, 1965, p. 325.

38. See Spencer, *The Goddess Revival*, pp. 110–29; Alvin F. Kimel, ed., *Speaking the Christian God*, Grand Rapids: Eerdmans, 1992.

39. 1 Timothy 3:16.

40. Isaiah 6:1–7.

41. Ezekiel 1:4–28.

42. Romans 16:25–26; Ephesians 3:3–9.

43. Ephesians 1:9; Colossians 1:26–27; 1 Corinthians 2:1.

44. 1 Corinthians 2:7; 14:2; 15:51; Ephesians 5:32; Colossians 2:2; Romans 11:25. See F. F. Bruce, *Paul and Jesus*, Grand Rapids: Baker Book House, 1974, pp. 27–29; Herman N. Ridderbos, *Paul: An Outline of His Theology*, Grand Rapids: Eerdmans, 1975.

45. 1 Corinthians 13:12.

46. See Vladimir Lossky, *The Mystical Theology of the Eastern Church*, Crestwood: St. Vladimir's Seminary Press, 1976.

47. Millard J. Erickson, *Christian Theology*, Grand Rapids: Baker, 1988, pp. 265–81.

48. B. B. Warfield, 'The Spirit of God in the Old Testament', in *Biblical and Theological Studies*, Philadelphia: Presbyterian and Reformed, 1968, p. 136. Also see Wilf Hildebrandt, *An Old Testament Theology of the Spirit of God*, Peabody: Hendrickson, 1995.

49. Warfield, 'The Spirit of God', p. 134.

50. Genesis 1:2.

51. Psalm 36:9; Job 36:13.

52. Job 33:4; Psalm 104:30.

53. Colossians 1:15–20.

54. Romans 8:18–23.

55. Acts 17:27–28. For background on this see F. F. Bruce, *Paul: Apostle of the Free Spirit*, rev. ed., Exeter: Paternoster, 1980, pp. 235–47.

56. See Amos Yong, 'The Spirit Bears Witness: Pneumatology, Truth and the Religions', *Scottish Journal of Theology*, 57/1, 2004, pp. 14–38.

57. John 6:1–15; Mark 6:30–46.

58. Mark 10:42–45.

59. Royce Gruenler, *The Inexhaustible God*, Grand Rapids: Baker, 1983; Ronald H. Nash, ed., *Process Theology*, Grand Rapids: Baker, 1987; Alan Gragg, *Charles*

Hartshorne, Waco: Word, 1973; Richard J. Bauckham, 'The New Age Theology of Matthew Fox: A Christian Theological Response', *Anvil*, 13/2 1996, pp. 115–26.

60. Leviticus 19:10; Numbers 35:6; Deuteronomy 10:18–19. Leon Morris, *The Gospel According to Matthew*, Grand Rapids: Eerdmans/Leicester: InterVarsity Press, 1992, pp. 638–39.

61. Colossians 3:17.

62. Luther, *Luther's Works*, Volume 23, pp. 132 and 134.

63. See Psalm 72:12–14 and Deuteronomy 17:20.

64. See Alvin C. Plantinga, *God, Freedom and Evil*, Grand Rapids: Eerdmans, 1977; C. S. Lewis, *The Problem of Pain*, Glasgow: Fontana, 1957.

65. Peter C. Craigie, *The Old Testament*, Nashville: Abingdon, 1986, pp. 221–27; Michael A. Eaton, *Ecclesiastes*, Leicester and Downers Grove: InterVarsity Press, 1983, pp. 117–29.

66. For more on these themes see Ross Clifford and Philip Johnson, *Riding the Rollercoaster: How the Risen Christ Empowers Life*, Sydney: Strand, 1998.

Chapter 3

1. Martin Buber, *I and Thou*, 2nd ed., NY: Scribner, 1958.

2. The best discussion of this issue is David Abram, *The Spell of the Sensuous: Perception and Language in a More-Than-Human World*, New York: Pantheon, 1996, pp. 93–135.

3. Hugh Brody, *The Other Side of Eden: Hunters, Farmers, and the Shaping of the World*, New York: North Point Press, 2000, p. 126; Jordan Paper, *Through the Earth Darkly: Female Spirituality in Comparative Perspective*, New York: Continuum, 1999, pp. 111–16, 129.

4. Ginsburg, *Ecstasies*, New York: Pantheon, 1991, pp. 127, 215–16.

5. E.R. Dodds, *The Greeks and the Irrational*, University of California Press, 1962.

6. Some of the best descriptions of these senses without resorting to metaphysical terminology such as mine can be found in Aldo Leopold's *A Sand County Almanac*, New York: Ballantine, 1966. See especially pp. 142–44, 158.

7. This statement is true for all British Traditional Wiccan Esbats, but may not hold for Wiccan Esbats of all other traditions.

8. Gus diZerega, 'Nature Religion and the Modern World', *Sacred Cosmos*, November, 2000.

9. This discussion is very brief. For a more detailed discussion of the meaning of the Sabbats, see diZerega, *Pagans and Christians*, pp. 64–70.

10. There is an account of such literal Pagan fundamentalism in Plato's Socratic dialogue *The Euthyphro*.

11. diZerega, *Pagans and Christians: The Personal Spiritual Experience*, Llewellyn, 2001, p. 69.

12. Daniel Botkin, *Natural History: The Lessons of Lewis and Clark*, NY: Oxford University Press, 2004, pp. 176–211.

13. Jim Lichatowich, *Salmon Without Rivers: A History of the Pacific Salmon Crisis*, Washington, DC: Island Press, 1999, pp. 33–41.

14. Colin Woodard, *Ocean's End: Travels Through Endangered Seas,* NY: Basic Books, 2001; Richard Ellis, *The Empty Ocean,* Washington: Island Press, 2004.

15. Psalms 19:1–4; 97:1; 98:4–8; 148.

16. Isaiah 14:7–8; 49:13; 55:12.

17. Proverbs 8:22–30; Job 38–42.

18. Walter Brueggemann, *Living Toward a Vision*, New York: United Church Press, 1976, p. 15.

19. Lynn White, 'The Historical Roots of our Ecological Crisis', *Science* 155, 10 March 1967, pp. 1203–07; Peter Singer, *Practical Ethics*, 2nd ed., Cambridge: Cambridge University Press, 1993, pp. 265–68; Steven M. Wise, *Rattling the Cage*, Cambridge, Massachusetts: Perseus, 2000.

20. Raymond Klibansky, *The Continuity of the Platonic Tradition during the Middle Ages*, Millwood: Kraus, 1982.

21. Thomas à Kempis, *The Imitation of Christ*, 3.31. Translated by Leo Sherley-Price, Harmondsworth: Penguin, 1952, p. 133.

22. Erica Fudge, *Perceiving Animals*, Urbana: University of Illinois Press, 2002; John Warwick Montgomery, 'Evangelical Social Responsibility in Theological Perspective' in *Our Society in Turmoil*, Gary R. Collins (ed.), Carol Stream: Creation House, 1970, pp. 17–19.

23. Kallistos Ware, *The Orthodox Way*, Crestwood: St. Vladimir's Seminary Press, 1990, p. 84.

24. R. C. D. Jasper and G. J. Cuming, *Prayers of the Eucharist*, 3rd ed, New York: Pueblo, 1987; Mother Mary and Kallistos Ware, *The Lenten Triodion*, London and Boston: Faber and Faber, 1987.

25. C. H. Lawrence, *Medieval Monasticism*, London and New York: Longman, 1984; Mary Low, *Celtic Christianity and Nature: Early Irish and Hebridean Traditions*, Edinburgh: Edinburgh University Press, 1996.

26. Lester K. Little, *Religious Poverty and the Profit Economy in Medieval Europe*, Ithaca: Cornell University Press, 1978; Roger D. Sorrell, *St Francis of Assisi and Nature*, New York: Oxford University Press, 1988.

27. Vladimir Lossky, *The Mystical Theology of the Eastern Church*, Crestwood: St. Vladimir's Seminary Press, 1976, p. 111.

28. E. G. Fairholme and W. Pain, *A Century of Work for Animals: The History of the RSPCA, 1824–1924,* London: John Murray, 1924.

29. Iolo A. Williams, *The Firm of Cadbury, 1831–1931*, London: Constable, 1931.

30. Andrew Linzey, 'C. S. Lewis' Theology of Animals', *Anglican Theological Review*, 80/1 (1998), pp. 60–81.

31. John W. Klotz, *Ecology Crisis: God's Creation and Man's Pollution*, St. Louis: Concordia, 1971; Francis Schaeffer, *Pollution and the Death of Man*, Wheaton: Tyndale House, 1970; Loren Wilkinson (ed.,) *Earthkeeping, Christian Stewardship of Natural Resources*, Grand Rapids: Eerdmans, 1980.

32. John Chryssavgis (ed.,) *Cosmic grace, Humble prayer: The ecological vision of the green patriarch Bartholomew I*, Grand Rapids: Eerdmans, 2003; Pope Benedict XVI, 'Message for the celebration of the World Day of Peace 2007'.

http://www.vatican.va/holy_father/benedict_xvi/messages/peace/documents/hf_ben-xvi_mes_20061208_xl-world-day-peace_en.html. Christian groups include: AuSable Institute http://www.ausable.org/au.main.cfm; A Rocha Christians in Conservation http://www.arocha.org/; Catholic Conservation Center http://conservation.catholic.org/; Christian Ecology Link http://www.christian-ecology.org.uk/; Evangelical Environmental Network http://www.creationcare.org/.

33. Tim Flannery, *The Future Eaters*, Sydney: Reed New Holland, 1994.

34. Jared Diamond, 'Ecological Collapses of Past Civilizations', *Proceedings of the American Philosophical Society*, 138/3 (September 1994), pp. 363–70.

35. Roland J. Fletcher, et al., 'Redefining Angkor: Structure and Environment in the largest low density urban complex of the pre-industrial world', *Udaya*, 4 (2003), pp. 107–121.

36. J. Donald Hughes, *The Mediterranean: An Environmental History*, Santa Barbara: ABC-CLIO, 2005.

37. Ronald Hutton, *The Pagan Religions of the Ancient British Isles*, Oxford and Malden: Blackwell, 1993, pp. 13–16, 252–53.

38. J. Donald Hughes, *Pan's Travail*, 2nd ed., Baltimore: Johns Hopkins University Press, 1996. Also see the UK documentary *Beasts of the Roman Games*, Channel 4 Touch Productions, 2004.

39. Lucius Annaeus Seneca, *Epistulae morales ad Lucilium*, 104.6.

40. On some (but not all) of these points see: Keith Suter, *Global Agenda: Economics, the Environment and the Nation-State*, Sutherland: Albatross/Oxford: Lion, 1995; Keith Thomas, *Man and the Natural World*, London: Allen Lane, 1983.

41. John Drane, *Cultural Change and Biblical Faith*, Carlisle: Paternoster, 2000, pp. 62–63.

42. In the following paragraphs I follow Drane, *Cultural Change*, pp. 63–64.

43. Genesis 1:1–2:25.

44. Genesis 3:1–24.

45. Genesis 4:8–16.

46. Genesis 5:1–11:32.

47. Drane, *Cultural Change*, p. 64.

48. Drane, *Cultural Change*, p. 65.

49. For example Hosea 4:1–3; Jeremiah 12:10–11.

50. Genesis 1:20, 24 and 2:19.

51. Genesis 16:13.

52. See Deuteronomy 17:20 and Psalm 72:12–14.

53. William Dumbrell, 'Genesis 2:1–3: Biblical Theology of Creation Covenant', *Evangelical Review of Theology*, 35/3 (July 2001), p. 227.

54. Gordon J. Wenham, *Genesis 1–15*, Waco: Word, 1987, pp. 29–34; Victor P. Hamilton, *The Book of Genesis Chapters 1–17*, Grand Rapids: Eerdmans, 1990, pp. 132–40.

55. Scott Bader-Saye, 'Imaging God Through Peace With Animals: An Election for Blessing', *Studies in Christian Ethics*, 14/2 (2001), pp. 1–13.

56. Genesis 9:8–17.

57. Exodus 20:10; 23:12; Leviticus 25; Deuteronomy 22:4; 25:4; Luke 12:6; 14:5; Matthew 6:26.

58. Isaiah 11:1–9; 65:17–25; also see Revelation 5:13–14.

59. Larry L. Rasmussen, 'Creation, Church and Christian Responsibility', in *Tending the Garden*, Wesley Granberg-Michaelson (ed.), Grand Rapids: Eerdmans, 1987, pp. 114–31.

60. B. B. Warfield, *Biblical and Theological Studies*, Philadelphia: Presbyterian and Reformed, 1968, pp. 133–138.

61. Romans 8:18–23.

62. Colossians 1:15–20.

63. Francis Bridger, 'Ecology and Eschatology: A Neglected Dimension', *Tyndale Bulletin*, 41/2 (November 1990), pp. 290–301.

64. See Ecclesiastes 3:1–8. The wisdom books include Job, Proverbs and Ecclesiastes.

65. Matthew 11:19.

66. Cheryl Forbes, *Imagination: Embracing a Theology of Wonder*, Portland: Multnomah, 1986; Leland Ryken, *Culture in Christian Perspective: A Door to Understanding and Enjoying the Arts*, Portland: Multnomah, 1986; Jane Stuart Smith and Betty Carlson, *The Gift of Music*, Westchester: Crossway, 1987.

67. Sebastian P. Brock and George A. Kiraz (eds), *Ephrem the Syrian: Select Poems*, Provo: Brigham Young University Press, 2007; Glen Cavaliero, *Charles Williams; Poet of Theology*, Grand Rapids: Eerdmans, 1983.

68. C. S. Lewis, *Surprised by Joy*, Glasgow: Fontana, 1959; J. R. R. Tolkien, 'On Fairy Stories', in *Essays Presented to Charles Williams*, C. S. Lewis (ed.), Oxford: Oxford University Press, 1947, pp. 38–89.

Chapter 4

1. These are all discussed at some length in *Pagans and Christians*, op. cit., pp. 3–49.

2. Hugh Brody, *The Other Side of Eden: Hunters, Farmers, and the Shaping of the World*, New York: North Point Press, 2000, pp. 86, 233, 242–46.

3. Trance is a difficult subject for those personally unacquainted with the experience to study. One good introductory discussion is Merete Demant Jacobsen, *Shamanism: Traditional and Contemporary Approaches to the Mastery of Spirits and Healing*, NY: Berghahn Books, 1999, pp. 8–17. But unfortunately Merete seems not to distinguish between working *with* spirits and *mastering* them. For an important corrective to this issue, and to some other common misunderstandings of shamanism, see Paper, 2005, op. cit., pp. 52–57, especially p. 56.

4. Paper, *Deities*, op. cit., pp. 53–54. See also Robert Torrance, *The Spiritual Quest: Transcendence in Myth, Religion, and Science*, Berkeley: University of California Press, 1994, 249–50.

5. Boyda, op. cit., pp. 96–97, 142–43.

6. Luther H. Martin, *Hellenistic Religions: An Introduction*, New York: Oxford, 1987, pp. 19–25.

7. William Irwin Thompson, *The Time Falling Bodies Take to Light*, New York: St Martin's Press, 1981, p. 103.

8. For a discussion of this process in ancient Greece, particularly with respect to bear spirits, see Paul Shepard and Barry Sanders, *The Sacred Paw: The Bear in Nature, Myth, and Literature*, New York: Arkana, 1985, pp. 110–20.

9. On Lithuanian and Latvian Paganism see Jonas Trinkunas (ed.), *Of Gods and Holidays: The Baltic Heritage*, Lithuania, Tverme, 1999, and Prudence Jones and Nigel Pennick, *A History of Pagan Europe*, London: Routledge, 1995, pp. 165–83.

10. Margot Adler, *Drawing Down the Moon: Witches, Druids, Goddess-Worshippers, and Other Pagans in America Today*, revised ed., Boston: Beacon, 1986, pp. 162–65.

11. Boyda, op. cit., p. 113.

12. I am grateful to Don Frew for this way of putting the matter.

13. This concept is explored in a Pagan context by Sabina Magliocco, *Witching Culture: Folklore and Neo-Paganism in America*, Philadelphia: University of Pennsylvania Press, 2004, pp. 122–81.

14. Aldo Leopold, *A Sand County Almanac*, NY: Sierra Club, 1966, p. 117.

15. *Pagans and Christians*, op. cit., pp. 212–15.

16. http://www.kansascity.com/mld/kansascity/sports/special_packages/oneil/

17. http://www.firedoglake.com/2007/01/14/give-it-up/

18. On personality types and mysticism see Leslie J. Francis, 'Psychological Type and Mystical Orientation', *Pastoral Sciences*, 21/1 2002, pp. 77–93. Also see Leslie J. Francis, *Faith and Psychology: Personality, Religion and the Individual*, London: Darton, Longman and Todd, 2005.

19. See Deuteronomy 6:4–5; Mark 12:30–31; Matthew 22:37–39; Luke 10:27–28.

20. On the place of imagination and culture in Christian theology see Michael Frost, *Seeing God in the Ordinary*, Peabody: Hendrickson, 2000.

21. Romans 12:1; Colossians 3:17.

22. See my remarks in Chapter 3 about humans as priests. On Israel as an entire nation of priests see Exodus 19:6; and for all Christians as priests see 1 Peter 2:4–9.

23. See Tilden Edwards, *Living in the Presence*, San Francisco: Harper, 1995; Richard Foster, *Prayer: Finding the heart's true home*, London: Hodder and Stoughton, 1992; Brother Lawrence, *The Practice of the Presence of God*, London: Hodder and Stoughton, 1981; Alister McGrath, *Spirituality in an Age of Change*, Grand Rapids: Zondervan, 1994; Peter Toon, *What is Spirituality and is it for me?* London: Daybreak, 1989; Bishop Kallistos Ware, *The Orthodox Way*, Crestwood: St. Vladimir's Seminary Press, 1990.

24. Ben Witherington, *Jesus the Seer: The Progress of Prophecy*, Peabody: Hendrickson, 1999; Anne Marie Kitz, 'Prophecy as Divination', *Catholic Biblical Quarterly*, 65 2003, pp. 22–42.

25. Deuteronomy 13:1–5; 18:18–22; Matthew 7:15–23; 1 Thessalonians 5:21; 1 John 4:1–3.

26. 1 Samuel 8.

27. 1 Samuel 10:9–12.

28. 1 Samuel 19:23–24.

29. 1 Samuel 28.

30. Deuteronomy 18:10–11.

31. 1 Samuel 28:15–17. The thought is paralleled in Isaiah 8:19.

32. See Joyce Baldwin, *1 and 2 Samuel*, Leicester: InterVarsity Press, 1988, pp. 87–164.

33. Matthew 7:21–23; Numbers 22–24.

34. Evangelicals are currently on a steep learning curve in their discernment about Pagan pathways. See Brooks Alexander, *Witchcraft Goes Mainstream*, Eugene: Harvest House, 2004; David Burnett, *Dawning of the Pagan Moon*, Eastbourne: MARC, 1991; Craig S. Hawkins, *Witchcraft: Exploring the World of Wicca*, Grand Rapids: Baker, 1996; Catherine Edwards Sanders, *Wicca's Charm*, Colorado Springs: Shaw Books, 2005; Aida Besançon Spencer, Donna F. G. Hailson, Catherine Clark Kroeger and William David Spencer, *The Goddess Revival*, Grand Rapids: Baker, 1995.

35. John 3:1–8.

36. Matthew 4:19; 8:22; 9:9; 16:24; Luke 5:27; John 1:43.

37. Matthew 11:29–30.

38. Matthew 7:16–20; Luke 6:43–44.

39. See, for example, Amos 5.

40. Matthew 5:21–22.

41. Luke 15:11–32.

42. Luke 6:27–28.

43. See Luke 6 and Matthew 5–7.

44. 1 John 3:17; 4:20.

45. Luke 10:25–37.

46. See UNICEF's website http://www.unicef.org/why/index.html

47. See Martin E. Marty and R. Scott Appleby (eds), *Fundamentalisms Observed*, Chicago and London: University of Chicago Press, 1991.

Chapter 5

1. Margaret Murray, 'The Witch-Cult in Western Europe: A Study in Anthropology', *FQ Classics*, 2007.

2. For perhaps the most extreme example regarding Buddhism see Brian Daizen Victoria, *Zen at War*, 2nd ed., Rowman and Littlefield, 2006.

3. Karen Armstrong, *The Battle for God*, New York: Ballantine Books, 2000, p. xv.

4. Armstrong, p. 69.

5. Gerald Gardner, *The Meaning of Witchcraft*, New York: Magickal Childe 1959, p. 189.

6. T. Honderich (ed.), *The Oxford Companion to Philosophy*, Oxford: Oxford University Press, 1995, p. 43.

7. David Tracy, 'Two Cheers for Thomas Aquinas', *The Christian Century*, March 6, 1974, pp. 260–62. Article available at http://www.religion-online.org/showarticle.asp?title=1608

8. Sallustius, *On the Gods and the World*. All quotations from Sallustius are taken from a version developed by Don Frew with the assistance of other scholarly Pagans. They used the three existing published English translations as well as the Greek original. At the time of writing their version is not easily available. But see Thomas Taylor's 1793 translation in *Collected Writings of the Gods and the World*, The Prometheus Trust: Somerset, UK 1994; Gilbert Murray, *The Five Stages of Greek Religion*, Doubleday: Garden City, NY: 1951; and A. D. Nock, ed., *Sallustius: Concerning the Gods and the Universe*, Chicago: Ares Publishers, Inc., reprint of Cambridge 1926 edition.

9. For an example of the blind literalism that could hide the understanding of even Classical mythology, see Plato, Euthyphro, in *The Trial and Death of Socrates*, 3rd ed., G. M. A. Grube, trans. John M. Cooper, revised, Indianapolis: Hackett Publishing Co., 2000. The problem is not just a Christian Fundamentalist failing, nor is it only recent.

10. Charles Taylor, 'Liberal Politics and the Public Sphere', Amitai Etzioni (ed.), *New Communitarian Thinking: Persons, Virtues, Institutions, and Communities*, Charlottesville, VA: University Press of Virginia, 1995, p. 197. Taylor's essay is wonderful.

11. Taylor, ibid., p. 198; Brody, ibid., pp. 133–34.

12. Taylor, ibid., p. 302n.

13. See John H. Lienhard, 'The Age of the Earth: Science, Religion, and Perception', Shell Distinguished Lecture Series, May 21, 1998. http://www.uh.edu/engines/shell.htm

14. Armstrong, p. xvii.

15. See Plato's dialogue *Phaedrus*.

16. Luke 9:58, NIV.

17. Richard Dawkins, *The God Delusion*, London: Bantam, 2006, pp. 31–46.

18. Basic introductory discussions about understanding and interpreting the literary genres of the Bible include Gordon D. Fee and Douglas Stuart, *How to Read the Bible for All It's Worth*, 2nd ed., Grand Rapids: Zondervan, 1993; Walter C. Kaiser and Moisés Silva, *An Introduction to Biblical Hermeneutics*, Grand Rapids: Zondervan, 1994; Tremper Longman III, *Literary Approaches to Biblical Interpretation*, Grand Rapids: Zondervan, 1987.

19. Gerhard F. Hasel, 'The Polemic Nature of the Genesis Cosmology', *Evangelical Quarterly*, 46/2 1974, pp. 81–102.

20. John Warwick Montgomery, *Cross and Crucible: Johann Valentin Andreae (1586–1654) Phoenix of the Theologians*, Vol. 1, The Hague: Martinus Nijhoff, 1973, p. 148.

21. For background see Humphrey Carpenter, *The Inklings*, London: Allen and Unwin, 1978.

22. John Drane, Ross Clifford and Philip Johnson, *Beyond Prediction: The Tarot and Your Spirituality*, Oxford: Lion, 2001.

23. John Meyendorff, *Byzantine Theology*, London and Oxford: Mowbrays, 1975, p. 180.

24. Meyendorff, *Byzantine Theology*, p. 185.

25. Meyendorff, *Byzantine Theology*, p. 185. Meyendorff's italics.

26. Meyendorff, *Byzantine Theology*, p. 187.

27. Garry W. Trompf, *Early Christian Historiography*, London: Continuum, 2000.

28. See John Warwick Montgomery, *The Shape of the Past*, rev. ed. Minneapolis: Bethany, 1975, pp. 43–45.

29. Charles Williams, *Many Dimensions*, Grand Rapids: Eerdmans, 1979, p. 54.

30. Charles Williams, *Descent into Hell*, Grand Rapids: Eerdmans, 1979.

31. Chad Walsh, 'Charles Williams' Novels and the Contemporary Mutation of Consciousness', in *Myth, Allegory and Gospel*, John Warwick Montgomery (ed.), Minneapolis: Bethany, 1974, p. 74.

32. Walsh, 'Charles Williams' Novels', p. 56.

33. See Robert Ackerman, *J. G. Frazer: His Life and Work*, Cambridge: Cambridge University Press, 1987. On Campbell, Jung and Eliade see Robert Ellwood, *The Politics of Myth: A Study of C. G. Jung, Mircea Eliade and Joseph Campbell*, Albany: State University of New York Press, 1999.

34. Mircea Eliade, *The Myth of the Eternal Return*, Princeton: Princeton University Press, 1971.

35. Carl G. Jung, *Man and His Symbols*, New York: Dell, 1964.

36. Stith Thompson, *Motif-Index of Folk Literature*, Indiana: Indiana University Press, 1994.

37. George Miller, 'The Apocalypse and The Pig: Or the hazards of storytelling', *The Sydney Papers*, 8/4 1996, pp. 39–49.

38. J. R. R. Tolkien, 'On Fairy Stories', in *Essays Presented to Charles Williams*, C. S. Lewis (ed.), Oxford: Oxford University Press, 1947, pp. 83–84.

39. C. S. Lewis, *God in the Dock*, Glasgow: Fontana, 1979, pp. 43–45.

40. Jeremiah 23:24; Isaiah 6:3; Habakkuk 3:3; Psalm 72:19.

41. Psalms 19:1–6; 97:6.

42. Proverbs 6:6–8; Job 39:26–28.

43. Luke 12:22–28; Matthew 5:45; Acts 14:17; Job 38:41.

44. Psalms 139:1–18; 71:6; Romans 1:20; Luke 1:41.

45. Some of these matters are helpfully discussed in Paul W. Barnett, *Is The New Testament Reliable?* Downers Grove: InterVarsity Press, 2003; John Drane, *The Bible Phenomenon*, Oxford: Lion, 1999.

46. See Ross Clifford, *Leading Lawyer's Case for the Resurrection*, Alberta: Canadian Institute for Law, Theology and Public Policy, 1996.

47. The former claim appears in the novel by Dan Brown, *The Da Vinci Code*, London: Corgi, 2004. The latter claim forms part of the thesis in Timothy Freke and Peter Gandy, *The Jesus Mysteries*, London: Thorsons, 1999.

48. John 1:1–14.

Chapter 6

1. *San Francisco Examiner*, 2/21/99.

2. Barbara A. McGraw, *Rediscovering America's Sacred Ground: Public Religion and Pursuit of the Good in a Pluralistic America*, Albany: SUNY Press, 2003, p. 79.

3. Michael Ventura, 'Listen to that Long Snake Moan: The Voodoo Origins of Rock and Roll', *Whole Earth*, Spring, 1987, Summer, 1987, Nos. 54, 55.

4. Terry H. Anderson, *The Sixties*, 2nd ed., NY: Pearson Longman, 2004, p. 162.

5. See for example, Rita M. Gross, *Buddhism After Patriarchy: A Feminist History, Analysis, and Reconstruction of Buddhism*, Albany: SUNY, 1993, and her dialogue with the Christian theologian Rosemary Radford Ruether, *Religious Feminism and the Future of the Planet: A Buddhist-Christian Conversation*, London: Continuum, 2001.

6. See especially her *Spiral Dance, A Rebirth of the Ancient Religion of the Great Goddess*, 20th anniversary ed., NY: HarperCollins, 1999.

7. Margot Adler, *Drawing Down the Moon: Witches, Druids, Goddess-Worshippers, and Other Pagans in America Today*, revised ed., Boston: Beacon, 1986, pp. 176–229.

8. I know of nowhere where quite this point is made, but evidence can be found in Luther H. Martin, *Hellenistic Religions: An Introduction*, New York: Oxford University Press, 1987, pp. 158–61. See also my 'Nature, Religion and the Modern World', *Sacred Cosmos*, November 2000. This article may be downloaded from my website: www.dizerega.com.

9. There are many good sources for exploring this point. See especially Evelyn Fox Keller, *Reflections on Gender and Science*, New Haven: Yale University Press, 1985, and Linda Jean Shepherd, *Lifting the Veil: The Feminine Face of Science*, Boston: Shambhala, 1993.

10. Andy Coghlan, 'Pro-choice? Pro-life? No choice', *New Scientist*, October 20, 2007, pp. 8–9.

11. Quoted in Stephanie Simon, 'Evangelicals battle over agenda, environment', *Los Angeles Times*, March 10, 2007. http://www.latimes.com/news/nationworld/politics/la-na-evangelicals10mar10,1,5976802.story?coll=la-news-politics-national

12. Starhawk offers a more gendered form of this basic myth in *The Spiral Dance: A Rebirth of the Ancient Religion of the Great Goddess*, New York: Harper and Row, 1979, pp. 17–18.

13. Buchanan is the exception as he is a practising Roman Catholic.

14. See 'Falwell apologizes to gays, feminists, lesbians', accessed at http://archives.cnn.com/2001/US/09/14/Falwell.apology/

15. Jennifer S. Butler, *Born Again: The Christian Right Globalized*, London: Pluto/Minneapolis: University of Michigan Press, 2006; Chris Hedges, *American Fascists: The Christian Right and the War on America*, New York: Free Press, 2007.

16. Flo Conway and Jim Siegelman, *Holy Terror*, Garden City: Doubleday, 1982; Marion Maddox, *God Under Howard: The Rise of the Religious Right in Australian Politics*, Sydney: Allen and Unwin, 2005.

17. Robert Booth Fowler, *A New Engagement: Evangelical Political Thought, 1966–1976*, Grand Rapids: Eerdmans, 1982.

18. Richard V. Pierard, *The Unequal Yoke: Evangelical Christianity and Political Conservatism*, Philadelphia: Lippincott, 1970; Robert E. Webber, *The Moral Majority – Right or Wrong?* Westchester: Crossway, 1981; Robert Zwier, *Born-Again Politics*, Downers Grove: InterVarsity Press, 1982; Jim Wallis, *God's Politics: Why The Right Gets It Wrong and The Left Doesn't Get It*, San Francisco: Harper, 2005; Randall H.

Balmer, *Thy Kingdom Come: How the Religious Right Distorts the Faith and Threatens America*, New York: Basic Books, 2006.

19. David W. Bebbington, *Evangelicalism in Modern Britain*, London: Unwin Hyman, 1989; Catherine Bramwell-Booth, *Catherine Booth*, London: Hodder & Stoughton, 1970; Samuel Escobar and John Driver, *Christian Mission and Social Justice*, Scottsdale: Herald, 1978; Will A. Linkugel and Martha Solomon, *Anna Howard Shaw: Suffrage Orator and Social Reformer*, New York: Greenwood, 1991; Norris Magnusson, *Salvation in the Slums: Evangelical Social Work, 1865–1920*, Metuchen: Scarecrow, 1977; Timothy L. Smith, *Revivalism and Social Reform*, Baltimore: Johns Hopkins University Press, 1980; Charles E. White, *The Beauty of Holiness: Phoebe Palmer as Theologian, Revivalist, Feminist and Humanitarian*, Grand Rapids: F. Asbury Press, 1986.

20. William G. McLoughlin, *Cherokees and Missionaries*, New Haven: Yale University Press, 1984.

21. James W. Skillen, *The Scattered Voice*, Grand Rapids: Zondervan, 1990, p. 18.

22. Noll, *One Nation Under God?* pp. 158–66.

23. David Kuo, *Tempting Faith: An Inside Story of Political Seduction*, New York: Free Press, 2006.

24. 'Stars of the Cathode Church', *Time*, February 4, 1980.

25. Noll, *One Nation Under God?* pp. 160 and 186.

26. Philip Jenkins, *Mystics and Messiahs: Cults and New Religions in American History*, New York: Oxford University Press, 2000.

27. Ronald A. Wells and T. A. Askew (eds.), *Liberty and Law*, Grand Rapids: Eerdmans, 1987.

28. Mark A. Noll, Nathan O. Hatch and George M. Marsden, *The Search for Christian America*, Westchester: Crossway, 1983.

29. Richard V. Pierard and Robert D. Linder, *Civil Religion and the Presidency*, Grand Rapids: Zondervan, 1988.

30. See Matthew 22:21; Mark 12:17; Luke 20:25.

31. See Luke 13:31–32; Matthew 11:7–8.

32. See Luke 10:29–37; Matthew 5:43–44.

33. John 6:1–15; Mark 6:30–46. Paul W. Barnett, *Jesus and the Rise of Early Christianity*, Downers Grove: InterVarsity Press, 1999, pp. 109–132.

34. John 18:36.

35. See Richard Bauckham, *The Bible in Politics*, London: SPCK, 1989; Jacques Ellul, *The Politics of God and the Politics of Man*, Grand Rapids: Eerdmans, 1972; N. T. Wright, *The Original Jesus: The Life and Vision of a Revolutionary*, Oxford: Lion, 1996; John Howard Yoder, *The Politics of Jesus*, Grand Rapids: Eerdmans, 1972.

36. Guy F. Hershberger (ed.), *The Recovery of the Anabaptist Vision*, Scottsdale: Herald, 1957.

37. Edwin S. Gaustad (ed.), *Liberty of Conscience: Roger Williams in America*, Grand Rapids: Eerdmans, 1991.

38. Wil A. Linkugel and Martha Solomon, *Anna Howard Shaw: Suffrage Orator and Social Reformer*, New York: Greenwood, 1991; Charles E. White, *The Beauty of Holiness: Phoebe Palmer as Theologian, Revivalist, Feminist and Humanitarian*, Grand

Rapids: F. Asbury Press, 1986; Patricia Grimshaw, 'Colonising Motherhood: Evangelical Social Reformers and Koorie Women in Victoria, Australia, 1880s to the Early 1990s', *Women's History Review*, 8/2 (1999), pp. 329–49.

39. Ruth A. Tucker and Walter Liefeld, *Daughters of the Church: Women and ministry from New Testament times to the present*, Grand Rapids: Zondervan, 1987.

40. Ann Brown, *Apology to Women*, Leicester: InterVarsity Press, 1991; Bonnidell Clouse and Robert G. Clouse (eds), *Women in Ministry: Four Views*, Downers Grove: InterVarsity Press, 1989; Ruth B. Edwards, *The Case for Women's Ministry*, London: SPCK, 1989; Alvera Mickelsen (ed.), *Women, Authority and the Bible*, Downers Grove: InterVarsity Press, 1986.

41. Karla Poewe, *New Religions and Nazis*, Milton Park: Routledge, 2006.

42. Jeffrey Kaplan, 'The Reconstruction of the Ásatrú and Odinist Traditions', in James R. Lewis (ed.), *Magical Religion and Modern Witchcraft*, Albany: State University of New York Press, 1996, p. 195.

43. Margot Adler, *Drawing Down the Moon*, Rev. ed., Boston: Beacon, 1986, p. 278.

44. Graham Harvey, *Contemporary Paganism: Listening People, Speaking Earth*, New York: New York University Press, 1997, p. 68.

45. Graham Harvey, 'Heathenism', in *Pagan Pathways*, Charlotte Hardman and Graham Harvey (eds), London: Thorsons, 2000, pp. 57 and 60.

46. Paul Tuitéan and Estelle Daniels, *Essential Wicca*, Freedom California: The Crossing Press, 2001.

47. I do not want to inflame matters by singling out individual Pagan and Christian storytellers but examples are cited in Sarah M. Pike, *Earthly Bodies, Magical Selves: Contemporary Pagans and the Search for Community*, Berkeley: University of California Press, 2001, pp. 87–122; Jason Bivins, 'Religious and Legal Others: Identity, Law, and Representation in American Christian Right and NeoPagan Cultural Conflicts', *Culture and Religion*, 6/1 (March 2005), pp. 31–56.

Responsive Thoughts

1. Some readers may recall the character 'Pat' from *Saturday Night Live*. Pat was an androgynous office worker who routinely unsettled his/her co-workers by refusing to confirm his/her gender.

Conclusion

1. For more on this issue see my *Pagans and Christians*, St. Paul, MN: Llewellyn, 2001, pp. 173–208.

2. diZerega, *Pagans and Christians*, op. cit., pp. 173–89.

3. 1 Corinthians 13:12.

4. Richard Bauckham, 'The New Age Theology of Matthew Fox: A Christian Theological Response', *Anvil*, 13, 2, 1996, p. 124. Bauckham's italics.

Further Reading

Paganism

Any Pagan's booklist will differ in part from others'. But this list covers many of the foundational books as well as many of the more recent studies of our religion, and I think most would be in any well-read Pagan's top twenty. I do not claim that I wouldn't alter this list a *little* bit were I to do it again in a week.

Foundational – if you read only one book, read this one

Margot Adler, *Drawing Down the Moon*, Penguin, 2006 (new edition).

This is *the* basic introduction to NeoPaganism in the United States. Adler covers virtually all the dimensions of NeoPagan religion.

The Founding Mothers and Fathers

Stewart Farrar, *What Witches Do: The Modern Coven Revealed*, 2nd ed., Phoenix Publications, 1983.

Perhaps the first public study of what it means to practise contemporary Witchcraft.

Stewart and Janet Farrar, *The Witches' Way*, Robert Hale, 1984.

One of the best if not the best early study of contemporary NeoPaganism by people who were there almost from the beginning.

Gerald Gardner, *Witchcraft Today*, Rider, 1954.

The founder of modern NeoPaganism. This was the first nonfiction book on contemporary Witchcraft.

Gerald Gardner, *The Meaning of Witchcraft*, Aquarian Press, 1959.

An early general overview of the subject.

Doreen Valiente, *Witchcraft for Tomorrow*, Robert Hale, 1978.

A basic introduction and overview of the Craft by one of its founders.

Doreen Valiente, *The Rebirth of Witchcraft*, Robert Hale, 1989.

Valiente was one of Gardner's High Priestesses and contributed heavily to the Craft. This is her final book on the subject.

History

Philip Heselton, *Wiccan Roots: Gerald Gardner and the Modern Witchcraft Revival*, Capall Bann Publishing, 2000.

A careful study of the evidence for and practices of England's New Forest Coven, which trained Gerald Gardner and is thus in many ways the seed coven of much modern NeoPaganism.

Ronald Hutton, *Triumph of the Moon*, Oxford University Press, 1999.

Jeffrey Burton Russell and Brooks Alexander, *A History of Witchcraft*, 2nd ed., Thames and Hudson, 2007 (British ed.: *A New History of Witchcraft*, Thames and Hudson, 2007).

Different Traditions and Contemporary Studies

Helen Berger (ed.), *Witchcraft and Magic: Contemporary North America,* University of Pennsylvania Press, 2006.

Judy Harrow, *Wicca Covens: How to Start and Organize Your Own*, Citadel Press, 1999.

Title says it all. A good book on what a coven is and how it works.

Sabina Magliocco, *Witching Culture: Folklore and Paganism in America*, University of Pennsylvania Press, 2004.

A clear and accurate description of modern NeoPagan practice, with a British Traditional orientation.

Ralph Metzner, *The Well of Remembrance: Rediscovering the Earth Wisdom Myths of Northern Europe*, Shambhala, 1994.

A contemporary study of northern European Pagan mythology and its relevance for today.

Sarah Pike, *New Age and Neopagan Religions in America*, Columbia University Press, 2004.

Pike situates NeoPaganism in the broader context of alternative American spirituality.

Jone Salomonsen, *Enchanted Feminism: The Reclaiming Witches of San Francisco*, Routledge, 2004.

A good study of the Reclaiming tradition whose roots are in the work of Starhawk. Reclaiming is the most socially and politically engaged NeoPagan tradition.

Starhawk, *The Spiral Dance: A Rebirth of the Ancient Religion of the Goddess*, 20th Anniversary ed., Harper, 1999.

Undoubtedly the single most important volume for introducing the most people to NeoPagan religion.

V. Vale and John Sulak, *Modern Pagans: An Investigation of Contemporary Pagan Practices*, Re/Search, 2001.

A good overview of the diversity of Pagan traditions, though dwelling on the edgier aspects of Pagan practice.

Pagan Philosophy/Theology

Chas Clifton and Graham Harvey (eds), *The Paganism Reader*, Routledge, 2004.

A good selection of a variety of Pagan source readings.

Gus diZerega, *Pagans and Christians: The Personal Spiritual Experience*, Llewellyn, 2000.

The first sustained comparison of Pagan and Christian religions on a variety of issues. This is complementary to but not simply a restatement of diZerega's arguments in this volume.

Jordan Paper, *The Deities Are Many*, SUNY Press, 2005.

Paper presents the most inclusive and academically thorough study of polytheism yet. Interestingly, he does not discuss NeoPaganism. Nevertheless, this book is central to many dimensions of NeoPagan thought and practice.

Christianity

The following list includes authors from evangelical, Protestant, Roman Catholic and Eastern Orthodox traditions. There are many topics not covered by this list and the inclusion of items here does not signify my complete agreement with what each author says. For deeper discussion on topics discussed throughout *Beyond the Burning Times*, refer to my chapter endnotes.

The Bible

Tremper Longman, *Reading the Bible with Heart and Mind*, Colorado Springs: NAV Press, 1996.

Christian Belief

Alister E. McGrath, *Theology: The Basics*, 2nd ed., Malden & Oxford: Blackwell, 2008.

R. C. Sproul, *The Mystery of the Holy Spirit*, Wheaton: Tyndale House, 1990.

John R. W. Stott, *Basic Christianity*, Rev. ed., Grand Rapids: Eerdmans, 1981.

Christian Celtic Spirituality

Timothy J. Joyce, *Celtic Christianity: A Sacred Tradition, A Vision of Hope*, Maryknoll: Orbis, 1998.

J. Philip Newell, *The Book of Creation*, Mahwah: Paulist, 1999.

Ray Simpson, *Soul Friendship: Celtic Insights into Spiritual Mentoring*, London: Hodder & Stoughton, 1999.

Esther De Waal, *Every Earthly Blessing: Rediscovering the Celtic Tradition*, London: Fount, 1991.

Christian Life

Richard Foster, *Prayer: Finding the heart's true home*, London: Hodder & Stoughton, 1992.

Michael Frost, *Exiles*, Peabody: Hendrickson, 2006.

Os Guinness, *When No One Sees: The Importance of Character in an Age of Image*, Colorado Springs: NAV Press, 2000.

Ruth A. Tucker, *Walking Away From Faith*, Downers Grove: InterVarsity Press, 2002.

Creation

Ian Bradley, *God is Green*, London: Darton Longman & Todd, 1990.

Vigen Guroian, *The Fragrance of God: Reflections on Finding God Through the Beauty and Glory of the Natural World*, London: Darton, Longman & Todd, 2007.

Alister E. McGrath, *The Open Secret: A New Vision for Natural Theology*, Malden & Oxford: Blackwell, 2008.

Stephen H. Webb, *On God and Dogs*, New York: Oxford University Press, 2002.

Jesus

N. T. Wright, *The Original Jesus*, Oxford: Lion, 1996.

Spirituality

Ray S. Anderson, *Living the Spiritually Balanced Life*, Eugene: Wipf & Stock, 2005.

Olive M. Fleming Drane, *Spirituality to Go: Rituals and Reflections for Everyday Life*, London: Darton, Longman & Todd, 2006.

Frederica Mathewes-Green, *The Illumined Heart*, Brewster: Paraclete, 2001.